THE LITERACY HOAX

The Decline of Reading, Writing, and Learning in the Public Schools and What We Can Do About It

by PAUL COPPERMAN

Morrow Quill Paperbacks
New York   1980

Library of Congress Cataloging in Publication Data

Copperman, Paul.
    The literacy hoax.

    Bibliography: p.
    Includes index.
    1. Academic achievement.   2. Education and state—United States.
3. Reading—Ability testing.   I. Title.
LB1131.C5477   1978b   371.2'6   78-18703
ISBN 0-688-03353-9
    0-688-08353-6 pbk.
BOOK DESIGN   CARL WEISS

Printed in the United States of America.

First Morrow Quill Paperback Edition

1 2 3 4 5 6 7 8 9 10

This book is gratefully dedicated to the staff of the Institute of Reading Development for providing me with the time and resources to conduct this investigation.

ACKNOWLEDGMENTS

I AM DEEPLY INDEBTED TO THE FOLLOWING PERSONS, WITHOUT WHOSE assistance I would not have been able to write this book: above all, Bob Beveridge, my research assistant, who started with me in the summer of 1974 and was with me at the finish in the spring of 1978; Dr. James Shanker, Department of Education, California State University, Hayward; Dr. Bjorn Karlsen, Department of Education, California State College at Sonoma; Tom Williams, Director of the Office of Research and Evaluation, Richmond Unified School District; Joe Spitzley, owner, Berkeley Franchise, Institute of Reading Development; Mark Herndon, owner, San Diego Franchise, Institute of Reading Development; Lynn Berntson, Director, Office of Measurement and Guidance, Palo Alto Office, Houghton Mifflin Publishing Company; Paul Kullman, Regional Manager, Addison-Wesley Testing Service; Robert Kellar, senior social studies editor, Addison-Wesley, Menlo Park, California; Andrew Copperman, Director, San Francisco Institute of Reading Development; Victor

Gross, doctoral candidate, Department of Education, University of California, Berkeley; Robb Schwartz, owner, Orange County Franchise, Institute of Reading Development; and the many teachers, students, parents, publishers, editors, and federal, state, and local school officials all over the country who gave generously of their time and energy to help me understand the workings of our educational system.

I would also like to thank the following persons for rendering editorial assistance when the book was in manuscript: Dr. James Highsmith, Department of English, Lone Mountain College, San Francisco, California; and Dr. Gerald Frank, San Francisco, California.

Because of the controversial nature of some of the material presented in this book, I wish to state explicitly that I bear full and sole responsibility for its conclusions and interpretations.

CONTENTS

LIST OF TABLES AND GRAPHS

《 9 》

10))

A NOTE ON THE REFERENCES

When a reference to a published document is made within the body of the text, the number in superscript refers to the numbered bibliography at the end of the book.

Preface to the Quill Edition

THERE IS CURRENTLY UNDER WAY A MASSIVE PUBLIC RELATIONS campaign designed to convince the American public that there has been no decline in the academic achievement of America's schoolchildren or in the quality of American public education. The key figures in this campaign include the national leadership of a number of the major professional educational associations, high-level executives in some of the major test-publishing organizations and educational foundations, and ranking officials in several of the state and federal educational bureaucracies. At stake is control over a national education budget of $165 billion a year. If the leadership of the education profession can convince the American people that public education has prospered under its stewardship, it will retain control over the biggest industry in our domestic economy. If this massive public relations campaign fails, it is possible that local communities and state legislatures will reassert a measure of control over public education.

The decline in the academic achievement of our schoolchildren is real, it is massive, and it will be tragic in its consequences. Its principal cause is a severe deterioration in the quality of public education. If the American people can find the will and the leadership, we can reassert control over the educational destiny of our schoolchildren.

Read my book. Then write your senators, your congressmen, your state legislators. Tell them you want public education policies changed, and tell them how. Attend school board meetings. Tell your elected school board members what policies you want instituted. Help assertive, policy-minded people get elected to local school boards. Consider running yourself.

The 1980's will witness massive battles over educational policy and over the control of public education. If you care about our children and our country, you will get involved.

INTRODUCTION

E VIDENCE PRESENTED IN CHAPTER ONE OF THIS BOOK INDICATES that between 1900 and the mid-1950's the academic achievement of America's students registered gradual improvement. This trend accelerated between 1957 and the mid-1960's as a result of the increased curricular rigor induced by *Sputnik*. In the mid-1960's heightened public concern about education broke the logjam preventing federal aid to education. For this and other reasons, our national education budget more than tripled between 1964 and 1976. This same period saw a sharp rise in the reading-readiness skills of our preschool children.

Yet the American educational system, flush with money and resources, enrolling children much better prepared than ever before in history, did not successfully teach these children their basic academic skills. Since the mid-1960's, academic performance and standards have shown a sharp and widespread decline. Today's eighth grader reads approximately as well as the average seventh grader just ten years ago and computes about as well as the average sixth grader of that period. On college admissions tests only about a quarter of our current high-school graduates attain the level recorded by the average high-school graduate in the early 1960's. The decline in academic achievement has been measured in locales as disparate as Iowa and Hawaii, California and New York, Minnesota and Idaho. The decline is as evident in middle-class and upper-middle-class students as it is in disadvantaged students, as pronounced in students with above-average or even superior intelligence as in students of average or below-average ability. The academic skills of America's young people in the late 1970's have deteriorated to the pre-*Sputnik* level of the early 1950's.

The decline in educational standards is as sharp as the decline in basic academic skills. The amount and quality of academic work demanded of public-school students has been cut sharply. For one thing, students are simply not taking as many academic courses as they did in the early 1960's. As a percentage of high-school enrollment, enrollments in English, history, science, and math are sharply lower. Even the enrollment figures underestimate the reduction in the academic courseload of the average student. Many traditional and rigorous courses have been replaced with fare best described as educational entertainment. Courses in film literature and science fiction are replacing English composition; courses in contemporary world issues and comparative revolutions are replacing world history. In these courses the amount of work assigned and the standard to which it is held are considerably lower than in the courses they replace.

Even in the more traditional classes, work demands and imposed standards have dropped considerably. Part II of this book reproduces a series of interviews with teachers and administrators from city and suburban high schools. The consensus of these teachers is that the average student is assigned 50 percent less reading and writing than in the early 1960's, and that standards for written work are correspondingly low. Chapter Two cites evidence that high-school textbooks in most subject areas have been rewritten with a sharply reduced reading level, usually one or more years lower than the grade for which they are intended. The same chapter discusses the phenomenon of grade inflation, which has seen the grades of high-school and college students improving even faster than their academic skills are declining.

With skills down, assignments down, standards down, and grades up, the American educational system perpetrates a hoax on its students and on their parents. I have taken the liberty of applying a name to this successful piece of deception: I call it the literacy hoax.

America's public schools and colleges enroll over fifty million students each year. The overwhelming majority of them are repeatedly informed that they are acquiring an adequate or even excellent education. These students believe their report cards, their grade slips, and their teachers, counselors, and professors when these agents of the educational system tell them they have adequate academic skills, and are doing adequate or excellent schoolwork. In fact, many of these students suffer from a delusion of adequacy, engendered by an educational system which is lying to them.

In June of 1972 a young white male who calls himself Peter Doe graduated from a public high school in San Francisco. His school records show that he has an average IQ, and that during his twelve years of public schooling he achieved average grades, never had any discipline problems, attended school regularly, and was promoted every year. His parents testify that they frequently complained to school officials that he did not seem to have adequate reading skills. They were repeatedly assured that he was reading at the average level and had no special or unusual problems.

The first job Peter obtained after graduation was selling shoes. He lasted less than a week in this job because his reading skills were so poor that he could not do the minimal amount of paper work the job required. His reading skills were subsequently tested, and it was discovered that he was reading at a fifth-grade level. Peter sued the San Francisco Unified School District for a million dollars, arguing that he should not have been passed along from grade to grade without being taught the skills he needed at each grade level, and further arguing that by repeatedly lying to his parents, school officials had effectively prevented them from helping him obtain the remedial assistance he needed. When the California Supreme Court refused to hear an appeal of two lower-court decisions dismissing the suit, public-school educators across the land breathed a collective sigh of relief, because from 10 to 15 percent of our recent high-school graduates read no better than Peter Doe.

What can a functionally illiterate young adult do in modern American society? Join the welfare ranks, try burglary or prostitution or perhaps armed robbery—or go to junior college? A recent report indicates that over 50 percent of the entering students at San Francisco's public two-year college read at a fifth-grade level or below.[90] Even the military has a hard time with these young people. A study recently reported by UPI indicates that over a third of the nation's naval recruits read below a tenth-grade level, and that 70 percent of these read so poorly they cannot complete their basic training.[70] The UPI story tells of a sailor who did $250,000 damage to a ship's engines because he could not read a repair manual. As a result of this incident and other, similar ones, the Chief of Naval Personnel has mandated a sixth-grade reading level as the minimum acceptable level for naval personnel, a standard which, of course, leaves out Peter Doe and over half the entering freshman class at San Francisco City College.

When one examines such a widespread phenomenon as the literacy decline of the past ten years, it is easy to become preoccupied with statistics and other abstract measures of performance. We forget that these statistics measure the ability of vulnerable human beings to survive and function in the world. Imagine how devastating it must be at eighteen years of age to discover that you are illiterate and incapable of holding a job. The declining scores reported in Chapter One presage a generation of pain.

This book is the personal statement of one individual who is concerned with the trends he sees developing in American education. I own and operate a private reading school, the Institute of Reading Development, with offices located throughout California. I train and supervise teachers who teach reading to junior-high, senior-high, and college students. For the past five years I have become increasingly concerned with the reading skills of our students. I have recently met high-school graduates in San Francisco who did not know where the Pacific Ocean was, or whether New York was east or west of California, or how to spell the name of our country. Each year I meet dozens of parents who are shocked to discover that their children read three, or four, or five years below grade level. In

1976 I worked with several dozen graduate students who were reading below an eighth-grade level, students who were obtaining their master's degrees or doctorates in fields as varied as sociology, education, linguistics, and psychology.

I did not initially intend to write a book. Because I wanted to know if the inadequate skills of my own students reflected a national pattern, I initiated a research project at my San Jose Institute in the summer of 1974. The purpose of this research was to develop an historical profile of reading achievement in the United States, especially since 1960. I anticipated that the study would be restricted to a review of the published research in the area. I was amazed to find that except for historical data on the Scholastic Aptitude Test, there was virtually no recent research that measured changes over time in the academic skills of America's students. Practically every other conceivable topic in education had been the object of study during the preceding ten years except this one—yet what could be more important?

Frustrated at my lack of progress, I decided to seek the advice of two evaluation experts I knew in the educational-testing industry. These are the people who develop the tests that would be used in the kind of study I was looking for, tests such as the Stanford Achievement Test, published by Harcourt Brace Jovanovich, or the Iowa Tests of Basic Skills (ITBS), published by Houghton Mifflin. When I contacted Lynn Berntson, Houghton Mifflin's West Coast measurement expert, I discovered that he had been personally interested in the topic of my research for some time, and had accumulated some information on the subject. He willingly shared his information, which included historical data on the ITBS, and several unpublished reports that would not normally have been available to me. His information indicated that academic skills at the late-elementary and secondary levels had declined significantly after the mid-1960's.

My interview with Harcourt's testing expert, Paul Kullman, was, if anything, even more productive. He started the interview by informing me that Harcourt had accumulated forty-seven years of historical statistics on reading achievement. Apparently, the statistics for the first twenty-seven years were not terribly accurate, but the data from 1953 through 1973 clearly indicated that reading and math skills had improved up to 1964, and had declined sharply thereafter. Not only did Kullman give me Harcourt's published information in this area, but he also gave me access to an unpublished Harcourt report which confirmed the sharp ten-year decline in basic academic skills.

I spent the first six months of 1975 completing this initial phase of the historical research. From Bjorn Karlsen, co-author of both the Stanford Achievement Test and Stanford Diagnostic Reading Test, I obtained data which confirmed the decline in basic academic skills, a decline which Karlsen calculates has been occurring nationwide at the rate of one month per year since 1964. Bob Beveridge, my research assistant, obtained every study measuring historical changes in academic achievement that had ever been published in this country. Although all of the major test publishers had refused our direct requests for historical statistics (including Harcourt and Houghton Mifflin), we were able to add the McGraw-Hill data to our file when Paul Kullman moved there from Harcourt. By putting together all of the various pieces of information, I was able to develop an historical profile of academic achievement in the United States since the late 1800's, a profile which becomes increasingly accurate as it approaches the present. I decided at that time, and continue to believe today, that America's parents must be apprised of the nature and extent of the current decline in basic academic skills. In June of 1975 I started writing Chapter One, which is my report on the skills decline affecting America's young people. This chapter, and indeed the entire book, was written without educational jargon and without complicated or confusing statistics.

I spent the next two years investigating the cause of the skills decline. Chapter Two describes and analyzes changes in course work and curriculum at the preschool, elementary, secondary, and university levels of our educational system, spotlighting those changes which I believe have directly contributed to the decline in academic achievement. This chapter also analyzes some of the consequences of federal intervention in the educational process. Federal money and intervention were supposed to solve our most pressing educational problems. Instead, they have proven to be a multi-billion-dollar source of fraud and political interference. This chapter concludes with a discussion of the battle over standardized testing, and its implications for future curricular change.

During the Bicentennial year of 1976, I worked on the final two chapters. While our politicians were proudly trumpeting America's accomplishments, I wrote my analysis of the underlying cause of the skills decline affecting her educational system. The analysis contained in Chapter Three stands at almost total variance to the basic philosophy that motivates most contemporary educational practices. Without hesitation, I can say that this analysis is the most important contribution of the book. The solution to our educational dilemma presented in Chapter Four follows directly from the model of effective education presented in Chapter Three. While the information and description presented in the first two chapters is time bound, the ideas and principles presented in Chapters Three and Four provide a blueprint for effective education at any time and any place. Where these principles are applied, education will accomplish its primary goals. Where they are ignored, as has been the case in our public schools since the early 1960's, education will fail.

Although my analysis of our educational system is completed in Chapter Four, I have included a second part to the book. Part II reproduces transcripts of interviews I conducted with students, teachers, school administrators, and reading experts while doing the research which led to this book. The reader may find some of these interviews to be quite interesting: the young man who talks about peddling drugs on a high-school campus; the evaluation expert who tells the inside story of the new math; a permissive teacher who describes his reaction to the discovery that his own child was being taught permissively; the educational consultant who explains what's wrong with big city schools, and how to fix them; an extremely successful elementary-school principal who discusses how he gets his school to function effectively. This material was included in the book so that the reader could participate intimately in my investigation of our public schools.

Today, anybody who watches the television news or reads newspapers or magazines on a regular basis is aware of the decline in reading, writing, and learning skills in our public schools. Note, however, that this decline did not become an important news story until late 1975, almost six months after I had completed my historical profile of academic achievement in the United States. It has been a source of much frustration and some fascination for me to see numerous pieces of the research in this book reported in the news media—as piecemeal studies published independently by other authors and researchers. Wiley and Harnischfeger completed their study of recent changes in academic achievement almost exactly the same time I did, and beat me into print by three years. Bob Beveridge and I completed our study of the reduction in the reading level of textbooks about a year before Jeanne Chall at Harvard even started her study, yet Chall, sponsored by the Educational Testing Service, beat us into print, and into the media, by over a year. But what these studies have not done, or really even attempted to do, is to present a complete and comprehensive study of our nation's educational problems. *Literacy Hoax* is such an attempt. I hope the reader finds it informative, entertaining, and useful.

I will conclude this introduction with a brief statement of the assumptions, values, and beliefs that influence my perception and judgment about education. I believe that the primary function of our schools is to teach students a body of skill and knowledge that will enable them to function in modern society. Far and away the most important of these skills are the primary academic skills: reading, writing, and computing. When an individual is sufficiently developed in these skills so that he can successfully apply them to socially required tasks associated with securing and maintaining employment, maintaining his health, taking advantage of the various services available in his community, and meeting his obligations of citizenship, he has reached a state of functional literacy. I believe virtually everyone has the intellectual ability required to attain this state of educational development.

There is a body of research which supports my belief that it requires a degree of competence in the primary academic skills to function in our society. A recent study indicates that it takes approximately a seventh-grade reading level to hold a job as a cook, an eighth-grade level to hold a job as a mechanic, and a ninth- or tenth-grade level to hold a job as a supply clerk.[144] I believe it is a reasonable inference that a job as a teacher, nurse, accountant, or engineer would demand a higher minimum level of reading ability. Innumerable studies have found high correlations between reading disability and criminal behavior or juvenile delinquency, including a recent study which indicates that as many as 85 percent of the youngsters who appear in juvenile court are disabled readers.[87] The recently conducted Adult Performance Level (APL) study shows that 40 percent of the adult population with incomes under $5,000 per year are functionally illiterate, compared to 8 percent of the population with incomes over $15,000 per year.[114] When I judge course work or curriculum, my first question is, Will this program promote the acquisition and development of the basic skills?

I believe the second function of our educational system is to promote the development of what I call higher literacy. I define higher literacy as the ability to apply primary academic skills to the cultural and intellectual record of the society: history, literature, science, and mathematics. Education to higher literacy helps an indivdual make sense out of the world in which he lives by training his intellect to understand the bonds connecting places, times, and events. By teaching him to recognize the consequences of past actions, this type of education refines his decision-making ability, and enables him more fully to realize his human potential. It allows him to participate actively in modern society, to feel that he is a part of the day-to-day events which shape his environment, and his life.

We live in a democratic society, one of the few free societies existing today, or indeed one of the few that has existed since the dawn of civilization. We jeopardize our freedom if we do not make every attempt to teach all of our citizens the knowledge they need to make the good choices that will keep our democracy operating. The decline of academic achievement, the perpetration of the literacy hoax—these are harbingers of Huxley's brave new world, and Orwell's world of 1984. Thomas Jefferson said it first, and said it best: "If a nation expects to be ignorant and free, in a state of civilization, it expects what never was and never will be." In judging course work and curriculum, my second question is, Does this program promote higher literacy?

Between illiteracy and functional literacy, between functional literacy and higher literacy, is a continuum of skill and knowledge. I believe the key to movement along this continuum is the acquisition and refinement of the primary academic skills: reading, writing, and computing. The past ten years have witnessed a sharp decline in the acquisition of these skills by America's young people, a decline tragic in its consequences for the individuals it affects, and for our society. I have written this book in the hope that an informed public and an informed educational community will together act to improve the education being provided America's youth.

PART

I

1

LITERACY

DECLINE

THE PAST TEN YEARS HAVE WITNESSED A SHARP AND WIDESPREAD decline in the primary academic skills of America's students. An historical profile of academic achievement in the United States since the early 1960's shows a startling pattern: the reading-readiness skills of preschool children have improved substantially; the academic skills of primary-grade (first to third grade) students have increased slightly; the reading, writing, and computing skills of late-elementary and secondary students have deteriorated sharply.

This chapter will briefly present an historical record of the academic achievement of America's students from the 1800's to the early 1960's, followed by a detailed presentation of the evidence of the massive decline in the primary academic skills since the mid-1960's. I wrote this chapter with two goals in mind: first, to present the historical record accurately and completely; second, to present it in such a way that no knowledge of statistics would be required of the reader. A reader who takes a few moments to examine the chapter's one graph and three tables will have no difficulty understanding the discussion presented in this chapter.

1800's TO THE EARLY 1900's

Until quite recently, literacy was considered an automatic result of education. To this day, the Bureau of the Census calculates the functional literacy rate as the percentage of the population fourteen years and older who have completed five years or more of school. According to this measure, literacy in the United States has increased steadily over the past two hundred years. As Table 1 indi-

TABLE 1

PERCENTAGE OF AGE GROUPS IN
SCHOOL OR COMPLETING SCHOOL

	Percentage of 5–17 age group enrolled in grades K–12	Percentage of 17-year-olds graduating from high school	Percentage of 18–21 age group enrolled in higher education	Percentage of age group 25 and older who completed 4 years of college
1840	38			
1850	45			
1870	57	2		
1890	69	4	3	
1900	72	6	4	
1910	74	9	5	3
1920	78	17	8	3
1930	82	29	12	4
1940	84	51	15	5
1950	83	59	27	6
1960	82	65	37	7
1970	87	76	46	11
1975	88	75	45	13

cates, American educational history has been characterized by increasing percentages of the appropriate age groups enrolling in and graduating from progressively higher levels of our education system.[31, 39, 56]

Table 1 reflects the establishment and development of the American system of mass public education. Throughout the 1800's and early 1900's, the goal of the American educational system was to provide eight years of public education to as large a percentage of the population as possible. The percentage of the school-age population enrolled in school increased from under 40 percent in 1840 to almost 80 percent in the 1920's, and this increase is matched by attendance figures which show the average student attending 78 days a year in 1870 and 140 days a year by the 1920's.[31] Although enrollment figures prior to 1840 and attendance figures prior to 1870 are not available, we know that the 1840 figures represent a significant increase over the early 1800's, and we know that school attendance was extremely irregular prior to 1850.[123]

When we attempt to compare the achievement of nineteenth- and twentieth-century students, we are confronted with two major problems. First, the differing percentages of the appropriate age groups enrolled in school tend to make comparisons misleading. For example, in making a comparison of the academic achievement of high-school graduates in 1870 and 1970, we would have to take into consideration the fact that the 1870 students represented only the upper socioeconomic classes, whereas the 1970 students were representative of the population as a whole. Thus, we would be comparing the academic achievement of a highly selective group of students in one time period with that of a nonselective group in another. For this reason, long-term historical comparisons are quite difficult to interpret.

The second problem in developing historical comparisons of academic achievement is even more troublesome. The United States is the only advanced country in the world without a uniform system of educational evaluation. Each state and frequently each school district is free to establish any system of evaluation it chooses. Until quite recently most states and school districts either conducted no evaluation of academic achievement at all or did not publish the results of their evaluations. Use of different educational tests in different time periods makes historical comparisons especially difficult.

Despite these two major and several minor evaluation problems, a number of researchers have attempted to measure and analyze historical changes in the academic achievement of America's students. A quite useful review and analysis of the most important of these studies was recently published by the noted authority on reading and measurement, Dr. Roger Farr.[50] In this report, Dr. Farr reviews four studies comparing the academic achievement of students in the mid-1850's and early 1900's. These studies compared the test scores on educational tests used in the 1840's and 1850's of students in Boston in 1845 and 1919, in Springfield in 1846 and 1905, in Cleveland in 1848 and 1947, and in Boston again in 1853 and 1929. In each of these four studies the students from the later period were academically far superior to the students in the earlier period. The evidence of these four studies is of an upward trend in academic achievement in the 1800's and early 1900's.

THE EARLY 1900's TO THE MID-1950's

Reference to Table 1 will show that the most significant educational trend from the early 1900's to the mid-1950's was the tremendous increase in the percentage of students graduating from high school. This figure increased from 6 percent in 1900 to over 60 percent by the mid-1950's. During this period the comprehensive high school evolved as the principal vehicle for the preparation of America's young adults for the worlds of work and higher education. The goal of America's educational system became the high-school graduation of as high a percentage of the population as possible.

The most comprehensive and accurate study analyzing achievement trends in this period was a renorming study conducted by the dean of American reading experts, Arthur Gates.[58] His investigation is called a renorming study because he developed his analysis by comparing norms—a technical-sounding word which means nothing more than average scores—of the 1937 and 1957 versions of the reading achievement tests that bear his name.

Gates's first finding was that public-school students in every grade were about six months younger in 1957 than in 1937, as a result of a change in the public-school policy regarding academic promotion. In the late 1930's, well over 30 percent of the students were forced to repeat at least one grade in the first six, a figure which had dropped to about 15 percent by the late 1950's, and was considerably less than 10 percent by 1970.[141]

Gates's findings regarding academic achievement must be interpreted in light of his findings regarding age differences. Comparing 1937 and 1957 students according to grade level, he found that the 1957 students scored an average of two months lower than the 1937 students. However, when he compared students of the same age, he found that students of the later period scored five months higher than their earlier counterparts. Since students started school at approximately the same age in both 1937 and 1957,[89] students of the same age in the two different periods had received approximately equal amounts of schooling. Gates concluded from this that the average gain of five months represented a real and significant improvement over the twenty-year period.

Gates's renorming study is the most important and most accurate study of the period, because a renorming study must attempt to test students who are representative of the national population. Thus Gates's crop of 107,000 students in 1937 and 31,000 students in 1957 were each representative of the national student population in those years.

Farr reviews an additional eighteen studies of academic achievement during this period. These studies indicate either no change or small improvements in the academic achievement of elementary and junior-high-school students between the period of the 1920's to 1940's and the mid-1950's. These studies did not take age into account, but if they had, they would have indicated improvements of between five months and a year.

Two important studies were not reviewed by Dr. Farr. The

first was a comparison of the IQ's of soldiers in World Wars I and II, which showed that the average soldier in World War II had a higher IQ than 83 percent of the soldiers in World War I, despite a sampling procedure which made the World War II group somewhat less selective.[75,151] (Follow-up research indicates that the IQ level of draftees has remained relatively stable throughout the 1940's, 1950's, and 1960's.[8]) The second study was the renorming study of the United States Army Tests of General Educational Development (G.E.D.), which compared high-school seniors in 1943 and 1955.[21] This study showed that 55 percent of the seniors in 1955 had better academic skills than the average senior in 1943, despite declining high-school dropout rates which would have tended to make the 1955 group less selective.

The best interpretation of the gains recorded during this period is that the educational standards established in the 1920's and 1930's were maintained through the mid-1950's, even though the schools were working with a younger and less selective group of students. We know that many average- and low-ability students who would have dropped out in the 1920's and 1930's were still in school in the mid-1950's. We also know that as a result of changing promotion policies, some students who would have been in the sixth or seventh grade in 1930 were in the eighth or ninth grade in 1955. Despite these very real challenges, the American educational system maintained its standards and significantly improved the academic achievement of America's students.

1957 TO THE EARLY 1960's

The closer we get to the present, the easier it is to measure accurately changes in academic achievement. The composition of the student population becomes much more stable, and the quality and quantity of educational evaluation improves markedly. A great deal of evidence exists that shows a sharp rise in the academic achievement of America's students during the post-*Sputnik* era, 1957 to the early 1960's. The two best studies analyzing changes in academic achievement during this period are renorming studies conducted by the educational-test publishing firms of Harcourt Brace Jovanovich and Houghton Mifflin.

Table 2 quantifies the changes in reading and math-computation skills of first- through ninth-grade students between 1958 and 1964. Harcourt developed these figures by comparing the norms (average scores) of the 1958 and 1964 versions of two of their most widely used achievement tests.[99] The unit of achievement on this table is months of improvement (education years are ten-month years, September through June, so one month equals one-tenth of a school year). Thus the table indicates that the average beginning eighth-grade student in 1964 scored six months higher in math computation, and eighth months higher in reading, than a comparable student in 1958. This means that the average beginning eighth grader in 1964 had math skills equal to the average student in 1958 who was six months through the eighth grade, and reading skills equal to the average student in 1958 who was eight months through the eighth grade.

TABLE 2

GAINS IN ACADEMIC ACHIEVEMENT, 1958 TO 1964
(*Unit of measure is months of improvement*)

Grade	Reading	Math Computation
9	+13	+6
8	+ 8	+6
7	+ 4	+6
6	+ 2	+6
5	+ 2	+7
4	+ 4	+6
3	+ 5	+5
2	+ 4	+3
1	0	0

Because of the vagaries of educational testing, it is wise to remain skeptical of the results of a study until it has been duplicated several times. Fortunately, the data in the table above are supported by at least ten studies with which I am familiar. The renorming study of the Iowa Tests of Basic Skills (ITBS), published by Houghton Mifflin, compares the academic achievement of third- through eighth-grade students in 1956 and 1964.[64] The results of this study produced in tabular form look quite similar to the table above. The main difference is that the figures in the ITBS renorming study are about 30 percent smaller, ranging primarily between two and four months. Dr. Farr reviews data from New Hampshire, Idaho, and West Virginia as well as three large public-school districts and a number of private schools distributed nationwide, all of which indicate the same pattern. Achievement test scores in these states and public and private schools rise sharply during the post-*Sputnik* era.

A good deal of the increase in academic achievement recorded during this period can be attributed to the raised educational standards induced by *Sputnik*. When the Russians successfully launched *Sputnik* in 1957, Americans were roused out of their complacency regarding their scientific, technological, and educational superiority. Congress rushed to pass the National Defense Education Act, whose primary purpose was to accelerate and improve the scientific education of America's most talented secondary students.

The Russian educational system, which was the object of so much discussion, comparison, and competition during this period, was and is characterized by enormous work demands and exceptionally high standards imposed on a very high percentage of their students. As this fact became widely known to the American people, they seized the *Sputnik* issue as a lever with which to pressure the American educational system to improve the quality of education for all children. America's educators responded by initiating curricular changes that attempted to supply what America's political leaders and people were demanding. Not only was the science and math curriculum strengthened, but also work demands and educational standards were raised for all students. America's students rose to the challenge presented by the more difficult curriculum by increasing their academic achievement.

THE EARLY 1960's TO THE MID-1970's

In 1964 the United States entered President Johnson's "Great Society" era. Coincidentally, academic achievement went into a sharp and massive decline nationwide. This decline has been so sharp and so widespread that it has not only wiped out the very substantial gains recorded during the post-*Sputnik* era, but it has also wiped out the significant improvement in reading-readiness skills recorded by preschool children after 1964. A renorming study comparing the 1964 and 1976 versions of the Metropolitan Readiness Tests indicates that over 80 percent of beginning first-grade students in 1974 had better reading-readiness skills than the average beginning first-grade student in 1964.[100] These gains disappear by fourth grade. The post-*Sputnik* gains disappear by ninth grade. By the time today's average student completes his secondary schooling, his reading, writing, and computational skills have developed no further than those of the average student in the early 1950's.

HIGH-SCHOOL GRADUATES

The most widely publicized evidence of the literacy decline of the past decade is the sharply declining scores on the Scholastic Aptitude Test (SAT), published by the Educational Testing Service (ETS) of Princeton, New Jersey, and administered by the College Entrance Examination Board (CEEB). This college admissions test is taken by approximately one-third of the high-school seniors nationwide, amounting recently to over a million students a year. The graph below shows the average score in each academic year from 1952 to 1977 for two measures, verbal and mathematical aptitude, for high-school seniors nationwide.[115]

This graph is very easy to interpret. The range of possible scores for an individual is from 200 to 800. When the scoring system for the test was devised in 1941, the average score for both verbal

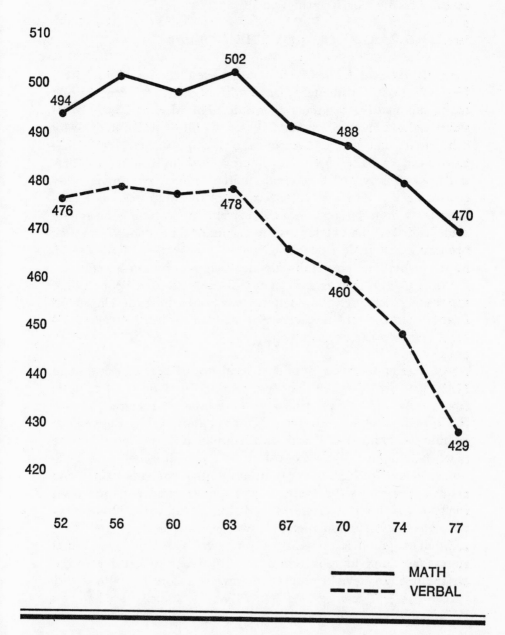

Graph 1

SAT SCORES, 1952 TO 1977

MATH

VERBAL

and math aptitude of the students taking the test in that year was set at 500. The test is designed so that although the language and questions are kept up to date, the same score recorded in two different years indicates the same level of skill.

The Educational Testing Service will not release data on the average scores or population composition of test takers between 1941 and 1952, because it claims that the composition of the test-taking population changed so drastically over this time period that score comparisons would be misleading. We do know that approximately 80,000 high-school seniors took the SAT in 1952, compared to only 11,000 students in 1941.[7,115] Their scores indicate no significant drop in math aptitude after 1941, but a drop in verbal aptitude of 24 points. The sharp increase in the number of students taking the test, combined with a sharply reduced high-school dropout rate over the same time interval, implies that the decline in the verbal-aptitude score should be attributed to a less selective test-taking population, rather than a general decline in verbal skills.

The pattern after 1952 is very clear in its message. Verbal and math aptitude vary somewhat over the next few years but show 2- and 8-point gains respectively by 1963. This increase took place despite a high-school dropout rate which declined from 40 to 30 percent, and despite a sharp increase in the percentage of high-school graduates taking the SAT, up from less than 7 percent in 1952 to approximately 30 percent in 1963.[165, 115] As both of these factors would tend to make the test-taking population significantly less selective, we can reasonably infer that America's high-school seniors significantly increased their academic achievement during this period.

Between 1963 and 1977 verbal- and math-aptitude scores dropped sharply, and at an accelerating rate. The drop in verbal aptitude averaged $2\frac{1}{2}$ points a year from 1963 to 1970, and $4\frac{1}{2}$ points a year from 1970 to 1977. Math aptitude dropped 2 points and $2\frac{1}{2}$ points a year over the same intervals. These declining scores are the harbinger of the first major skills decline in American educational history.

The SAT is a technically excellent educational test, and its continued development has occasioned very real contributions to the field of psychometry. Nonetheless, ETS investigated the possibility that the declining test scores could be attributed to test construction error which was making it more difficult to obtain high scores, or to changes in the composition of the test-taking population—perhaps a significant increase in the percentage of minority students or students from lower socioeconomic groups taking the test. The study of test construction error, completed in 1977, was actually the third such study. The first of these studies, completed in 1966, had demontrated that between 1941 and 1963 there had been no drift in scoring procedure.[143]

The second and third studies, however, indicated that there had been a scoring drift between 1963 and 1973, which had caused an 8- to 12-point error in both verbal and math scores, in the opposite direction of the one anticipated.[103, 115] Thus, the real drop in verbal aptitude between 1963 and 1977 was not 49 points, it was approximately 59 points, and the real drop in math aptitude was not the indicated 32 points, but 42 points. The 59-point drop in verbal aptitude means that 75 percent of the high-school seniors taking the test in 1977 scored below the average recorded in 1963.

The CEEB study of compositional changes in the test-taking population concluded that a significant portion of the score decline between 1963 and 1970 resulted from an increase in the percentage of poorer youths, minority students, women (who score sharply lower than men in math), and low-ability students taking the test.[115] The same study concluded that the compositional effects were only a minor factor in the much sharper score decline recorded after 1970. Since the available data demonstrate quite conclusively that the changes in the test-taking population between 1963 and 1970 were not nearly as great as similar changes between 1952 and 1963 (when SAT scores went up), I believe the CEEB report exaggerates their importance. During the 1970 to 1977 score decline, high-school dropout rates remained stable, the percentage of high-school graduates taking the SAT declined significantly, the percentage of minority students remained constant, and the average family income of SAT takers increased sharply. It is an inescapable conclusion that the level of academic achievement attained by America's high-school graduates declined materially betwen 1963 and 1970, and that this decline accelerated sharply between 1970 and 1977.

A score of 600 or better on the SAT is generally considered to indicate academic excellence. It is thus distressing to note that between 1966 and 1977, the only years for which data are available, the percentage of students scoring above 600 on the verbal part of the test declined 36 percent, and the percentage scoring above 700 declined 48 percent.[34,73] The corresponding declines on the mathematical aptitude section were 11 percent and 15 percent. Since the number of students taking the SAT remained relatively constant during this period, the effect of this trend was to sharply reduce the number of well-prepared students entering America's universities and colleges.

An interesting sidelight to this decline is showing up at the University of California. Prior to 1968, a student attending one of the campuses of the University of California was automatically exempted from remedial English composition, more familiarly known as "bonehead English," if he scored higher than 600 on the English achievement test, which is also produced by ETS and is similar to the verbal section of the SAT. Despite the fact that the cutoff score for exemption was reduced to 550 in 1968, the percentage of freshmen required to take this course increased from less than 35 percent in the early 1950's to well over 50 percent in the mid-1970's.[76] In August 1976, the University of California proposed abolishing "bonehead English" as a separate course and merging it with freshman English, which is required of all entering students. When a majority of students require remedial assistance, it is no longer labeled remedial.

Confirmation of the SAT trends comes from the American College Testing Program, which produces the second most widely used college admissions test, the ACT. Whereas the SAT takers are concentrated in the East, the almost one million students who take the ACT each year come primarily from the South, the Midwest, and the Far West. The ACT is composed of four academic subtests, English, math, social studies, and natural sciences. Data, available only since 1965, indicate that academic skills peaked in 1966 and have declined sharply since in English, math, and social studies.[52] The magnitude of the declines on these subtests is similar to the recorded declines on the SAT verbal and math subtests, and the percentage of high-school graduates taking the ACT also follows the pattern of the SAT.

The SAT and ACT data imply that the academic skills of today's high-school graduates lag far behind the skills of high-school graduates just ten to fifteen years ago. The data imply the same thing about today's college freshmen when compared to college freshmen of a dozen years ago. The percentage of high-school graduates and SAT takers going immediately on to college has increased slightly during the period of the test-score decline, implying that a higher percentage of less well prepared students is actually entering college. When the American College Testing Program conducted a study of the scores of ACT takers who actually enrolled in college, they found that the scores of enrolled students declined slightly more than the average ACT scores.[52]

Even the cream of the nation's students, its graduate students earning master's and doctoral degrees, recorded a sharp decline in academic skills over the past decade. Scores on the verbal and math subtests of the Graduate Record Exam, the graduate-school entrance exam published by ETS, show 37- and 22-point declines respectively between 1965 and 1975.[97] My experiences with graduate students with severe reading deficiencies, mentioned briefly in the Introduction, are apparently not unique.

ELEMENTARY AND SECONDARY STUDENTS

The SAT and ACT data provide us with a great deal of information about the academic competence of our nation's students when they complete their secondary schooling. As I stated at the beginning of this section, a renorming study of the Metropolitan Readiness Tests indicates that today's preschool children are far better prepared academically than were preschool children a dozen years ago. We can follow the pattern of academic achievement of America's students between preschool and graduation by examining the results of the Harcourt renorming study of the 1964 and 1973 versions of the Stanford Achievement Test.[139] Table 3 measures the decline in reading and math skills in grades one through eight over the indicated time period.

TABLE 3

DECLINE IN ACADEMIC ACHIEVEMENT,
1964 TO 1973
(Unit of measure is months of loss)

Grade	Reading	Math Computation
8	−8	−18
7	−5	−14
6	−7	−12
5	−4	− 9
4	−5	− 4
3	−4	− 2
2	+1	+ 4
1	+3	not available

According to the figures in this table, eighth-grade students in 1973 read about as well as seventh graders in 1964, and compute about as well as sixth graders at that time. Note that the achievement decline is reduced in the lower grades, and is actually an achievement increase in grades one and two. The table indicates that it takes three years before the gains recorded by preschool children are wiped out. Comparison of Tables 2 and 3 shows that by 1973 the post-*Sputnik* gains have been wiped out for all grade levels four through eight.

The pattern revealed in this renorming study has been uncovered in a number of other studies. Although the magnitude of the decline is usually less than in the Harcourt study, most studies of changes in academic achievement in the past fifteen years show improvement in grades one and two, and sometimes in grades three and four, and increasingly substantial declines in grades four and higher. A renorming study of the 1964 and 1971 versions of the

ITBS shows this pattern,[64] as does a renorming study of the 1968 and 1973 versions of the Comprehensive Tests of Basic Skills, published by McGraw-Hill.[165] The ITBS study indicates that the achievement decline has been as pronounced among high-ability students as among students of average ability.

It is interesting to note that the decline in academic skills seems also to have affected both Canada and England. A renorming study of a Canadian achievement test indicates that the skills of Canadian students deteriorated badly between 1968 and 1973, with the declines ranging from 1.5 months in third grade to 6.1 months in eighth grade.[78] A 1971 English study reports that academic skills peaked in 1964 after fifteen years of improvement, and declined the equivalent of several months between 1964 and 1970.[140]

A NATIONAL PATTERN

Many parents will be interested in data which trace the academic achievement of students in private school between 1934 and 1974.[25, 50] The data show that test scores of students in grades one through eight remain relatively stable to 1963. Slightly overlapping data for students in grades seven through twelve show a slight decline in test scores from the mid-1940's to the mid-1950's, followed by a sharp rise during the post-*Sputnik* period. From 1966 to 1974 first and second graders record small gains, third-grade scores remain stable, and students in the higher grades show progressively larger declines. A parent considering withdrawing his child from one of these private schools because of this information might consider the following fact: after ten years of declining test scores, the average student in one of the private schools in this study still scored about two grade levels above the national average in most subject areas.

It is very interesting to note that the pattern of change described above shows up in the records of virtually every state office of education that makes its data available for analysis. The most interesting records to me are those of California and Iowa—California because my teachers and I must struggle every day with the products of California schools, and Iowa because for over thirty-five years Iowa has possessed an extremely effective and honest system of educational evaluation.

Because the office of Superintendent of Public Instruction in California is an elective one, public education in California tends to be highly politicized. The results of the yearly statewide evaluation of academic achievement of California students are used as political ammunition in the various disputes surrounding public education in the state. Since the department and the Superintendent are always involved in educational and political controversy, and the statewide evaluations are conducted by the department under the Superintendent's supervision, a cynical observer might suspect that the data interpretation by the department might be slanted to make the department, and their boss, look good.

The California record shows a familiar pattern.[145] Second- and third-grade students record slow but steady improvement in their reading skills from 1966 through 1976. Sixth-grade students record sharp drops in most areas of academic achievement, including reading, from 1969 through 1973, after which their test scores increase slightly, although this latter trend must be interpreted with extreme caution as the achievement test used after 1973 is highly suspect. Twelfth graders record a precipitous drop from 1969 to 1976. The California data show the same pattern revealed by the ITBS renorming study: the achievement of above-average students is falling as fast or faster than the achievement of average or below-average students. Although the State Department of Education does not publish an analysis of achievement trends prior to 1969, careful examination of the available statistics indicates that the decline in sixth-grade scores actually started in 1963.

One of the problems in interpreting California data is that the State Department of Education has changed the tests mandated for local use four times in the past dozen years. Since it is difficult to compare scores achieved on different tests, these changes in test procedure make historical comparison of academic achievement of California students rather difficult. One never knows exactly what motivates these changes, but we do know that when California changed from the Stanford to the Cooperative reading test in 1970, its national percentile ranking jumped from 38 to 50, as a result of differences in the way the norms for the two tests were developed. The latest change, in spring, 1975, was to a very poor, locally developed test, which was not even constructed by professional psychometrists. The second- and third-grade levels of this test are identical, and the twelfth-grade level measures eighth-grade achievement. Since the test has not been nationally standardized, it is exceedingly difficult to obtain accurate comparisons of the achievement of California's students with students in the rest of the nation.

The California situation is especially interesting because the office of Superintendent of Public Instruction has been filled by two consecutive outspoken and highly political educators. Max Rafferty, the Superintendent from 1963 to 1970, is an extremely conservative educator who is a major proponent of the back-to-basics movement in education. He was defeated for reelection in 1970 by the incumbent Superintendent, Wilson Riles, a highly articulate liberal educator who has developed tremendous political influence in California and throughout the nation. Riles cites the improvement in test scores of second- and third-grade students as proof of the effectiveness of his policy of focusing an extra fifty to one hundred million dollars a year on students in grades one through three. He neglects to mention that the pattern of change in test scores in California is the same as the national pattern of change as described in the preceding pages, that it became firmly established under his predecessor, and that it probably has nothing to do with his policies whatsoever.

The Iowa situation stands in marked contrast to California. Iowa tests students in grades three through eight with the ITBS, and students in grades nine through twelve with the Iowa Tests of Educational Development (ITED), and has done so continuously for over thirty years. Although these tests are commercially published and widely used throughout the country, they were originally developed at the University of Iowa, which still supervises their administration to Iowa students. This has tended to keep politics out of educational evaluation in Iowa. Twenty continuous years of ITBS data are available, as are a dozen years of ITED data,[106] which gives us an opportunity to examine changes in academic achievement in an extremely stable population between 1955 and 1974.

I would expect most readers to be able to predict the pattern of change in academic skills over this time period. The academic skills of Iowa students in all grades climbed steadily between 1955 and 1965. From 1965 to 1974 third-grade students recorded small gains in reading and math computation. Students in fourth grade and above recorded declines in all skills tested after 1965, and the decline accelerated after 1970. Students in the higher grades recorded significantly greater declines than students in the lower grades. Eighth-grade students recorded a gain of 5.0 months in reading and 5.5 months in math computation between 1955 and 1965, and then lost 5.5 and 7.3 months respectively between 1965 and 1975.

In March of 1975 the Adult Performance Level (APL) study, mentioned in the Introduction, was published at the University of Texas.[114] Its authors had conducted a unique investigation into the functional literacy of American adults, by testing thousands of adults with tasks designed to determine if they could function in modern society. The researchers discovered that over twenty million adult Americans, about 20 percent of the adult population, were functionally incompetent. These individuals could not perform the simplest societally required tasks, such as reading a want ad or a W-2 form, addressing an envelope, or calculating the change due on a purchase of a specified amount. Another 34 percent of the adult population, about 39 million adults, were found to be barely functional in these basic skills.

During the period after the report's publication, public discussion included such facts as that 11 percent of the nation's high-school graduates were functionally incompetent, and another 37 percent barely competent, while corresponding figures for college graduates were 2 percent and 17 percent. However, one key fact uncovered by the report was discussed hardly at all. In analyzing the levels of functional competence of different age groups in the adult population, the researchers discovered that the age group 30–39 was much more competent than any other group, and that the literacy characteristics of the groups 18–29 and 40–49 were very similar. This means that the group of adults who completed (or would have completed if they had not dropped out) twelfth grade between 1964 and 1975 had a much higher rate of functional incompetency than the group who completed their secondary schooling between 1954 and

1963, and about the same rate as the group completing school between 1944 and 1953. These figures support my estimate that the average level of academic achievement of today's students has deteriorated to the level achieved by students in the early 1950's.

Another series of studies confirming the indicated pattern of decline has recently been reported by the National Assessment of Educational Progress (NAEP), a federally funded project attempting to measure changes in academic achievement in several subject areas.[108] In a 1976 study, NAEP found that fourth-grade students improved their reading skills from 1971 to 1975. The study also found that the reading skills of eighth and twelfth graders remained relatively stable over the time period, although both groups recorded a small decline on test items that measured advanced comprehension skills. In a 1975 study, NAEP reported that the writing skills of fourth graders improved between 1969 and 1974, but the writing skills of eighth and twelfth graders declined over the same time period. A 1974 NAEP study reported a sharp drop-off in the science knowledge of students at all three grade levels between 1970 and 1973. Finally, NAEP reported devastating declines between 1969 and 1976 in the knowledge of eighth and twelfth graders regarding American government and political processes.

In the study mentioned previously, Dr. Farr attempted to obtain recent achievement data from all 50 states and from 100 of the largest public-school districts in the country. Some of the problems associated with this kind of research are evident in the response statistics he reports. Of the 100 public school districts, only 45 responded to his repeated requests for information. Forty of these reported that they did testing, but only 12 of them sent him the achievement scores he requested. Only 6 of the 12 districts volunteering data reported scores over at least a four-year period. Only 17 of the 50 states sent Farr the statistics he requested, and only 8 of the states reported scores over at least a three-year period. Farr remarks that the scores he reports may appear more positive than a representative sample would have shown, because some school districts and states may have been so worried about adverse criticism that they did not provide data which indicated declining achievement.

In order to obtain achievement scores from the six districts that would cooperate, Farr had to promise not to publish their names. All we know is that the five largest of the six districts responding, including two serving cities over two million in population, reported steady declines between the mid-1960's and early 1970's. The smallest district, reporting almost unusable data, indicated no change over the time period.

I was able to obtain follow-up information from several of the eight states which disclosed their scores to Farr, as well as fairly complete information on high-school graduates in Minnesota.[106, 143, 163] Of these nine states, the New Hampshire scores stop in 1964 and indicate an increase from 1959 to that date, and the Iowa data have already been reported. Reports from the remaining states show that the previously indicated pattern of decline occurs in Minnesota, Ohio, Idaho, Hawaii, West Virginia, and New York. A peak of academic achievement was recorded in each of these states sometime during the mid-1960's, after which skills deteriorated at varying degrees of rapidity. The upper grades usually reported sharper declines than the lower grades. Only Alabama reported little change over this time period.

Interestingly, Dr. Farr has turned into one of the biggest apologists for our public schools. In this report and others, he tends to minimize the importance of the achievement decline. In reading his report, one is immediately struck by the fact that his figures and his conclusions are only tangentially related. His figures show significant and widespread declines during the past dozen years, yet in his conclusion he speaks only of a small and temporary drop-off in skills. Although his survey of the historical literature is excellent, his research of the recent period is inexcusably poor. He makes no reference to the ACT or SAT data, nor does he use any of the renorming studies published after 1960; indeed he states that he considers such reports to have little value. Yet he depends heavily on Gates's renorming study for his analysis of the pre-1960 period.

A study which deserves at least a brief mention was presented in the form of a series of articles in the August 1976 *Los Angeles Times*.[97] Education journalists Jack McMurdy and Ian Speich reported that thirteen of sixteen states which supplied them with usable data showed a definite downward trend at the late-elementary and secondary levels, while three showed small, short-term increases at several grade levels. They also reported that a similar proportion showed either no change or measurable improvement in grades one to three.

The final two studies which I will mention are historical studies of academic achievement, both of which make use of some of the information reported in this chapter, and both of which were published in the second half of 1975. The first report, by David Wiley of the University of Chicago and his associate Annegret Harnischfeger, is a quite useful technical analysis of some recent academic achievement data.[165] Wiley and Harnischfeger conclude that the academic skills of American students have deteriorated significantly during the past few years.

The second study is a rather speculative analysis by Frank Armbruster of The Hudson Institute.[8] Armbruster analyzes test scores from twenty-two states, most of which display the pattern reported by Farr, *i.e.*, the bulk of the information is worthless for historical comparisons, but the statistics which can be analyzed indicate a sharp decline in academic skills at the late-elementary and secondary levels. In his analysis of the New York State figures, Armbruster makes the interesting observation that students in rural areas, suburbs, and small cities are all experiencing a more rapid falloff in reading and math ability than students in New York City. This pattern reinforces the message of the ITBS renorming study and the California data, that the decline in academic achievement is not restricted to economically disadvantaged, low-ability students. Like other researchers, Armbruster concludes that academic skills have been deteriorating badly since the mid-1960's.

Some obvious questions are raised by the material presented in this chapter. What is the cause of the literacy decline? Why are skills up in the primary grades and down sharply thereafter? How do we reverse the trend of declining academic achievement?

2

FROM

MISS GRUNDY

TO

JOHNNY CARSON

IN RECENT YEARS THE CONVENTIONAL WISDOM REGARDING THE EF-
fects of public schooling has undergone a shift of almost 180
degrees. Until the 1960's, most educators assumed that twelve years
of formal schooling had such a powerful effect on a child's intellectual development that it completely overrode the influences of
his socioeconomic background. The publication of the Coleman
report in 1966 [33] and the subsequent reanalyses of its data by
Mosteller and Moynihan in 1972 [105] and Jencks et al. also in 1972 [75]
subjected the educational and intellectual communities to the influence of a radical and powerful concept, that the influences of a
child's family, socioeconomic class, and peer group were so potent
that twelve years of formal schooling had only a minimal effect on
his cognitive development. Largely as a result of the failure of compensatory education, discussed later in this chapter, this new view
of the comparative influence of school and nonschool factors had
become dominant among professional educators by the mid-1970's.

Like most violent swings of the educational pendulum, this one has swung quite far past the truth. In fact, careful study of the above-listed reports leads one to conclude that schooling does make a big difference in a child's intellectual development, but that its effects are modulated by nonschool factors. It is my perspective that three separate but related factors contribute to educational results: the innate ability of the student; the quality of support, encouragement, care, and training provided him by his family and the society at large; and the quality and quantity of his schooling. There is nothing in any of the above-listed studies to lead one to believe that a deterioration in the quality and quantity of schooling will not lead directly to a decline in academic achievement. Indeed, two recent studies by University of Chicago researcher David Wiley and associate Annegret Harnischfeger indicate that a decrease in the quantity of schooling results directly in a sharp deterioration in academic achievement.[164, 166]

The most likely explanation for the achievement decline cited in Chapter One is a reduction in the quantity and quality of education provided to America's young people over the past dozen years. The purpose of this chapter is to describe and analyze the curriculum changes of the past decade that have contributed directly to the achievement decline. My analysis is guided by a fundamental principle of education. In the domain of academic achievement, children tend to learn what they are taught. Conversely, in the same domain, children tend not to learn what they are not taught. Preschool and primary-grade children are learning more today because they are being taught more. Intermediate, secondary, and college students are learning less today because they are being taught less.

MONEY

The United States spends a lot of money on education. As a matter of fact, our total national education budget of well over 130 billion dollars in 1976–1977 is approximately as big as the rest of the world's education budget combined. To put this figure in perspective, note that in 1976, the total expenditures of the American public for automobiles were 72 billion dollars, the total sales of primary iron and steel by the American steel industry were 61 billion dollars, and the total expenditures of the Defense Department were 93 billion dollars.[120, 141]

The reader should note that the federal, state, and local figures reported in Table 4 represent only the money paid directly to schools.[39] They do not include such education expenditures as money for the G.I. bill, money for the training of government employees, or money spent by the military for teaching basic literacy. The total federal education budget in 1976 was 26.6 billion dollars, and the total state and local education budget was probably over 90 billion dollars. Nor do the figures in Table 4 include the estimated 100 billion dollars a year spent for training by private industry.[113] Thus, our real national education budget is probably double the 131-billion-dollar figure presented in the table.

The twenty-five-year spending trend exhibited in this table reflects the increased importance given to education in our national life. The total school-expenditures figures represent 3.4 percent of our GNP in 1950, 6.1 percent in 1964, and 7.9 percent in 1976.[39]

After taking inflation and the growth of the student population into account, we find that the average elementary and secondary student in 1977 received about two and a half times the amount of real-dollar services as a comparable student in 1950, and about one and a half times the amount of real-dollar services as a comparable student in 1964. What did we get in return for our increased educational investment?

PRESCHOOL

The first finding of Chapter One that requires analysis is the sharp improvement in reading-readiness scores recorded by preschool children between 1964 and 1974. The major finding of the 1976 renorming study of the Metropolitan Readiness Tests was that over 80 percent of the preschool children in 1974 scored above the average established by preschool children in 1964.

TABLE 4

EDUCATIONAL EXPENDITURES, 1950 TO 1977

	1949–1950	1963–1964	1976–1977
Average per pupil yearly expenditure (public schools)	$ 259	$ 559	$ 1,580 (1975–76)
Average classroom teacher's salary, in public elementary and secondary schools	$3,010	$5,995	$12,524 (1975–76)
Average elementary and secondary pupil/teacher ratio	28:1	26:1	20:1 (1975–76)
Total school expenditures, public and private, in billions of dollars			
Elementary and secondary	6.7	24.6	81.9
Higher education	2.1	11.3	49.2
Total	8.8	35.9	131.1
Source of income for school expenditures			
Federal		3.3	13.8
State	not	10.6	45.9
Local	available	12.7	37.4
Other		9.3	34.0
Total		35.9	131.1

The Metropolitan Readiness Tests measure the following abilities, which have been judged by reading experts to affect significantly the acquisition of basic reading and arithmetic skills: simple phonics, *i.e.*, knowing the sounds of letters; auditory discrimination, *i.e.*, the ability to hear differences and similarities in spoken words; visual discrimination, *i.e.*, the ability to see differences and similarities in printed words; listening skills, *i.e.*, the ability to understand simple material presented orally; quantitative skills, *i.e.*, knowledge of the numbers, counting ability, addition, subtraction, reasoning ability. The tests also include an optional copying exam, to test visual-motor coordination.[107]

How can we explain the enormous improvement in the scores of 1974 preschool children over comparable children in 1964 on a test composed of such items? The pedagogical principle introduced at the beginning of this chapter offers the most likely explanation. A much higher percentage of children in 1974 had been taught these items. Between 1964 and 1974 there was an enormous expansion of enrollment in preschool educational programs, and during the same period the character of preschool instruction changed to include much more overt academic training. Also during this period, the television show "Sesame Street" quite consciously attempted to teach children the basic reading-readiness skills.

Between 1964 and 1974, enrollment in preschool programs increased from 25 percent to 45 percent of the three- to five-year-old age group.[39] Three-year-olds increased their enrollment from 4 percent to 20 percent, four-year-olds from 15 percent to 38 percent, and five-year-olds from 58 percent to 79 percent. Most of the enrolled three- and four-year-olds were in private nursery schools, whereas most of the enrolled five-year-olds were in kindergarten. About 10 percent of the roughly four and a half million children enrolled in preschool programs were enrolled in Head Start, a federally funded educational program designed to raise the academic performance of economically disadvantaged preschool children.

Prior to the mid-1960's, the primary goal of preschool child care was the normal and healthy psychosocial development of young children, to be achieved through peer-group play and other guided play activities. Subsequent to this period, an increasing percentage of early-chlidhood education specialists recommended that a major goal of preschool education should be the accelerated academic development of young children. "Sesame Street" and Head Start, with their explicit educational goals, were concrete manifestations of this philosophical shift.

Reading- and arithmetic-readiness activities and materials have been infused into the kindergarten curriculum. All of the major elementary-school textbook publishers have produced special readiness programs to be used at the kindergarten level. Other educational firms have rushed to capitalize on the federal money available in this area for disadvantaged children, by producing a variety of toys, games, books, and gimmicks designed to help poor children develop readiness skills. Many of these and similar materials are now marketed directly to parents who want to accelerate their children's educational development. Private nursery schools have been quick to pick up these commercially published programs, materials, and games, and many of them use an educationally oriented curriculum as a major sales point in their advertising.

"Sesame Street" first came on the air in 1969, very rapidly capturing a major share of the preschool viewing audience. A recent study indicates that as many as half of all American children three to five years old watch the program regularly.[91] There is little doubt that the program increases the reading-readiness skills of viewing children. An ETS study showed that children who watch the program score considerably higher on readiness tests than comparable children who do not watch the program.[12]

I believe that the increased amount of educational instruction experienced by preschool children over the past dozen years explains the sharply raised scores on reading-readiness tests. I must caution the reader, however, that I consider some of this instruction, especially out-of-the-home group instruction, to be a mixed blessing for preschool children. While there is evidence that reading-readiness instruction in kindergarten can have long-term benefits if followed up by teachers in all subsequent grades,[95] the preponderance of recent research indicates that most of the gains experienced by preschool children in group educational programs disappear by the end of first or second grade. For example, the Ohio State-Westinghouse Learning Corporation study [162] of Head Start shows that participating children outscore their nonparticipating peers on reading-readiness tests prior to first grade, but that their peers catch up within one or two years. In his analysis of the long-term effectiveness of group preschool educational programs for disadvantaged children, Cornell's noted expert on early childhood education, Urie Bronfenbrenner, writes:

> Early intervention produces substantial gains in IQ as long as the program lasts. But the experimental groups do not continue to make gains when intervention continues beyond one year, and, what is more critical, the effects tend to "wash out" after intervention is terminated. The longer the follow-up, the more obvious the latter trend becomes.[23]

The noted reading authority George Spache, in a recent review of the pertinent literature, concludes that the long-term benefits of preschool reading instruction have not been established.[138] Another study on the same subject with a somewhat more aggressive message was recently published by Raymond Moore.[104] Moore contends that the short-term gains experienced by middle-class children in group preschool programs are outweighed by negative long-term effects. He suggests that out-of-the-home group preschool programs are hazardous to the long-term cognitive and emotional development of children, citing the cases of Hungary and Czechoslovakia, both of which have recently decided to cut back or eliminate their day-care programs for young children as a result of independent investigations which revealed that institutional care damages preschool children. Moore also cites a number of studies which show that students whose reading instruction is delayed until second grade need only a few years to catch up and surpass students whose reading instruction started in first grade. Interestingly, both Moore and Bronfenbrenner cite extensive research which shows that by sharply increasing the quality of maternal care, some children's IQ's can be permanently raised as much as 30 points.

I have raised the issue of the long-term effect of preschool educational programs because the pattern uncovered by researchers in this field is so similar to the pattern of change in academic achievement discussed in Chapter One, *i.e.*, sharp gains in readiness scores achieved by preschool children, which wash out within the first few years of school. I suspect that the patterns are similar because the same forces which cause the short-term cognitive gains to wash out in the early-childhood education experiments have caused the nationwide improvement in reading-readiness skills to wash out by fourth grade.

What are these forces? Moore suggests that unless a child has achieved adequate levels of maturation in the areas of vision, hearing, motor coordination, nervous system and cerebral cortex development, and social-emotional processes, institutional education is likely to cause serious mental and physical strain, which will show up later in retarded educational development. Other researchers, especially those in compensatory education, suggest that the washout of the educational gains is caused primarily by sociological factors, such as peer-group pressure, television, poor schooling, and inadequate educational reinforcement in the home. My own feeling is that out-of-the-home group preschool educational programs are not needed by most children, are damaging to some, and are probably helpful only to those children with physical or mental handicaps, or who come from disturbed or extremely deprived homes. The most effective way to foster a preschool child's intellectual and educational development is to ensure the high quality of his in-home experiences—verbal, educational, emotional, kinetic, and artistic.

ELEMENTARY SCHOOL

We know from Chapter One that the average level of academic achievement of first- and second-grade students increased from the early 1960's to the early 1970's. Over the same time interval, the achievement level of third-grade students probably increased slightly, while that of fourth graders held steady, although different studies report both small increases and small decreases for students in these two grades. Fifth- and sixth-grade students recorded a sharp deterioration in academic achievement over the time period, especially in computation and reading.

What caused the pattern of differential change? At least part, and probably a major part, of the increase recorded in grades one and two can be attributed to a carry-through of the gains in readiness skills discussed in the past few pages. The washout of these gains in grades three and four, and the substantial deterioration thereafter, must be interpreted in the light of curriculum changes in elementary education over the past dozen years.

The past decade has witnessed a bewildering number of innovations in elementary education. These include team teaching, open-space schools, open classes, heterogeneous grouping, nongraded classes, student tutors, closed-circuit television, teaching machines, computer-assisted instruction, individualized instruction, extensive use of teacher aides, the new math, increased phonics in the major reading textbooks, and the abandonment of reading textbooks by a significant percentage of primary-grade teachers. Probably the easiest way to make sense of these changes is to interpret them in terms of the basic shift in educational philosophy that has occurred in elementary education since the early 1960's.

While a philosophic shift was changing much of the focus of preschool education from the emotional development of children to their intellectual development, a reverse shift was occurring in elementary education. The primary goals of elementary education—teaching young children reading, writing, computing, citizenship, and basic subject matter—were replaced with a combination of psychological goals and restructured intellectual goals. The psychological goals included the development and maintenance of self-esteem, enthusiasm for life and learning, and independent judgment. The new cognitive goals included creativity, intellectual open-mindedness, and the mastery of the concepts that underlay traditional subject matter. Mastery of the basic skills was retained as an important goal, but curriculum and teaching methodology that were seen to be in conflict with the new psychological and intellectual goals were either abandoned or restructured.

Certain practices that had been common in the past, such as rote memorization of facts and the kind of repetitive drill used in teaching the multiplication table, were felt to be especially inhibiting to the achievement of the new psychological and cognitive goals. The goal of the new math was to teach children the concepts underlying the basic arithmetic operations. The goal of the new science curriculum was to teach children how to think like scientists. The goal of the new curriculum was to encourage each child to think for himself, to set his own learning goals, to pace his own learning activities, and to experience repeated success. The new curriculum attempted to do away with competitiveness, to meet the needs of each individual child, and to structure the school day so that each child's energy, basic curiosity, and zest for life were permitted expression and fulfillment. Virtually all of the curricular changes cataloged at the beginning of this section were developed to accomplish these new goals.

The problem with the new curriculum was that it did not include enough teaching. Recent research implies that the curricular reforms of the past dozen years led directly to the achievement decline experienced by late-elementary school students. Furthermore, there is no evidence of compensating gains in the areas of self-esteem, creativity, anxiety reduction, and general psychological health. As lovely as the goals of the new curriculum sound, it is impossible to escape from the reality of the pedagogical principle with which I started this chapter. The new curriculum sacrificed too much teacher direction, teacher input, and teacher discipline. One of the most serious charges that can be leveled against America's educational leaders is that they encouraged the implementation of wholesale curricular reform before the reforms had been proven successful, and, in many cases, before they had even been tested. What is perhaps even worse, when they were given several billion dollars to develop and test new educational programs, their experiments did not even approach compliance with basic principles of educational research.

BEGINNING READING INSTRUCTION

There have been several widely adopted changes in beginning reading instruction during the past decade. One of these has been the widespread use of commercially published individualized programs, which will be discussed shortly. A second is an entire constellation of changes associated with federally funded compensatory education, which will be described later in the chapter. The third change is distinctly positive, and probably has contributed to the increased reading ability of primary-grade students. This change is the sharply increased amount of phonics in the primary-grade reading textbooks (called basal reading series) published by all of the major publishers. This change was at least partially induced by the public response to Rudolf Flesch's book, *Why Johnny Can't Read,* which accused America's educational leaders of abandoning an effective phonics method of beginning reading instruction in favor of the ineffective whole-word or look-say approach.[54] When follow-up research in the 1960's substantiated some of Flesch's claims,[27, 152] all of the major publishers significantly increased the phonics content of their basal readers.

Another change in beginning reading instruction was symptomatic of the times that produced it. The hostility toward institutional authority which characterized American education in the late 1960's was manifested in a movement against the use of all commercially published basal readers. The sociological charges leveled against these readers included allegations that they were racist and sexist and that they promoted an uncritical acceptance of middle-class American values. The educational charges included Flesch's complaints, assertions that they were boring and unmotivating, and claims that their vocabulary level was so low and the reading passages so simplified that they couldn't possibly accomplish their purpose. While some of the critics wanted the readers improved, others recommended they be completely replaced with a variety of suggested methods and materials. One such critic was Herbert Kohl, whose book *Reading, How To,* purported to teach anyone how to teach reading to children of any age and any socioeconomic background.[84]

Some of the complaints about basal readers are justified, but generally speaking they do excellently the job they are designed to do. They provide a complete program for student *and teacher,* for teaching the several hundred items and basic skills necessary in beginning reading instruction. These skills include the sounds of the letters, a basic sight vocabulary of several hundred words, the sounds and meanings of endings, prefixes, roots, and suffixes, proper interpretation of punctuation, and a host of others. The publishers who develop these basal readers are extremely careful to introduce all of the skill components in the correct order, and to provide the necessary review.

If a teacher is highly trained and experienced, there is no doubt that he can teach beginning reading effectively without basal readers. However, the majority of teachers attracted to the type of undisciplined counter-culture approach recommended by Kohl and others of his ilk are neither highly trained nor experienced. The danger in the present situation is that many school administrators permit their teachers to use any method they prefer. While it is impossible to estimate the number of teachers who have abandoned basal readers in the past ten years, the movement away from basal readers by untrained and unqualified teachers is sufficiently dangerous to warrant corrective action on the part of elementary-school administrators.

THE NEW MATH

The new math was an attempt to teach students the basic concepts underlying mathematics, and in so doing to teach them to think mathematically. Promoters of the new math promised that improved understanding of mathematical concepts and processes would lead to better computational skills. As one who has undergone a great deal of training in this field, and who loves mathematics, I am extremely sympathetic to these goals. However, program selection in education must be based on an evaluation of student outcomes, not curricular goals. On this basis the new math has been an unmitigated disaster for America's students. It was introduced nationwide before it had been adequately tested, and its principal effect was an immediate falloff in computational skills among children subjected to it. The ensuing brouhaha involving parents, teachers, administrators, and various curriculum experts resulted in a wide variety of attempts to modify the math curriculum so as to retain the new math but increase computational ability. In my opinion, the resulting chaos contributed even further to the massive decline in computation skills reported in Chapter One.

There were three serious problems with the new math. The first was that it was not based on sound pedagogical principles. The new math attempted to replace rote memorization with conceptual understanding, and thus eliminated a great deal of repetitive drill from the math curriculum. Its developers failed to realize that repetitive drill and memorization of basic facts result in the ability to gain immediate and automatic access to certain basic stored information, an ability which is the basis of any skill. Its developers also committed a basic error in requiring young children to learn the theoretical basis of a simple skill before mastering the skill itself. Finally, research by Piaget implies that the level of intellectual development required for the mastery of basic mathematical concepts does not occur in most children before fifth or sixth grade, yet the new math was introduced in the primary grades.[118]

The second problem would have guaranteed the failure of the new math even if the first problem had not existed. The overwhelming majority of elementary-school teachers have had inadequate training in mathematics, and thus did not understand what they were expected to teach. A program that attempts to transmit knowledge not possessed by the teacher is doomed to fail. As this fact became clear to curriculum directors and textbook publishers across the country, they compounded their error by attempting to make the new math teacher-proof. This involved developing self-explanatory materials and mechanical, repetitive techniques which were based on underlying mathematical principles. Unfortunately, the new techniques were far more complicated than the old ones had been, the teachers still didn't understand what was going on, and an entire generation did not learn how to compute.

The third problem was an analogue of the second. Parents did not understand the new math, and were thus unable to help their children, as they had in the past. How many elementary-school pupils will struggle to learn something neither their teachers nor parents really understand?

Indicative of the weakness in our current method of mathematics instruction was a report comparing the math achievement of Vietnamese refugee children with white, middle-class children in San Diego in 1975, shortly after the end of the Vietnam War.[153] According to this report, these lower-middle-class refugee children, products of Vietnamese public schools which averaged seventy-five pupils per class, scored in the ninety-third percentile in mathematics achievement. Their middle-class American peers scored in the twenty-ninth percentile on the same nationally standardized math tests.

A friend of mine is an evaluation expert for one of the major textbook publishing companies. About ten years ago the company developed a new math series for sale to the State of California. The evaluation people within the company argued fiercely with the textbook people that children using the series would be crippled in their acquisition of computational skills. They were overruled, the books were widely used by California (which tends to be attracted to the latest educational fad), and, sure enough, my friend's evaluations show that school districts that use the series experienced a sharp decline in computation skills. (For a fascinating inside view of the new math, read Interview 12.)

OPEN EDUCATION

The open education movement has been one of the most powerful forces in elementary education during the past decade. The philosophy of open education stresses the psychological and cognitive goals listed at the beginning of this section, and provides a blueprint for classroom organization and procedure which is designed to promote their achievement. This blueprint includes the following major points: children are to be permitted to study the things that interest them, virtually whenever they want to do so; a wide variety of learning activities are to be made available to students within the classroom; during their learning activities children may move freely around the classroom, interacting with other students as they desire; the teacher is to behave in a democratic, nonmanipulative, warm, and respectful way toward his students, providing them with pleasant and enjoyable educational experiences.

This pattern of classroom organization is usually contrasted with the traditional pattern of organization, characterized by firm teacher direction of student learning, no student freedom of movement or discourse, education of the whole class together or in no more than a few distinct subgroups, and a rigid organization of classroom time and space. The past ten years have witnessed a decided shift away from the traditional and toward the open form of classroom organization.

The open-education movement in the United States was greatly influenced by a similar movement in British elementary education and by the popular writings of a number of extremely liberal educators, including A. S. Neill, Charles Silberman, Jonathan Kozol, Ivan Illich, John Holt, Herbert Kohl, James Herndon, Neil Postman and Charles Weingartner, and George Dennison. The 1960's opened with the publication of A. S. Neill's *Summerhill: A Radical Experiment in Child Rearing*, which is still today the educational bible of the counter culture.[110] This book describes the operation of Neill's private British school, Summerhill, which catered primarily to students with a history of discipline problems. Neill used his book to promote the principles of what came to be known as the free-school movement, including complete democracy between students and teachers, total freedom for students (including the freedom not to attend classes), abolition of tests and grading, and a general denigration of scholarship and intellectual training in favor of creativity and self-directed play.

Neill's book has had a tremendous influence in the United States, spawning hundreds of free schools around the country. I have had the opportunity to observe a number of these schools in operation, and have worked with many students who have gone through them. It is my experience that many children who attend these schools are not taught their basic skills adequately, nor are they taught any significant body of organized intellectual knowledge. Many of the students coming out of these schools are intellecutally crippled for life.[168] Indeed, Neill himself became so concerned about the damage his followers were doing that he wrote a sequel to *Summerhill* entitled *Freedom—Not License!*, in which he urged free-school teachers not to confuse educational democracy with educational anarchy.[111] Unfortunately, his second book was not as influential as his first.

Whereas Neill, Kozol, Dennison, and Illich advocate abandoning the public schools in favor of "free," "alternative" educational institutions, a more influential group of educators has advocated that free-school methods and philosophy (open education) be incorporated into the public schools. The most prominent of this second group is journalist Charles Silberman, whose book *Crisis in the Classroom: The Remaking of American Education* lavishly praised both the progressive wing of British elementary education and the open-education movement in the United States.[135] Silberman's book, elegantly written, funded with $300,000 of Carnegie Commission money and carrying with it the prestige of that organization, is one of the most damaging pieces of educational writing to have been published in the past twenty years. It is damaging because the prestige of the Carnegie Commission created an aura of acceptability, even inevitability, about a number of Silberman's proposals which have proven to be extremely detrimental to academic achievement. These include some of the basic guidelines for the open-classroom system of organization, and a number of suggestions for modifying the secondary curriculum, which, unfortunately, as the next section of this chapter indicates, have been widely adopted.

The most influential of the other educators writing in this area are John Holt and Herbert Kohl. Holt's first book, *How Children Fail*, was a perceptive analysis of the anxiety created in children by traditional forms of classroom organization and procedure.[67] Its major weakness, a weakness that became increasingly obvious in Holt's subsequent writing, was that he was unable to suggest either workable reforms or viable alternatives to the system he criticized so harshly. Kohl's first book, *36 Children*, was one of the first books to demonstrate the inadequacy of the education available in most inner-city schools.[82] His subsequent writing deteriorated badly, and his 1969 book on open education, *The Open Classroom*, is a hostile, rebellious, and damaging work in which he consciously demonstrates to teachers how they can abrogate their authority in every conceivable kind of classroom.[83]

A 1976 British study,[18] comparing the effects of the progressive education Silberman praised so lavishly with more traditional methods, shows quite conclusively that the traditional method produces greater academic achievement. The book's author, Neville Bennett, approached his four-year study with an admitted prejudice in favor of open education. He found to his surprise that traditional methods produced greater learning in every variable tested. These included not only reading, arithmetic, and English, where the gains ranged from three to five months over the course of a single year, but also such areas as imaginative use of language and creative writing.

Bennett also discovered that certain groups did especially poorly in open classes, and conversely exceptionally well in traditional classes. High-achieving students performed better than expected in traditional classes, and worse than expected in open classes. The same was true of students who were anxious about school. Bennett found that all students engaged in much more work activity and much less pupil interaction in traditional classes. This was especially evident in the two groups cited above, and also among low-achieving students. He found, for instance, that anxious students engaged in four times as much work activity in traditional as in open classes, and in the latter they tended to gossip, gaze into space, and engage in negative behavior.

Bennett did find one teacher who used the open-education approach yet whose students made excellent academic progress. In examining this particular case, he discovered that this teacher devoted as much time to teaching math, reading, and English as the traditional teachers, and that her teaching was clearly structured and ordered.

Bennett's conclusion is a direct analogue of the principle with which I started this chapter. He concludes that students tend to learn more when they do more schoolwork, and that they also tend to learn more if their teacher clearly structures and orders their learning activities. I must say that I find it somewhat odd that it requires a four-year study to arrive at this conclusion. What is even stranger is that Bennett's conclusion stands in sharp contrast to the dominant ideas in American elementary education.

A 1977 U.S. Office of Education study confirms Bennett's findings.[142] This report analyzes the effectiveness of different kinds of instructional programs with disadvantaged children. The study found that highly structured programs which emphasize basic skills are much more successful than other types of programs in helping disadvantaged children develop these skills, and also much more sucessful in helping these children develop self-esteem and a good self-concept. Open-education programs tend to produce poor results in both areas, although a few teachers are able successfully to use open-education methods. I believe an objective reading of the available research supports the following general conclusions: for the average teacher, traditional methods produce better results than open methods; it takes an exceptionally talented, organized, and experienced teacher to produce good results with open methods, but it can be done.

Open education has caused a certain amount of the deterioration in academic skills experienced by late-elementary school students during the past dozen years. In its concern for children's short-term enjoyment, it sacrifices too much teaching, and in so doing jeopardizes their long-term educational development. Open-education advocates have missed the following point entirely: it is the learning of socially useful skills which builds a good self-image and a feeling of independence; letting children do as they please and telling them how important and good they are do not create these feelings.

Probably the most destructive effect of the open-education movement has been its impact on the training of new teachers. A friend of mine who is a professor of education at a California university recently refused to certify one of his graduate students with a teaching credential until she passed an eighth-grade-equivalency spelling test. The young woman was doing her practice teaching with third-grade students, and the professor had noticed that she misspelled many third-grade spelling words on the board. Her response to the professor's demand was to file a grievance procedure with the university, alleging prejudice, demeaning behavior, and unprofessional conduct on the part of the professor.

When I told this story to the director of my Berkeley Institute, he countered with the story of one of his students. It seems that this youngster's teacher had marked only two answers wrong on a twenty-five-problem math assignment, although thirteen of the answers were incorrect. When the student's father challenged the teacher on this incident and numerous similar ones, the teacher had very aggressively argued, "Don't correct him, you'll turn him off." In an analogous incident, a young elementary-school teacher responded to my criticism of her terrible spelling by asserting that her deficiency was "a plus factor for my students, because it forces them to develop dictionary skills and an attitude of self-reliance."

What characterizes each of these stories, and hundreds of similar ones I have heard over the past few years, is the aggressiveness with which these teachers defend their sloppy and inadequate teaching. While bad teaching has always been with us, it has rarely been so aggressive in its own defense. I am afraid that for many of its practitioners, the open-education philosophy is little more than incompetence masquerading as ideology.

Despite its primarily negative impact, the open-education movement has made two contributions which I hope will be with us after its other excesses have long since disappeared. First is a focus on the necessity for teacher kindness. While this focus has been so extreme it has bordered on the insipid, it provides a quite valuable contrast to some practices which were unabashedly cruel and vicious. In my opinion, teacher discipline and direction are essential to education, but cruelty is antithetical to it.

The second contribution is a recognition that physical mobility is a necessary component in the lives of young children. In my opinion, it is ludicrous to expect a child of six or seven to sit still for six hours a day. While the open-education philosophy permitting unrestricted physical movement and social interaction clearly leads to classroom chaos, this contribution should not be totally dismissed. An effective compromise could be alternating periods in the day, including several in which all of the students were working at their desks at teacher-directed tasks, and several which permitted student mobility, some in organized-play activities, perhaps some in the type of student-directed learning activity which characterizes open education. This pattern of curricular organization would be gradually replaced by the more traditional pattern over the first four years of school, since by fourth grade children have much longer attention spans and do not need to move around nearly as much.

FORMAL SYSTEMS OF INDIVIDUALIZED INSTRUCTION

The remaining major curricular reform of the past decade was the wide adoption of various formal systems of individualized instruction. The systems are sequentially organized packets of teaching materials in various subjects and skill areas. Each packet represents one learning stage in a particular skill. Students are supposed to master each packet under their teacher's supervision before proceeding to the next. By monitoring the student's performance at each learning stage, the teacher is supposed to ensure that every student properly masters each stage of skill development before proceeding to the next. These systems are self-paced, which means that although all of the students go through all of the lessons in the same order, each student goes through at his own pace.

These systems have a number of theoretical advantages. They should ensure that slow students are not pushed so fast that they skip essential stages of learning, and that fast students are not compelled to go so slowly that they become bored. The programs are supposed to promote the mastery of skill and subject matter, and are supposed to reach every student. Finally, because the primary agent of instruction is the individual who develops the self-paced materials, students supposedly experience the advantage of expert instruction.

From the plethora of *should's* and *supposed to's* in the preceding paragraph, the reader can probably surmise that I do not believe these programs fulfill the promises of their promoters. My experiences with them have convinced me that the formal programs of individualized instruction currently in use suffer from a number of very serious practical and theoretical drawbacks. The most obvious of these, to anyone who has observed a number of classes being taught with one of these systems, is the state of near chaos they so frequently seem to engender. The systems provide few mechanisms for teacher control or supervision of student behavior. At any given moment every student in the room may be engaged in an entirely different activity. The teacher cannot know whether each student is proceeding properly with his learning activity, or merely socializing with another student.

I have witnessed many classrooms in which the mode of instruction was individualized instruction, which were enveloped in such total anarchy that very little learning was taking place. The possibility that students might prefer to run wild rather than learn in a solitary, self-disciplined manner was apparently not anticipated by the designers of these systems, but that possibility should certainly not surprise anyone who can remember his own early school years.

The most serious weakness of these systems is what they do to the teacher. He becomes little more than the overseer of a process in which he hardly participates. Even his title reflects this role change, as many of these systems refer to the teacher as facilitator, coordinator, or manager. I believe that young children learn better if they are taught by a good, sensitive, and responsive teacher, than if they are taught by supposedly teacher-proof materials in a learning system that has relegated the teacher to a managerial position in the educational process. I am convinced that children need the emotional contact with a responsive human being in order to learn.

On a theoretical level, the systems of individualized instruction seem to be based on an atomistic or behavioristic psychology of learning, which holds that the way to teach a skill is to teach its component parts one at a time. Most teachers, on the other hand, believe in a cognitive psychology of learning, which holds that children learn best through generalizations and principles that communicate the mature skill to be mastered, supported by extensive practice in its component parts. For most skills, including reading, I side with the teachers.

Like most of the other major innovations of the past dozen years, the formal systems of individualized instruction were implemented without adequate prior evaluation. The situation in California is a case in point. In 1973 the State Department of Education adopted regulations which virtually forced school districts receiving federal or state compensatory money to institute these programs in the primary grades.[2] These regulations were the bureaucratic interpretation of a state law passed the previous year, which in large part was motivated by a State Department of Education task-force report on early-childhood education, a report which did not even investigate the impact of such programs on educationally disadvantaged youngsters.[20, 43a] The pandemonium resulting from the introduction of these formal systems of individualized instruction into volatile, hard-to-control, inner-city schools has been an educational tragedy of the first magnitude.

In a 1976 report on the effects of educational innovation, the American Institutes of Research (AIR) found that the degree of innovation tended to be negatively correlated with reading and math achievement.[71] One of the major findings of this report was that the degree of formal individualization of instruction also tended to be negatively correlated with reading and math achievement. (On a more positive note, the AIR study found that the reading achievement of primary-grade students was positively correlated with the amount of time devoted to reading instruction, verifying David Wiley's reports cited at the beginning of the chapter.)

One of the nation's leading authorities on educational evaluation, Michael Scriven, has recently expressed his skepticism regarding the validity of most evaluations of the formal programs of individualized instruction.[131] Scriven argues that as a result of inadequately designed evaluations, we simply do not know how effective these programs are. He also argues that their development costs, which are borne by the public in the form of federal grants to program developers, are very high, and their purchase price is much higher than that of traditional programs. Furthermore, their administrative complexity requires the use of a teacher aide (usually salaried) in every classroom in which one of these programs is implemented. Scriven is neither for nor against individualized instruction. He is just pleading for more careful educational evaluation and cost analysis prior to program adoption and implementation.

It almost goes without saying that I have cited Scriven's remarks to back up my concern that we are subjecting American children to a bewildering variety of educational innovations without adequate prior evaluation. Except for the increased amount of phonics in basal readers, each of the educational innovations discussed in this section was adopted without proof of its educational effectiveness. Furthermore, I believe that each of these untested innovations has contributed to the decline in academic skills recorded by late-elementary school students over the past dozen years. The material presented in this section points up the need for a system of educational evaluation that will permit a determination of program effectiveness prior to decisions regarding program implementation.

JUNIOR AND SENIOR HIGH SCHOOL

The achievement decline of the past dozen years has been most pronounced at the secondary level. The reading, writing, and computing skills of America's secondary-school students have dropped sharply in virtually every section of the country. By junior high school the declines in reading and math skills measure from one to two years. At the end point of the public schooling process, high-school graduation, only about a quarter of our nation's students are as academically well-prepared as the average student of a dozen years ago.

After two years of investigation I am convinced that the single most important factor in the massive falloff in academic skills is the deterioration of the secondary-school curriculum. The pedagogical principle on which I have based my curriculum analysis is tragically applicable at the secondary-school level. Students do not know as much when they complete their secondary schooling because they have not been taught as much. Two factors enter into this. First, enrollment in rigorous, academic subject matter is sharply off. As a percentage of their course work, students are taking much less science, math, English, and history. Second, in the academic classes students do take, the amount of work assigned and the standard to which it is held have deteriorated badly. The writing skills of today's students have deteriorated because their teachers assign much less discursive writing. Their reading skills are weaker for the analogous reason, and also because the reading that is assigned is written at a much simpler level.

The curricular changes which occurred at the secondary level are most easily interpreted in light of their social and historical milieu. In the early 1960's, the schools were reaping the harvest from the curricular toughening induced by the post-*Sputnik* concern for academic rigor. Courses were demanding, standards were high, and parents, students, teachers, and administrators were relatively unanimous about the goals of the educational process. Many of the secondary-school teachers were veterans of World War II or Korea, or were long-term career teachers. They were highly mature and experienced, and believed firmly in high academic standards, heavy work demands, and classroom discipline.

The postwar baby boom exploded into our junior and senior high schools in the 1960's. High-school enrollment went from nine and a half million in 1959 to fourteen and a half million just ten years later.[39] In order to meet the expanded enrollment, the number of high-school teachers was increased from 575,000 to 960,000 over the same time period. These new teachers were the first generation of public-school teachers in the United States who were a product of the Affluent Society. They had experienced neither economic depression nor war, and indeed were themselves subject to many of the influences that affected their students in the late 1960's. The stage was set for an academic tragedy of historic proportions, as the nation's high-school faculty, about half of whom were young and immature, prepared to meet the largest generation of high-school students in American history.

Sparked by Vietnam, the assassination of the Kennedys and Martin Luther King, and the legitimatizing of civil protest and civil disobedience in the antiwar and civil-rights movements, the youth rebellion started in the middle 1960's. The most important and most ignored factors causing the youth rebellion were the exploding population of adolescents which fueled it, and the sharply decreased ratio of mature, authoritative adults to adolescents, which might have been able to control it. The result of the social and population factors was an almost uncontrollable psychological revolt against authority by America's young people.

In the nation's high schools, youth's revolt against authority was manifested in demands for student control of the educational process, including curriculum control. Demands were made to make course work more relevant, by replacing history with current events, biology with ecology, British, American, and world literature with contemporary literature, social studies with psychology and sociology, reading with group discussion, and term papers with group projects. These changes were resisted by the older faculty for several years.

By virtue of their increasing numbers, the younger faculty assumed a position of influence, even dominance in many schools, by the late 1960's. Generally speaking they sympathized with the rebelliousness of their students and considered the standards of the older faculty to be outmoded and irrelevant. In addition to the fact that they were a product of the same social environment and influenced by many of the same factors as their students, the younger faculty were heavily influenced by the writings of the liberal educators briefly discussed in the previous section.

By the early 1970's the curriculum reforms demanded by students, younger faculty, and liberal educators were instituted wholesale, without, of course, any attempt to determine the effect of these changes on academic achievement. The new high-school curriculum is a smorgasbord of unrelated courses. The curriculum of virtually every academic department has fragmented. In many schools students are no longer required to take six sequential semesters of English. Instead, they may choose such courses as composition, American literature, or British literature, or, if they prefer, film appreciation, feminist literature, or science fiction. Previously mandatory one- or two-year surveys of American or world history have disappeared or become optional. Even attendance is now optional for eleventh- and twelfth-grade students, as many schools permit and even encourage their juniors and seniors to attend school half a day and work at some part-time job the other half.

The new high-school curriculum has attempted to accommodate to students' immediately perceived concerns. We have replaced items of long-term educational value with items of short-term interest and entertainment value. We have replaced Miss Grundy with Johnny Carson, and America's young people will pay for this change the rest of their lives.

READABILITY

Readability is the analysis of written material to determine its level of vocabulary and syntactic difficulty. A number of years ago, reading experts, textbook publishers, and curriculum experts reached a consensus regarding the level of vocabulary and complexity of written material that should constitute the standard for each grade level. Thus, a readability analysis of a textbook will produce a grade-level score, which will estimate the grade level the book is good for.

When marketing a textbook to schools, publishers almost always indicate the readability level of the text. When a teacher refers to a book as having been written at the sixth-grade level, he means that its readability level, as determined by the publisher, is sixth grade. In calculating readability, most publishers use a simplified formula which takes only two factors into account, average sentence length and the percentage of words in the text unknown to most fourth graders.[36] Because the calculations do not take the subject matter of the material or the individual interests of potential readers into account, the publisher's readability level can only be taken as a rather gross estimate. For instance, the readability level of this book is about 14, which implies that a person needs to read at a college level to be able to comprehend it. Clearly, however, such is not the case. Someone who is interested in the subject matter of this book who reads at a high-school level can read the book with adequate comprehension if he wants to do so, provided he is willing to apply a certain amount of time and effort to the task.

Readability is one of those technical subjects that would not normally be of interest to most parents. Unfortunately, one of the most widespread movements in public education today requires that the subject be brought into the arena of public discussion. Over the past ten years, most of the major textbook publishers have instituted a conscious policy of rewriting their textbooks in order to reduce their readability to a level two years below the grade for which they are intended. Thus, eleventh-grade American history books are being rewritten to a ninth-grade level, and twelfth-grade American government texts are being rewritten to a tenth-grade level. This movement to reduce the readability levels of textbooks is widely known and accepted among secondary-school teachers and administrators, yet most parents have not been informed of it.

The following letter from Anne Thomas, social-science editor at Ginn and Company, one of the largest textbook publishing companies in the nation, is representative of the correspondence I have in my files from the major publishing companies.

Ginn and Company

April 10, 1975

Dear Mr. Copperman:

With the exception of the effort to advance studies in the period after Sputnik, the history of reading level in American textbooks has been a constant spiraling downward. Listed below are Ginn's history texts considered most popular for the periods which you query.

TWENTY YEARS AGO—From the early 1900s until the 1950s Ginn's most popular history text was *A History of Our Country* by David Saville Muzzey. The reading level of that edition is 14.9, and is based on sentence length.

TEN YEARS AGO—In the 1960s the above book was revised under the title of *Our Country's History* and the name of Arthur S. Link joined that of Muzzey as author. Effort was made at this time to drop the reading level from a 14.9 to one that ran between a 9 and 10. You will note that in addition to reorganizing of some material, sentences were shortened throughout.

TODAY—Ginn's most popular current history text is *Episodes in American History* by Robert E. Burns, et al. This is concept and inquiry oriented, and the reading level averages 9.3. It is currently being revised and the reading level dropped.

During the same period in the 60's as the Muzzey-Link book was lowering reading level, we brought out a book called *The Growth of American Democracy* by Arthur S. Link. This was aimed at above average students and was part of the trend to encourage students toward higher achievement. The reading level of the Link book is 12. This book never achieved great popular appeal on the high school level.

> *Sincerely,*
>
> ANNE THOMAS/Editor
> Social Science Dept.

In 1975, my research assistant, Bob Beveridge, conducted an historical analysis of changes in the readability levels of the most widely used eleventh-grade American history textbooks in the mid-1950's and the mid-1970's. The pattern reported by Ginn above reflects the findings of our study—there was a one- to four-year reduction in the readability levels of the most widely used books. A 1977 CEEB-commissioned study duplicated a great deal of this research, and confirmed many of our findings.[115] According to this report:

> . . . a constantly increasing percentage of textbook space is taken up by pictures, larger print, wider margins, shorter words and sentences and paragraphs; the amount of exposition is decreasing, the amount of narrative going up.
> . . . student testing is being reduced to an "objective answer" basis, meaning that students will find less reason to learn to write: "generally, the assignments in the Reading, History, and Literature textbooks [ask] only for underlining, circling and filling in of single words."

The study confirms what we know from the reports of textbook writers enjoined by publishers to "make it simple" and from the echoing reactions of better students that what they are reading at school is "simpler stuff than we read in the newspapers."

Why are the textbook publishers pursuing this policy? I have talked and corresponded with representatives of more than twenty of the largest textbook publishers in the country. In every case they indicated they were rewriting their textbooks at lower readability levels, and in every case they cited the same reason. They can no longer sell a textbook that has been written with a readability level higher than two years below the grade for which it is intended. Publishers who have attempted to buck this trend have seen their sales dwindle.

The question of the policy change thus becomes one for the schools. I have asked many secondary-school teachers and administrators why they will only purchase books written with reduced readability. They tell me that the books are easier to read, and therefore students are more likely to read them. They say that books written at grade level turn the students off, even the better readers. They tell me that students reading below grade level will not even try to read a book written at grade level.

Nowhere did I encounter any discussion of the possible consequences of reduced readability on the long-term development of reading ability. The educational research in this area is inadequate and throws virtually no light on this question. The published research is almost exclusively concerned with the short-term effects of high-readability materials on below-average students. Even with this group, the question of long-term effects of reduced readability is never raised.

Recently a Minnesota researcher compared the reading ability of students in two hundred Minnesota elementary-school districts with the readability level of the textbooks they were assigned.[129] She found that 75 to 90 percent of the above-average readers were assigned textbooks with a readability level below their reading ability. With the lack of educational stimulation and challenge this situation implies, combined with the fact that the situation will worsen sharply when these youngsters enter junior high school, how long will these above-average students remain above average?

Several other facets of the readability situation deserve comment. The textbooks written two years below grade level are not designed for poor readers. These books are referred to as *regular* textbooks and are designed for and marketed to school districts whose students read at or above grade level. The publishing companies market entirely different textbooks to inner-city schools and to other schools with a significant number of poor readers. These different textbooks fall into three categories. First are the *low*-level textbooks. These are books specifically designed for high-school use but written at a fifth-, sixth-, or seventh-grade level. Robert Kellar, senior social-studies editor for Addison-Wesley Publishing Company, who acted as a consultant for this phase of the research, estimates that these low-level books currently occupy about 10 percent of the market for high-school American history books. He anticipates they will expand their share of the market to 35 percent within the next five to ten years, and he also indicates that the same trends are current throughout the secondary-level social-studies curriculum.

The second kind of book used for this purpose, called an *adapted* version, is actually just a special type of low-level book. This is a textbook designed to look exactly like a regular textbook, with the same title, author, and format, but with the vocabulary and sentence length reduced, or adapted, to a fifth-, sixth-, or seventh-grade level. The idea behind the development of these books was that in the same classroom, some students could use the regular book, others the adapted version, and only the teacher would be the wiser.

The third type of book used for this purpose is a textbook originally developed and marketed for use at the *junior*-high-school level. For example, a salesman for Rand McNally informed my research assistant that the Oakland, California, school district purchases primarily eighth-grade American history books for their eleventh-grade students. Kellar estimates that these books currently comprise another 10 percent of the high-school history textbook market, but he believes that their share of the market will gradually be taken over by the low-level texts.

I recently visited the social-studies library of a high school that had asked me to conduct a reading workshop for some of its teachers. I was quite shocked to find that they had replaced *all* of their regular textbooks with one or another of the three types discussed above. The department chairman claimed that fewer than a dozen students a year who passed through his school had sufficiently developed reading skills to handle a textbook written at higher than a seventh-grade level. He also stated that virtually all of the high schools in the area used low-level texts. I later found that the best high school in the district, one which drew its students exclusively from an upper-middle-class community, had also replaced over half of its regular textbooks with one or another of the three types of books discussed above.

A number of examples of reduced readability have recently surfaced at the college level.[132] The Association of American Publishers (AAP) found that college students across the country were having difficulty reading their pamphlet *How to Get the Most Out of Your Textbook*. When a readability analysis showed the pamphlet was written at twelfth-grade level, the AAP had it rewritten to a ninth-grade level. In a very similar incident, McGraw-Hill discovered that college students were having difficulty with the materials used in its basic-skills program, so rewrote them to a seventh- and eighth-grade level. A recent article in the educational literature complained that the textbooks being used at the City University of New York (C.U.N.Y.) were written at a college level, even though C.U.N.Y.'s new open-admissions policy had resulted in the enrollment of several thousand students reading below a ninth-grade level.[86] The article's author urged the publishing industry and the university to develop and use materials with reduced readability. In fact, most good, four-year colleges have not adopted books with reduced readability, but many two-year colleges and open-admissions colleges have. A readability analysis of the books used by a two-year college near one of my California offices reveals that less than a third were written at a college level.

At the elementary-school level, a number of companies are publishing textbooks with greatly reduced readability, and compensating for the reduced content with the addition of filmstrips, audio cassettes, and modular kits. I have frequently heard publishers' representatives justify these books with the assertion, "It isn't fair to penalize children just because they can't read." For example, Houghton Mifflin recently published a new-math curriculum for use in grades one through eight, with minimal reading.[37] The intention of the program is to give students who read very poorly an opportunity to learn math. The consultant who explained this program to me admitted that math without reading was not terribly useful, but he insisted it was better than math with reading that students could not understand.

I find the prospect of the elimination of reading from major areas of the curriculum, all in the name of fairness, to be a rather frightening proposition. Even though the schools may claim they are trying to be fair to their low-ability students, they are in fact reducing the educational opportunities of all their students. The chairman of the math department for a California junior high school told me that even though most students in his school were not having difficulty reading their math textbooks, the State Department of Education was pressuring him to replace his math textbooks with the Houghton Mifflin math textbooks discussed above. According to their formulas, the students in his school "needed" the reduced readability books. Interview 10 records the remarks of another math teacher, who makes the point that students today are extremely weak at solving word problems. He feels acutely frustrated in his teaching because his students cannot put the two processes, reading and computation, together.

The movement toward low-readability books is the path of least resistance for our schools. It reinforces the literacy hoax, by convincing functionally illiterate students and their parents that the students can perform adequately. The proper response to the skills decline is not a compensating decline in curricular rigor, but a full-scale effort to teach students their basic academic skills.

In this matter of reduced readability, I see five very destructive tendencies which seem to affect the entire decision-making process in American public education. First, there was no discussion with parents prior to the decision to reduce readability. Second, there was no research conducted to determine the long-term effects of the curriculum change before it was instituted. Third, the decision to reduce readability levels to extremely low levels for below-average readers tends to conceal a serious education problem, rather than confront it. Fourth, the decision to reduce readability levels for average and above-average readers seems to have been based on a fear of student resistance to hard work. Fifth, the total impact of the decision-making process was to reinforce the literacy hoax. As long as these tendencies dominate the decision-making process in American public education, our schools will fail to provide our children with the quality of education they deserve.

ABILITY GROUPING

Until the mid-1960's, the United States operated a dual system of school organization, heterogeneous grouping in elementary school, and homogeneous grouping by ability in junior and senior high school. There was, and remains, relative unanimity in the community at large and among professional educators that the proper setting for an elementary-school child's optimum psychological and social development is a classroom which contains a cross section of children from the child's community. In order to promote the optimum intellectual development of children within the classroom, certain periods of the day are reserved for whole-class instruction, and other periods are reserved for small-group instruction. The small groups are achievement-based, as, for example, in beginning reading instruction, where the class is usually divided into three groups composed of students making progress at below-average, average, and above-average rates.

At the secondary level, school organization changes drastically. Students have a specialized teacher in each subject, and the secondary-schooling process is seen by most educators as requiring more discipline and more hard work than schooling in the earlier years. Until the mid-1960's, there was general agreement among secondary-school educators that the elementary-school practice of grouping students based on academic achievement should be continued, and expanded, at the secondary level. Thus, students were usually grouped for each subject based on three factors: their prior achievement in the subject area; their mastery of the skills needed to learn the subject; and their learning ability. These factors were measured by standardized educational tests of aptitude, achievement, and intelligence, comments of past teachers, and grades from past course work.

The traditional system of organization, as described above, worked quite well for students who were in the above-average classes. They generally received stimulating and challenging instruction which pushed them to fulfill their educational potential. Such was not always the case for students placed in average or below-average classes. The instruction given to students in these classes was sometimes unchallenging and inadequate, and their educational development suffered for it.

In the middle and late 1960's, the civil-rights movement attacked homogeneous grouping by ability as a mechanism by which minority children were denied access to quality education. Representatives of civil-rights organizations pointed out, correctly, that virtually all minority children were assigned to average or below-average classes. Between 1964 and 1974 the civil-rights movement, bolstered with favorable court decisions [65] and substantial support from the society at large and from within the educational community, successfully influenced most secondary schools in the country to replace homogeneous ability grouping with heterogeneous grouping.

The sequential, optional, and difficult nature of the math and science curriculums insulated these fields from being substantially affected by this change. A student who barely passes beginning algebra or biology is unlikely to sign up for advanced algebra or chemistry. Thus, this major organizational reform barely affected the teaching practices of most math and science teachers.

The same cannot be said for the English and social-studies curriculums. Most high schools require students to take three years each of English and social studies. Most English and social-studies teachers had accommodated themselves to these requirements by developing different curriculums for different ability groups. The civil-rights organizations hoped that once ability grouping was eliminated, English and history teachers would use their most stimulating and challenging curriculum in all of their classes. Failing that, these organizations were fairly confident that the quality of instruction given to the new heterogeneous classes would be superior to that previously given to the below-average classes.

In fact, what happened was that most English and social-studies teachers employed the curriculum they had previously used with their average-ability classes. The teachers found that even with their middle-range curriculum, many students resisted the increased standards and work demands. The teachers were usually unable to compel these students to work, and thus lost a certain amount of their classroom authority and control. High-quality instruction to an exacting educational standard virtually disappeared from the English and social-studies curriculums of schools with a significant number of below-average sutdents, and discipline problems increased substantially.

Was the disappearance of the high-level English and social-studies curriculums necessary? Under the circumstances that have existed in most of this nation's high schools since the mid-1960's, the answer to this question is unfortunately yes. As Chapters Three and Four discuss fully, the key to effective education is a combination of high academic standards and heavy work demands imposed by the teacher on his students. The teacher must have parental, community, and administrative support in order to make his demands and standards stick, and in order to handle the resistance of his students to hard work.

Instead of obtaining support from the necessary societal forces, the teachers found themselves abandoned. The civil-rights movement actively promoted student and community resistance to their authority, the legal profession stripped them of legal authority and protection, school administrators refused to back them up for fear of student, community, and legal reprisals, and the society at large ignored them. Because the replacement of ability-grouped classes by mixed-ability classes was not accompanied by increased support to their authority, most teachers were unable to apply their high-level work demands and standards to their new classes. When they attempted to do so in the absence of the necessary support, they could not deal with the massive resistance they received from students who were unused to being subjected to these types of demands.

By the early 1970's, heterogeneous grouping was the dominant pattern of secondary-school organization, even in areas not directly affected by the civil-rights movement. The lobbying effort in favor of heterogeneous grouping by the National Council of Teachers of English (NCTE), the professional association of English teachers, combined with the fact that it had become established in virtually all metropolitan areas of the country, influenced secondary-school officials to accept the change. The effects of this change in most areas in which it has become established are similar to those described above. The high-level English and social-studies curriculums have tended to disappear, and discipline problems have tended to increase.

As the reader undoubtedly suspects, I strongly favor a return to ability grouping. I believe that homogeneous grouping by ability at the secondary level promotes the optimum intellectual development of students at all ability levels. In their educational focus, civil-rights organizations are attempting to promote the educational development of that minority of American children who do not have white skin. In restructuring American education toward that end, they are reducing the educational opportunities of another minority, the minority of students with above-average ability. If the ideal of equal educational opportunity means anything, surely it must mean that our brightest youngsters are also to be given a chance to fulfill their educational potential. Too much of current educational practice is based on the assumption that bright children already have so much going for them that their needs can be ignored. Our society can ill afford to waste the best minds of a generation in order to promote an experiment in social engineering.

I have spent many hours talking to intelligent young high-school students and observing their high-school classes. Many of them have never been in a course that challenged their ability. They do not know what it is like to take a class in which more than a few students participate in class discussions. Many of these youngsters have become very lazy in their work habits and attitude toward life, while others are extremely bitter about the quality of their education. Our society has cheated these young people out of the education they deserve.

Some of the most painful situations are those of bright, academically inclined black and Mexican-American students whose peer groups look down on their intellectual ability. Because these students are in classes with average- and below-average-ability black and Mexican-American students, peer-group pressure often prevents them from participating in class discussions or projects, or even doing their homework. Heterogeneous grouping is tearing these kids apart.

In Chapter Three I develop an educational philosophy which stands in stark contrast to the dominant educational philosophy of our day. I believe the key to the maximum educational development of all children is sharply increased teacher authority, backed by administrative, parental, and community support. A teacher with authority can impose heavy work demands and high standards on all of his below-average, average, and above-average classes, which will push all of his students to fulfill their educational potential.

ENROLLMENT TRENDS

The past dozen years have witnessed a sharp drop-off in enrollment in rigorous academic course work. Table 5 gives the approximate percentage of ninth- through twelfth-grade students enrolled in various courses in 1960 and 1972 for the country as a whole.[116] The data is only approximate because if one student was taking two English courses simultaneously, it would show up as if two students were each taking one course.

Table 5 shows that during the most recent period, the academic year 1972–1973, approximately 71 percent of the students were taking English, 26 percent were taking United States history, and 5 percent were taking geography. The table indicates that the average high-school student took 25 percent less English, 35 percent less world history, 35 percent less government and civics, 29 percent less geography, 19 percent less science, and 12 percent less math in 1972 than a comparable student in 1960. Although there is no national data available after 1972, there is evidence that the trend reflected by these figures has accelerated sharply since. The *Los Angeles Times* reports a 77 percent drop in California students taking English composition between 1972 and 1975, and smaller enrollment drop-offs in algebra, geometry, trigonometry, basic English, and American literature.[97] I think it is reasonable to associate these sharp enrollment declines with the equally sharp achievement declines cited in Chapter One.

Table 5 also shows that students are replacing these academic courses with—nothing. They are not replacing academic course work with business or vocational courses; indeed total enrollment in these two areas is down 12 percent.

There are two mechanisms, rare in 1960, common in 1972, and sharply expanded since, which have permitted the shrinkage of the average student's courseload. The first is the system of flexible class scheduling. Flexible scheduling was developed in reaction to the traditional system of high-school class scheduling, which required every student to be at school from 8:30 A.M. to 3:00 P.M. every day. Students attended school for six consecutive one-hour periods, with a half-hour break for lunch, the schedule being identical every day of the week. Silberman, other liberal educators, younger faculty, and students complained that such a system was needlessly rigid.

The system of flexible scheduling proposed by the critics and adopted by the schools allows leeway in the frequency and length of class meetings. Courses have the same schedule of class meetings each week, but they may meet from one to five times a week, and from one-half hour to two hours each meeting. Thus a student might have French on Mondays, Wednesdays, and Fridays, from 9:00 to 10:30 A.M., art on Tuesdays and Thursdays from 1:00 to 3:00 P.M., and American history Monday through Friday from 11:00 to 12:00 noon. Because the schedule's flexibility opened up holes in the student's day, during which he was not enrolled in any classes, his physical presence was usually not required at school during those periods. Since there was no longer any necessity to fill six

TABLE 5

PERCENTAGE OF NINTH- THROUGH TWELFTH-
GRADE STUDENTS ENROLLED IN COURSES,
1960 AND 1972, UNITED STATES

	1960–1961	1972–1973
English	95	71
Social studies		
United States history	24	26
World history	20	13
Civics and government	23	15
Geography	7	5
Sociology and psychology	5	10
Science		
General science and earth science	23	12
Biology	22	21
Chemistry	9	8
Physics	5	4
Math		
General math	17	14
Algebra	29	26
Geometry	14	11
Trigonometry	3	3
Foreign language	28	25
Industrial arts and vocational education	28	30
Business, typing, etc.	48	37
Home economics	23	24

periods a day with classes, the minimum number of classes students were permitted to take was usually reduced to four.

If high-school students were mature, self-disciplined adults, flexible scheduling would have worked. In fact, flexible scheduling has wreaked serious and permanent damage on many of the vulnerable students who populate our high schools. The sharp drop-off in the average student's academic and total courseload is only one result of this academic reform. Another is a sharp escalation in absenteeism.

In 1975, I spent several months visiting public high schools that used flexible scheduling. I estimate classroom absenteeism in these schools at over 40 percent. This does not mean that 40 percent of the enrolled students did not show up for school each day. Rather, most students attend their first class in the day, and usually the ten-minute homeroom period around eleven o'clock, when attendance is taken, but they are very likely to skip one or several periods during the rest of their day. They are especially likely to skip classes which occur right after any empty places in their schedule.

The holes in the students' schedules, during which they are not required to be anywhere, are an invitation to educational disaster. They promote absenteeism, but far more dangerous is that they promote drug-taking during school hours. The most frightening and depressing aspect of my visits to metropolitan high schools was my talks with stoned-out kids who told me they got stoned every day, at school, during the empty periods in their schedule. Taking drugs regularly is serious enough; taking them daily during school hours precludes any educational development.

These holes in the students' schedules have also contributed to the sharp escalation in school violence and crime, which is discussed further in Chapter Three. A student with nowhere to go is far more likely to get into trouble than a student who is in class. In schools with flexible scheduling, teachers and school officials cannot know whether a student or group of students walking the halls or loitering on a stairway are potential troublemakers, or are merely waiting for their next class. Thus school officials do not try to control out-of-class school behavior, and this lack of regulation is an invitation for nonstudents to come aboard and cause trouble.

The second mechanism which permits students to carry a lighter courseload is the new and increasingly widespread practice of permitting high-school juniors and seniors to attend school half a day and work at a part-time job the other half. School officials who are promoting this practice, which they call work experience, claim that it fits in with the concept of career education currently being heavily promoted by the United States Office of Education (USOE). Career education is the concept that public schooling should prepare an individual to function in society. The goal of work experience is to provide students with the opportunity to learn how to behave appropriately in work situations, and teach them certain work-related skills.

Over 20 percent of the juniors and seniors in a high school near one of my offices leave school in the afternoons to go to work. Statewide and nationwide the analogous figure seems to be between 10 and 15 percent.[61] Most of the federally funded work-experience programs are designed for vocationally oriented students, but state and local programs are geared to a broad range of students. In the school cited above, the work-experience students are representative of the student body as a whole, which is an upper-middle-class college-bound student body.

Work experience has several obvious nonacademic benefits which make it appealing to school officials. The schools do not lose any state money for those students attending only a half-day, because they receive full school credit for the time they are on the job. The absence of a significant number of juniors and seniors from school for a half-day eliminates some potential discipline problems for school officials, and permits both smaller classes and fewer teaching periods for teachers. Some students undoubtedly benefit from the practice, in a nonacademic way. This category includes potential dropouts and students who are habitually absent. Since the alternative to work experience for these students might be no school at all, it can hardly hurt and may even help.

Despite their utility for school officials and marginal students, work-experience programs are very damaging to most of the middle-range and above-average-ability students who participate in them. I have known personally a number of intelligent, college-bound students who became involved in work-experience programs. They chose to take work experience because they wanted some part-time income, and preferred to cut back on their course work rather than on their social life. Not one of these young people learned anything more useful in these programs than how to pump gas or wait on tables. Their high-school studies tended to suffer, and they took far fewer academic courses than I believe they should have. When they entered college, they tended to avoid classes for which they were not prepared and were thus restricted in their educational and career options.

I place full blame for the damage done by these programs on high school-officials who were seduced by their nonacademic benefits, and on high-school counseling staffs who encouraged their middle- and upper-range students to participate in them. An academic education is of intrinsic value, and the type of menial work most high-school students can find in its place is a poor substitute. Even the extrinsic benefits, the reading, writing, and computational skills, and the subject knowledge, are far more useful in the long run than a brief head start in the world of work. For the great majority of students, and certainly for most college-bound students, the work-experience choice has led to a decline in academic achievement.

Although the primary focus of this chapter is the effect of curricular change on the development of basic academic skills, I believe the enrollment decline has another serious implication which deserves at least brief comment. The reader will recall the 35 percent declines in world history and civics and government enrollments between 1960 and 1972. A 1975 report by the Organization of American Historians (OAH), which analyzed trends in history enrollment and instruction at the secondary and university levels in each of the fifty states, confirms the sharp decline in high-school history enrollment.[79] According to this report, the primary trend of the past ten years has been the replacement of history in the high-school curriculum with multicultural and ethnic studies, current events, consumer affairs, ecology, sociology, and psychology. The basis of the enrollment decline in history, and civics and government as well, is the widespread feeling on the part of students, counsellors, and administrators that these subjects are not practical or relevant.

Many of the high-school students I have taught in the past few years could not tell me who fought against the United States in World War II, and the overwhelming majority of them could not give me the political, economic, or historical background of that war. Very few of the college students I have taught recently could tell me what happened at the Bay of Pigs, and even fewer knew what happened in Munich in 1938. Recall also the 1977 NAEP study showing extremely sharp declines in the knowledge of eighth and twelfth graders regarding American government and political processes. We jeopardize our existence as a democratic society by not *requiring* our young people to acquire the knowledge that will enable them to meet their obligations of citizenship.

ENGLISH CURRICULUM

This section is devoted to a description of the changes that have occurred in English instruction, because I believe they have contributed more to the deterioration of the reading and writing skills of secondary students than curricular changes in any other subject. I am not including a description of instructional changes in social studies, science, or math, because such a description would quickly become repetitive and redundant. Many of the changes in the English curriculum have direct parallels in the other fields, especially social studies, the most important being the sharp drop-off in enrollment, the replacement of rigorous and required courses with electives of dubious educational value, and the great reduction in the amount of assigned reading and writing. The reader will have an opportunity to learn more of these changes as he reads the interviews with high-school teachers in Part II.

Table 5 indicates that the average high-school graduate took four years of English in 1960 and only three years in 1972. The effect of this change was probably matched in magnitude by the effect of changes in the English curriculum over the same time interval. The curriculum changed in content, in organization, and even in intent.

The most common organizational pattern in the early 1960's was a mandatory sequence of six semesters, taken by all freshmen, sophomores, and juniors, followed by a number of one-semester options for senior English, including creative writing, journalism, public speaking, debating, classical literature, advanced composition, and poetry. In some schools students who were not college-bound were permitted to opt out of senior English entirely, but this practice was not widespread. The six required semesters almost always included a year of composition, a year of American literature, and a semester of British literature. Within a given school district, the content of the six required semesters varied little from teacher to teacher.

The pattern as described above has been replaced in many, probably most, high schools around the country. The pattern I will describe as having replaced it is not universal, but is typical of the organizational patterns now in use. It is the English curriculum of the suburban California high school I attended in the early 1960's.[72] Students at this school are required to take three mandatory semesters of English in ninth grade and the first semester of tenth grade. These three semesters usually include basic composition, the reading of some contemporary fiction and nonfiction and a little American and British literature, creative writing, and public speaking.

Students are also required to take three additional semesters of English anytime in their last two and a half years of school. For these three semesters they may choose any three courses from a list of electives which includes the options previously described as available for senior English, plus American literature, British literature, composition, grammar, science fiction, feminist literature, tutoring, philosophy, satire, semantics, Shakespeare, sports literature, communications, drama, the hero in literature, popular culture, advanced composition, mass media, mythology and folklore, survey of the novel, the short story, Afro-American literature, and one course called survival English, which seems, as best as I can determine, to be the development of counter-culture cognitive processes.

The weakness in the current elective system is that it enables a student to avoid the kind of rigorous work he needs to develop his primary academic skills. A 1977 study by the Massachusetts Department of Education found that where enrollment in these specialty types of English electives remained constant, SAT scores did not decline significantly, but where enrollment in these electives increased, SAT scores declined sharply.[161] As interesting as many of the above-listed electives appear, most of them do not provide the type of disciplined training that students need in order to develop their skills. With reasonably judicious selection, students can get through high-school English without reading more than three or four books or writing more than three or four papers. I have known a number of high-ability but somewhat rebellious young people who made these kinds of choices, only to find their educational options severely limited at the college level. *I do not believe young people should be given the freedom not to learn.*

In addition to the options described above, this school and many others with which I am familiar permit their students to choose their teachers for the three mandatory semesters of English. Each English teacher publishes a brief course description and assignment sheet, and students are free to choose whichever program sounds most appealing. I need hardly say that this procedure turns all six required semesters into electives.

The weakness in this system is that it turns teaching into a popularity contest. A teacher who does not have sufficient student sign-ups will be pressured by school officials to jazz up his instruction, reduce his assignments, show movies—anything to even out course enrollments. I know of an excellent but very tough English teacher in a San Francisco high school who never has more than a dozen students per class. The students will not sign up for her classes because they will not work as hard as she demands, and the school cannot fire her or force her to change because she earned tenure before the new English curriculum was instituted. In that same school, the overwhelming majority of students take a semester course in film appreciation as one of their six required semesters. The work in this course consists entirely of watching and discussing a movie a week, and completing a fill-in-the-blank movie critique form supplied by the teacher.

For the reader who remains skeptical that high-school English can be anything but composition and literature, I present the following from the published course description of a freshman English course offered at my old high school:

ENGLISH 1 AND 2—THE PEOPLE'S ENGLISH

Most English classes reverse the natural order of things; English 1 and 2 manage to keep a proper perspective. The emphasis of the class is on listening/speaking, reading and writing in that order. Students are encouraged to have an open-minded, multi-valued approach to learning and to the environment around them.

. . . Five specific skills will be the focus of the class—1) question-asking, 2) information gathering, 3) critical thinking, 4) problem-solving and 5) communicating (sending and receiving thoughts and feelings accurately). By working on these skills students will become more self-confident, effective communicators, self-reliant and self-directed.

. . . By actively questioning people, seeking out information in the community, etc., the Freshmen will practice the skills and perfect them.

. . . Teacher aides will be incorporated as part of the class. Older students—"the cream-of-the-crop"—will help the teacher and individualize and personalize the class.

. . . The atmosphere of the class is such that learning should be fun and rewarding: a worthwhile activity, not drudgery.

. . . Little or no outside work will be given—students put in a six or seven hour day at school as it is. . . .[72]

Another ninth-grade English course at the same school publishes the following assignment sheet:

A "thought sheet" is required once a week. This is basically a journal entry where the student is asked to focus on ONE THOUGHT ONLY from a whole week of thoughts and to organize one or two paragraphs around this thought.

As I have indicated several times, I believe an academic education is of intrinsic value. It is tragic that American literature and

British literature have now become largely optional. In several high schools in which I have made specific inquiry, less than 20 percent of the students took the one-semester course in American literature during their four years, and less than 10 percent took the semester course in British literature. The English language has the greatest literary heritage of any language in the history of the world. Many of our young people are no longer even exposed to Shakespeare, Milton, Mark Twain, Carl Sandburg, Robert Frost, Jack London, Charles Dickens, Robert Louis Stevenson, Jonathan Swift, or Herman Melville.

Contrast this situation with that of the average Russian student. Soviet education is usually noted for its emphasis on science and mathematics, and for the volume of work assigned in these areas. It is true that every Russian student must take several years each of biology, chemistry, physics, and math, and that they attend six days of school a week and average five hours of homework a night.[74, 150] It is also true, however, that Russian students must take several years each of Russian history, world history, and geography, and *eight years of Russian and world literature.* The average Soviet high-school student is assigned a minimum of thirty books a year in his literature courses, and reports indicate that the average number of books read is closer to one hundred per year. Examination of the mandatory Soviet literature curriculum reveals that the average Russian student reads more English and American literature by the time he graduates from high school than his American counterpart.

The new English curriculum fares no better when scrutinized from the standpoint of its development of reading and writing skills. The consensus of secondary-school teachers, counselors, and administrators with whom I have talked is that the average student today is assigned barely more than half the reading assigned to the average student in the early 1960's. Because reading is a self-reinforcing activity, this reduction is probably multiplied in its effect on students' reading habits. The more an individual reads, the more fluid and pleasurable the process becomes, and the more likely he is to continue reading. Conversely, an individual who does not read often will find the process to be labored and awkward, and consequently he will tend to avoid reading. By cutting the volume of assigned reading in half, English teachers have reinforced the nonreading tendencies of many students.

Another change in the nature of English instruction has probably had an even greater impact on the development of reading skills than the reduction in assigned reading. In the early 1960's most teachers assigned several specific books to a class each semester. This gave the entire class the opportunity to discuss each book. It also enabled the teacher to focus the students' attention onto those elements of the book he considered important.

The current practice is to allow each student in a class to choose several books from a master list. Many teachers allow students to read anything they want. Some teachers justify these practices by asserting that students should have the freedom to read anything they want. Others simply say that any attempt to compel all students in a class to read the same books will create too much student resistance.

I strongly disapprove of these practices, as a result of my own experience teaching reading at the secondary and college levels. If a teacher has an approach to the art of reading he wants to impart, it is absolutely essential to build that approach through the sequential assignment of certain specific books. The teacher brings out certain elements in the first book. He gets the students to notice these same elements in the second as well as to see some new ones. In this way students learn to see pattern and depth in their reading. The teacher actually trains perception and cognition by focusing on specific incidents in specific books.

An even better case can be made that the new English curriculum has directly caused a deterioration in the writing skills of American students. Writing instruction in the early 1960's tended to be rather mechanical. Teachers focused on such aspects of the writing art as grammar, punctuation, syntax, and spelling. This type of instruction was fiercely criticized in the late 1960's as stifling creativity and fostering an imitative kind of writing. In my opinion, some of the criticism was well-founded, especially for bright students, but as usual the baby went out with the bath water.

The writing curriculum that developed in the early 1970's

was extremely concerned with encouraging students to express their feelings in writing. It was felt that such expression would be creative, nonimitative, and nonmechanical. Teachers tended to stop criticizing their students' writing out of concern that criticism would inhibit them from openly expressing their feelings. Many English classes resembled sensitivity training groups, as teachers attempted to help their students recognize and express their feelings. The amount of discursive writing was reduced sharply, as was focus on the mechanical aspects of writing. The standard writing assignment in the early 1960's was one logically organized composition a week. By the early 1970's, it was one creative paper, due at intermittent intervals, which would not be criticized. (A recent study conducted by the National Assessment of Educational Progress reported that most eleventh-grade students are given less than one writing assignment every two weeks.[115])

This new writing curriculum permits students to avoid serious writing. It panders to the contemporary philosophy that only enjoyable activities are of value, and that struggle and hard work are outmoded concepts promoted by old-fashioned people. Without extensive and repeated practice and criticism, a person cannot learn to write. Young people took advantage of the new writing curriculum and produced undisciplined, unedited garbage, which their teachers accepted in the name of respect for individual differences. Chapter One made reference to the NAEP study showing a deterioration in writing skills from 1969 to 1974, and the steadily increasing percentage of students required to take remedial writing at the University of California. The same pattern exists at virtually every university in the country. Reports from Michigan State, University of Oregon, Temple, City College of New York, Wisconsin, Stanford, Harvard, Georgia, and many others all show the same pattern. The top products of our secondary schools, America's college freshmen, write very poorly.

A 1977 CEEB analysis of the SAT score decline confirms the trends discussed above. This report states:

> Our firmest conclusion is that the critical factor in the relationship between curricular change and the SAT scores are (1) that less

thoughtful and critical reading is now being demanded and done, and (2) that careful writing has apparently about gone out of style.
. . . Homework has apparently been cut about in half.[115]

Perhaps the single clearest and most damaging manifestation of the new English curriculum was a document published by the Conference on College Composition and Communication (CCCC), which is an arm of the NCTE. This 1975 report, entitled "Students' Right to Their Own Language," is essentially an educational manifesto.[35] It asserts that the only substantive difference between the dialects of English spoken in the black inner-city ghettos or the poverty-stricken areas of Appalachia and among the educated and professional classes in this country is the amount of social prestige attached to the latter. The report concludes that to force poor or minority students to write exclusively in standard American English is an act of political repression and racism. The report goes on to urge all English teachers to encourage students to write in their own dialect.

In the following quotation from the CCCC statement, the letters EAE stand for "Edited American English," which is the form of standard American English used in written communication:

> EAE is important for certain kinds of students, its features are easily identified and taught, and school patrons are often satisfied when it is mastered, but that should not tempt teachers to evade the still more important feature of language.

I would like to ask the report's authors, If EAE is only important for certain kinds of students, who are the other students for whom it is not important? I would daresay, Not the authors' own children. Clearly they are referring to lower-class black and Mexican-American children, and other economically and educationally disadvantaged young people.

I doubt the report's authors consulted with the parents of those children for whom EAE is supposedly unimportant. I have found, in discussion with many black and Mexican-American parents, that they hate—and "hate" conveys only a mild sense of their feelings—the policy and attitude expressed in the CCCC report. These parents want their children to learn how to write and speak in standard English, so that they can prosper in our society. The authors of this document and those teachers who are attempting to institute its policy are consigning their minority students to another generation of educational and economic poverty. This document and the policy it espouses are a travesty of the most basic principles of education.

I believe that an overwhelming majority of the nation's parents, black, Mexican-American, and white, would violently disapprove of most features of the new English curriculum if they were aware of them. The dominant principle in this curriculum is to give students what they demand. We have a curriculum without standards, with insipid content, that neither exposes students to their cultural heritage nor trains them in the reading and writing skills they will need to function in society. I am convinced that the deterioration in the secondary-level English curriculum bears a significant share of the responsibility for the achievement decline experienced by America's secondary students over the past dozen years.

GRADE INFLATION

While courses were getting easier and reading and writing assignments were being reduced, high-school grades were moving upward. The following graph depicts the percentage of A's and B's, or C's, awarded throughout high school to representative groups of first-time college freshmen from 1966 to 1977.[5] By 1977, over 81 percent of the high-school grades reported by these students were A's or B's, less than half of one percent were D's, and less than .05 of one percent were F's.

Verification of this pattern comes from the two major college entrance testing programs. ACT reports an increase in the average high-school grade-point average from 2.59 on a four-point scale in 1966 to a 2.85 in 1976.[52, 4] Grade inflation during this period occurred in each of the four subjects investigated, English, math, social studies, and natural sciences, but was most pronounced in English. The reader will recall from Chapter One that the national average of ACT scores dropped sharply during this same period. High-school grades reported by ETS show a similar increase.[34]

In a study of high-school students discussed more fully in

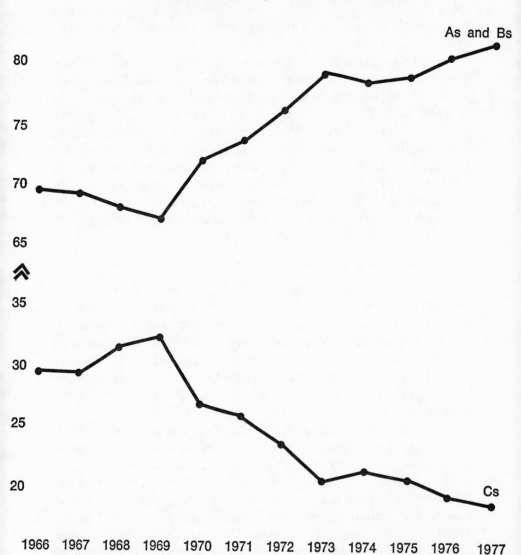

Graph 2

**PERCENTAGE OF As AND Bs,
OR Cs, AWARDED THROUGHOUT
HIGH SCHOOL, 1966 TO 1976**

As and Bs

Cs

80

75

70

65

35

30

25

20

1966 1967 1968 1969 1970 1971 1972 1973 1974 1975 1976 1977

Chapter Three,[53] Sanford Dornbusch asked the opinion of a large number of metropolitan high-school students about the grading practices of their teachers. About half the students reported that even if they did poor work or did not try, they would receive average or above-average grades. Dornbusch's data indicate that a student who does a minimal amount of work will not receive a low grade, as long as he does not cut an excessive number of classes.

A rather tragic example of grade inflation was featured in a September 1976 issue of *Newsweek* magazine.[154] The valedictorian of Western High School in Washington, D.C., was refused admission to George Washington University because he scored only 280 on the math section of the SAT, which placed him in the bottom 5 percent of college-bound seniors in the nation, and 320 on the verbal section, which placed him in the bottom 13 percent. Because they were puzzled by the discrepancy between his high grades and low SAT scores, George Washington privately administered to this student a series of educational tests, without time limit. The result confirmed the SAT pattern; this high-school valedictorian suffered from severe educational deficiencies. The following quotation from Joseph Ruth, admissions dean at George Washington, could have served as an introduction to my discussion of the literacy hoax:

> My feeling is that a kid like this has been conned. He thinks he's a real scholar. His parents think he's a real scholar. He's been deluded into thinking he's gotten an education.

The student involved was admitted to Boston University, the University of Pittsburgh, and Howard University. Lest the reader think this story a fluke, the *Washington Post*, in a follow-up story, reported that the valedictorian of Frederick Douglass High School in Baltimore scored 270 on the math section of the SAT, and 350 on the verbal section.

Grade inflation is caused by the same forces that have caused the other major changes in the secondary curriculum during the past dozen years. Graph 2 shows the outcome of the conflict between younger and older faculty on this and other issues. The slightly declining grades between 1966 and 1969 were recorded during the period when older high-school teachers were still dominant on most high-school faculties. The sharply increasing grades recorded thereafter indicate the ascendance of the younger faculty with their more liberal educational philosophy. A high-school administration that permits some teachers to grade easier than others, and also permits students to choose their teachers, puts an irresistible pressure on the rest of the faculty to relax their grading standards. Teachers that hold to older, stricter grading practices experience a decline in enrollment for their courses. Easing up on their grading becomes a matter of job survival.

Grade inflation is teaching America's young people that good work and hard work are almost pointless. Throughout their secondary schooling they are learning that there is only a very tenuous relationship between effort and reward. This is a very dangerous lesson to teach and bodes ill for the future of our country.

COLLEGE AND UNIVERSITY

For two reasons I intend to make the analysis in this section rather brief. First, my primary concern in this chapter is to explain the school-related causes of the achievement decline discussed in Chapter One. Since the great bulk of the evidence of the achievement decline pertained to late-elementary- and secondary-level students, the cause cannot logically be sought in the educational environment of older students. Second, virtually all of the changes at the secondary level, philosophical and curricular, have their analogues at the college level. A detailed presentation of much of this evidence would quickly become redundant.

Most readers will recall the turbulent period of the late 1960's and early 1970's, during which campus demonstrations, riots, strikes, and teach-ins seemed to be featured on the evening news almost every night. During the four years I attended the University of California at Berkeley in the middle and late 1960's, there was a campus-wide student strike an average of twice a year. For a minority of students, a college education during this period meant four years of picket lines, police confrontations, revolutionary rhetoric, and very little disciplined learning. The rest of us got by as best we could, occasionally being drawn into the various conflicts, more frequently having our studies inadvertently interrupted by police riot squads or revolutionary student groups keeping our classes from meeting.

Although the total chaos which reigned at Berkeley from 1964 to 1972 was matched only at about a hundred campuses around the country, most of the nation's colleges and universities experienced some form of academic turmoil. Unfortunately, a great deal of this turbulence manifested itself in innovations of little educational value, which have been quite difficult to eliminate. In the mid-1970's Berkeley was offering a course in comic books, Wayne State a course in monster literature, Michigan State a very popular course in "Star Trek," Ithaca College a course entitled "Why the Sky Is Blue and Things Like That," Boston College a course on "The God Question," the University of South Florida a course on the literature of terror and horror, and the University of Wisconsin had created a Division of Contemporary Trends, which was specifically designed to teach classes requested by students. A comparable level of academic rigor was achieved in such courses as urban affairs at City University of New York or criminology at Berkeley, which combined left-wing political indoctrination with some ineffective community social-action work. Both types of program are symptomatic of a severe and continuing deterioration in academic standards which the student rebellion brought in its wake.

One manifestation of this deterioration in standards is the reduction in requirements for graduation. A recent study commissioned by the Carnegie Foundation for the Advancement of Teaching shows an average 23 percent reduction in course requirements for a degree between 1967 and 1974.[19] The study indicated that the percentage of colleges requiring a foreign language declined from 73 percent in 1967 to 53 percent in 1974; for English the reduction was from 90 percent to 72 percent; for mathematics it was from 33 percent to 20 percent. The reduction in course requirements was matched by an increase in electives. Although this study did not report changes in history requirements, the OAH study mentioned earlier indicated that university requirements for history courses and enrollments in those courses dropped sharply nationwide during the period covered by the Carnegie study.[79] The Carnegie Foundation report concludes:

> General education is now a disaster area. It has been on the defensive and losing ground for more than 100 years. It represents the accretions of history more than a thoughtful concern for specialized current needs.[26]

An elective-oriented college curriculum evolved to meet the educational needs of well-prepared college students in the first half of this century. The rapid expansion of electives during a period when large numbers of poorly prepared students are entering college threatens to distort completely the historical concept of a college-educated person as somebody who possesses at least a minimal amount of academic skill and knowledge. It tends also to reinforce the literacy hoax, as indicated by the APL statistics reported in Chapter One, which show that 2 percent of the nation's college *graduates* are functionally incompetent, and another 17 percent barely competent. (I write this a few days after the director of my San Francisco Institute reported that he had to turn away a junior-college student applying to take our reading program, because the young man was reading only at a 2.4 grade level.)

Confirmation of the decline in English requirements comes from a recent study by Ron Smith of Utah State University.[137] He compared the 1967 and 1973 English composition requirements of approximately five hundred colleges and universities around the country. His study shows that in 1967, 93 percent of the nation's colleges required their freshmen to take at least one course in English composition, and 78 percent required them to take at least two, compared to 76 percent and 45 percent respectively in 1973. Smith also reports that an increasing number of students have been exempted from the composition requirements each year. That an increasing percentage of college graduates write poorly is the result, at least in part, of the reduction in these requirements.

A recent survey of faculty members at the nation's colleges and universities underscores this and other problems.[88] More than three-quarters of the professors believe that the required core curriculum needs to be expanded. Eighty percent of this group believe "there has been a widespread lowering of standards in American higher education." There is a virtual consensus that undergraduate students are "seriously underprepared" in the basic skills of written and oral communication, and slightly over half cite a comparable decline in the quality of their graduate students.

One specific manifestation of the deterioration in standards cited by the nation's professoriat is the extreme form of open admissions adopted by a number of colleges and universities during the past decade. This policy change was the college-level analogue of the elimination of ability grouping at the secondary level. It was promoted and demanded by the civil-rights movement, which saw restrictive admissions policies, like ability grouping, as a mechanism that prevented a disproportionate number of minority students from obtaining access to the training that they needed in order to succeed in modern American society.

One decidedly beneficial result of this pressure was to eliminate racial discrimination as a factor in college admissions policies. As a result, the percentage of minority college students rose from 6.8 percent in 1960 to 13.4 percent in 1974.[141] On the negative side of this ledger, and potentially extremely dangerous for both the civil-rights movement and the American system of higher education, is the degradation in academic standards caused by the adoption of extreme forms of open admissions by a number of public universities.

There is nothing inherently wrong with open admissions, nor is there an inherent conflict between open admissions and the maintenance of high academic standards. A number of the large midwestern universities, such as Ohio State University and Indiana State University, are compelled by the laws of their respective states to admit every applicant who has graduated from a high school in their state. These colleges maintain their academic standards by requiring all freshmen to take several difficult courses in writing, literature, history, and science. As many as a third to a half of each entering freshman class drops out or fails before the end of the first year. Many of these students return with increased maturity and self-discipline at a later date, and succeed on their second try. This form of open admissions gives everyone a chance at a college education, yet safeguards the integrity of the institution and the education of the disciplined and prepared students by maintaining the academic standards of the course work.

Unfortunately, this form of open admissions is rarely acceptable to the civil-rights movement, especially its radical wing. Many civil-rights organizations claim that academic standards are merely a middle-class tool which is intended to restrict the access of minority people to decision-making positions in the society. A classic case of the type of open admissions I consider to be educationally very destructive is the policy adopted by the City University of New York (C.U.N.Y.). C.U.N.Y. is the nation's third-largest university system, enrolling about 250,000 students a year. It has historically been one of this country's great universities, ranking with the University of California system, not only in size but in academic excellence. The C.U.N.Y. adoption of open admissions in the fall of 1970 came as an accommodation to a series of vicious assaults on the university and individual faculty members and administrators by a number of political organizations, including civil-rights groups, revolutionary student organizations, and far-left political groups. An excellent chronicle of the events of the 1969 through 1972 period is available in C.U.N.Y. professor Louis G. Heller's work, *The Death of the American University*.[62]

The open-admissions policy adopted by C.U.N.Y. was designed to satisfy the demands of the radical wing of the civil-rights movement. C.U.N.Y. reduced the educational standards of its course work to encourage open-admissions students not to drop out. C.U.N.Y. also adopted the policy of not failing any open-admissions student for two years, no matter how poorly he might be doing. As a result of these policies, the level of course work degenerated to junior-high-school and high-school levels. Numerous reports indicate that many faculty, administrators, and students were demoralized by these politically motivated changes.[94] The end result was that a post-1970 C.U.N.Y. degree is worth considerably less than its pre-1970 counterpart.

One incident from this ongoing tragedy deserves special comment. During the 1975 New York City fiscal crisis, C.U.N.Y. was hit with a budget cut of 100 million dollars on a 570-million-dollar budget. In order to save money, the board of higher education proposed the elimination of open admissions, and the institution of an admissions standard of an eighth-grade reading level. For a short while this eighth-grade reading level became an issue over which educational conservatives and liberals did battle, the conservatives pushing for an eighth-grade standard as better than nothing, the liberals arguing that it was too restrictive. In the midst of this debate, David Lavin, a C.U.N.Y. sociologist, published a report which indicated that the adoption of a minimum eighth-grade reading level would knock 72 percent of the blacks, 65 percent of the Puerto Ricans, and 20 percent of the whites right out of the university.[41] Shortly after this report was published the conservatives gave up the fight, and an eighth-grade reading level did not become a criterion for admissions to C.U.N.Y.

This kind of extreme open-admissions policy destroys the educational fabric of a university. Universities and colleges are extremely meritocratic institutions, rather like professional athletic teams. They reward academic and intellectual excellence, and flunk out academic incompetence. They require a meritocratic structure in order to accomplish the task society assigns to them. When a university is forced by political exigencies to reward mediocrity and even incompetence, it must do so by reducing the standards and work demands it imposes on all of its students. In so doing it prevents its most able students from achieving to the limits of their abilities, and denies the society the efforts of its potentially most productive citizens.

The real victims of schools that have reduced their academic standards are their students. Unless they are forced to take them, how favorably are employers or graduate schools going to look on C.U.N.Y. graduates in the near future? Several medical schools have informed me that they will not even consider the applications of students who have attended schools they believe have reduced their academic standards. Schools that cheapen their degrees serve neither the interests of the society nor the interests of the overwhelming majority of their students.

While this extreme form of open admissions is not in society's best interest, it is unarguable that it is in society's interest to increase the pool of skilled, qualified minority college students. Thus some kind of modified open-admissions policy, without a reduction in academic standards, combined with a program of intensive basic-skills instruction for minority students who are able to benefit from such a program, would seem to be the indicated blueprint for this nation's public universities, at least until our inner-city schools significantly increase the quality of the education they offer.

From my own experience I can testify that many students can make significant improvement in their reading and study skills in a relatively short program. Bright, motivated students, with good vocabularies, can realistically expect to make strong and permanent gains in reading comprehension. Unfortunately, this does not happen in every case. Low-ability students and those with poor vocabularies have a great deal of difficulty. Even worse are the students who have the attitude that society owes them an education. Society owes people access to an education; the achievement of an education is an individual task which requires sustained, disciplined effort over a period of many years.

The most important manifestation of the deterioration in academic standards is sharp and continuing grade inflation, which is even greater at the college level than the analogous phenomenon at the high-school level. The faculty survey cited earlier in this section reported that 94 percent of the nation's college and university professors believe that grade inflation is an important problem at their own institutions, and two-thirds admit to assigning higher grades than their students deserve.[88] The following graph charts the rise in average college grades among a representative group of over one hundred colleges nationwide between 1960 and 1975. It was derived from data reported by Professor Arvo Juola of Michigan

State University.[77] The graph shows grade inflation of about .4 of a grade point on a four-point scale, most of which occurred between 1968 and 1973. The grade-point average of a university in a given year is the average of all grades assigned that year (including physical education), where A is assigned a value of 4.0, B is 3.0, C is 2.0, D is 1.0, and F is 0.0.

Confirmation of the above trend comes from a 1975 study by the University of California at Berkeley, which showed that the average undergraduate grade-point average at twenty-three of the nation's biggest universities went from 2.49 on a four-point scale in 1963 to 2.94 in 1974.[147] The study showed that the percentage of A's increased from 16 percent to 34 percent over the eleven-year time span, while the percentage of C's dropped from 37 percent to 21 percent. These figures are reinforced by the Carnegie Foundation report cited earlier, which shows that the percentage of A's and B's awarded to undergraduates nationwide increased from 54 percent in 1969 to 74 percent in 1976.[26]

Data are available for several dozen individual colleges, all of which confirm the upward trend in grades over the past dozen years. In 1974, 75 percent of the grades at American University were A's or B's, as were 81 percent of the grades at Vassar and Dartmouth, and 85 percent of the grades at Amherst. In 1975 Harvard graduated over 83 percent of its seniors with honors, and the average grade-point average at Stanford was 3.41 on a four-point scale. Ohio State University graduated more students with straight-A averages between 1971 and 1975 than it did in its first one hundred years of existence. Dickinson College in Pennsylvania eliminated its Dean's List in 1975 when approximately a third of the student body earned the qualifying 3.5 grade-point average. The University of Michigan reported that its freshman class in 1974 had earned the highest grade-point average in the school's history, and was the academically weakest freshman class in more than two decades. I have seen reports indicating sharp grade inflation at Kent State, University of Wisconsin, University of California at Berkeley, University of Illinois, Yale, Temple, Bowdoin, Kenyon, UCLA, University of Virginia, University of North Carolina, University of Min-

Graph 3

AVERAGE GRADE-POINT AVERAGE
AT OVER 100 AMERICAN COLLEGES
AND UNIVERSITIES, 1960 TO 1975

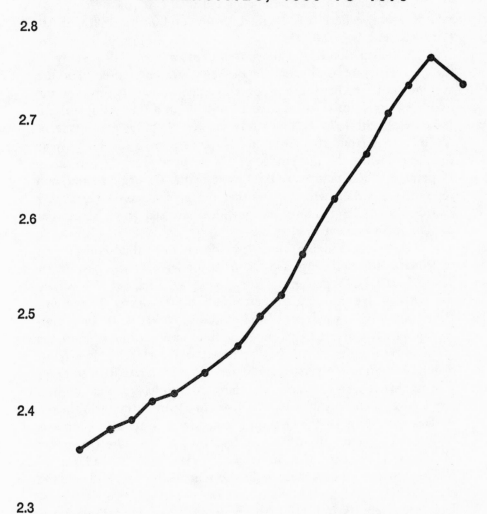

nesota, and many others. To compensate for the reduced standards at American universities, Phi Beta Kappa, the national student honor society, has recently been compelled to upgrade sharply its own standards for eligibility.

Grade inflation is indicative of a real and continuing deterioration in academic standards at American universities. The Vietnam War and the student rebellion have been over for years, yet grade inflation is worse today than it was at the height of those twin conflicts. Its cause is not difficult to fathom. With a completely free elective system, professors are afraid to grade hard for fear they will not keep their students, and their jobs. Now that many colleges use student evaluations as a basis for tenure decisions, professors must use their grading practices as one element in an educational popularity contest. What's true for professors applies to departments and colleges as well. With departments competing for reduced budgets, which department is going to compel its faculty to tighten up its grading standards and scare away potential students? With a shrinking potential student population, which college is going to jeopardize its enrollment by cracking down on the grading practices of its faculty?

The political pressure caused by the extreme form of open admissions discussed earlier also forces grades up. If the incompetent must be given a C, then the competent get the A's and B's formerly reserved for the superior. Many colleges which have retained selective admissions criteria enroll a large number of special students who do not meet those criteria. Faculty are under intense political pressure to award B's and C's to these students, no matter what the quality of their work. Sometimes this situation creates a double standard for grading; more frequently it just forces up the grades of all the students.

Another factor which tends to push up grades is the system of Pass/No Credit (P/NC) grading, which, according to an unpublished report by the Carnegie Council on Policy Studies in Higher Education, has been adopted as a grading option by over 80 percent of the colleges and universities in the country. A student who registers to take a course P/NC either passes the course or gets no credit;

in either case it does not affect his grade-point average. At a northern California college, a student enrolled in and passed 42 units of course work in one semester. Several of the courses for which he registered were offered at the same time. (It takes 120 semester units to graduate from college.)

A good deal of the course work available to students is both trivial and easy. How can one get anything but an A or B in a course on science fiction or comic books? Admittedly these are extreme cases, but the proliferation of "relevant," student-oriented courses adds to the upward pressure on grades. This factor is tied to what is probably the key to the entire process, the changing values of the faculty, especially the younger faculty. The older, pre-1965 faculty, many of whom were scholars of merit, most of whom had matured through the depression and World War II, believed in and promoted the value of scholarship and intense intellectual effort. A great many of the younger faculty simply do not believe in the paramount values of intellectual accomplishment and hard work. Many of them promote a form of modern egalitarianism, which holds that the efforts of all individuals are inherently equal. As an example of this kind of attitude, a young psychology professor who read this chapter when it was in draft form criticized it as being based on a model of deficits, rather than differences. He was, of course, correct. (See Interview 8.)

The egalitarianism of many of the young faculty is really a manifestation of their own resistance to authority, and their unwillingness to assume the authoritative role which society intends for its teachers. The very concept of standards and hard work are predicated on an underlying authority relationship between faculty and student. It is no wonder that college is easier and standards relaxed, when a significant percentage of the faculty refuses to assume the authority assigned to it.

Grade inflation penalizes the superior, the talented, and the hardworking, and rewards the mediocre, incompetent, and lazy. It produces a kind of intellectual fantasyland, where everybody is superior. It teaches America's brightest young people that there is no particular merit attached to hard work. It is a measure of the deterioration of our institutions of higher education.

The phenomenon of grade inflation deserves one final comment. Reference to Graph 3 will show that in 1975 the average grade-point average of America's college students declined slightly for the first time in fifteen years. This finding was heralded in the academic community as an indication that the deterioration in academic standards had ended. Yet reference to the same graph will show that in 1975 grade inflation was worse than at any time in history except for the one year 1974. (Also note that ACT and ETS data, and Graph 2, indicate that grade inflation among high-school students actually accelerated in 1976 and 1977.)

I expect the same kind of wishful thinking to explode into the media the first time the SAT scores go up by a few points. If they should go up two years in a row the media pundits will be telling us that the achievement decline has ended. The American public needs to be forewarned that a one- or two-year trend reversal will not signal the reconstruction of our public schools. A real danger in the present situation is that both trends will reverse slightly and then stabilize, leaving us with a permanently deteriorated educational system.

COMPENSATORY EDUCATION

The academic achievement of the average black or Mexican-American youngster falls far behind that of the average white student. By the end of elementary school the average minority student has fallen almost two years behind the national average in reading and math computation, and by the end of high school the gap is three to four years. Data reported in the APL study cited in the Introduction and Chapter One show that 44 percent of the nation's black adults and 56 percent of the nation's Mexican-American adults are functionally illiterate, compared to 16 percent of the nation's white adults. The APL study also shows that the educational deficits are translated directly into economic deficits.

Starting in 1965, the federal government, in conjunction with a number of state offices of education, instituted wide-scale educational programs designed to help minority and other educationally disadvantaged children improve their academic performance. These took the form of special preschool programs, most notably Head Start, and special reading and math programs in elementary school. These programs are generally subsumed under the heading of compensatory education, which communicates the intent of the programs to help children compensate for the environmental deficiencies which have contributed to their educational deficiencies.

Compensatory-education programs are designed primarily to serve this nation's five to six million educationally disadvantaged children (out of a total elementary-school population of almost twenty-five million). The label "educationally disadvantaged" describes a child who attends a school that has a large enrollment of children from poor families, and who scores significantly below the national average on tests of academic achievement. The federal government allocates about 60 percent of its elementary- and secondary-school expenditures, or about 3.5 billion dollars a year, to pay for compensatory education. The figures for state contributions to compensatory education are difficult to obtain, but the best estimate seems to be about half a billion dollars a year. These four billion dollars a year pay only for the extra services provided to educationally disadvantaged children, and may not be used by local school districts to pay the normal, day-to-day costs of their education.

A dozen years and 50 billion dollars later, we are in a position to evaluate the effectiveness of the major compensatory-education programs. In the next few pages I will review a number of studies which demonstrate unequivocally that these programs have failed. The educational gap separating minority and white students is approximately as wide today as the day the first dime of compensatory-education money was allocated.

I have included such an evaluation in this chapter for several reasons. Compensatory education brought in its wake wide-scale curricular reforms which affected the entirety of public education, and thus the academic achievement of all this nation's children. These programs started when the academic skills of America's students were at their historical peak and expanded steadily during the period when these skills were declining. We need to ask if the extensive federal and state intervention in local education, which is the hallmark of compensatory education, contributed to the achievement decline of the past dozen years.

We also need to examine the programs themselves in order to isolate the factors that caused their failure. As a nation we are morally obliged to help educationally disadvantaged children achieve the skills that will enable them to function in society. The failures of the past dozen years have caused widespread demoralization in the ranks of the teachers in our poverty areas and inner cities. We must provide these teachers with an acceptable analysis of previous program failure and a rationale for future program conduct.

Finally, I have included this section because it contains some very important lessons for anyone concerned with solving the educational problems of our society. If we are to avoid the errors of the past dozen years as we confront the pressing educational problems of the next dozen, we need to know what not to do. A neurotic is defined as someone who cannot learn from his mistakes. I am writing this section in the hope that our society is sufficiently healthy that, knowing our mistakes, we will not be forced to repeat them.

The first major independent evaluation of compensatory education was an analysis of Head Start in 1969 by Westinghouse Learning Corporation and Ohio State University.[162] Their study showed that Head Start produced virtually no long-term effects in students' learning abilities or attitudes toward school. Results for the summer-school version of Head Start were so negative that the Westinghouse authors recommended its immediate discontinuation. Some short-term gains were recorded as a result of the full-year program, but these gains disappeared by the time the students had completed second grade. Students who had participated in Head Start displayed the same pattern of deficits in reading and arithmetic as comparable students who had not participated.

A number of other evaluations of Head Start since 1969 have reproduced these findings, including a 1975 General Accounting Office (GAO) report to Congress.[122] The 1975 GAO report indicates that in the face of these evaluations, the response of Head Start administrators has been to redefine the program's goals from cognitive learning to social competence. Social competence is defined as a child's everyday effectiveness in dealing with his environment and later responsibilities in school and life. Not too surprisingly, program administrators have unanimously declared Head Start to be successful along this objectively unmeasurable parameter. Funding for Head Start has increased from 300 million dollars per year prior to the Westinghouse study to about 400 million dollars per year by 1976. (In 1969 Congress established the Follow Through program, which was expressly designed to maintain the improvements achieved in Head Start. A massive 1977 evaluation indicates that Follow Through has failed, and that, indeed, Follow Through produces more negative than positive effects.[142])

The Elementary and Secondary Education Act (ESEA) of 1965 funds compensatory education through local school districts. Title I of ESEA provides about two billion dollars per year for programs to develop the academic skills of educationally disadvantaged children. The first major attempt to evaluate these programs came in a 1968 U.S. Office of Education (USOE) report.[44] The report concluded that participating students were not closing the educational gap separating them from the national average. In 1969, a Health, Education, and Welfare Department (HEW) analysis of 189 Title I programs selected in a manner likely to be biased toward higher scores reported that 58 of the programs showed gains in reading, 50 showed losses, and 81 showed no change.[119]

Other evaluations of Title I programs since 1969 also indicate they have failed. The most recent evaluation was published by the General Accounting Office in December of 1975.[10] The GAO reported that 50 percent of the students in the Title I programs it evaluated were learning to read at a faster rate than before enrolling in the program, one percent were learning at the same rate, and 49 percent were learning at a slower rate. The GAO also reported that 70 percent of the participating students did not reach grade level while in the program, and that almost 60 percent of the students who did achieve grade level while in the program fell below grade level once the program was ended.

A 1974 Rand Corporation analysis of compensatory programs concluded that they had failed to help disadvantaged youngsters reach grade level in cognitive skills. The report's conclusion reads:

> Without exception, all of the large surveys of the large national compensatory education programs have shown no beneficial results on average, as measured by achievement tests or IQ scores.[11]

Why has compensatory education failed? As I mentioned in the very first page of this chapter, the reanalyses of the Coleman report by Mosteller and Moynihan in 1972, and Jencks *et al.* also in 1972, indicated that the influences of a child's family, socioeconomic class, and peer group were so potent that twelve years of formal schooling could have only a minimal effect on his cognitive development. The implied message of these reports was that compensatory education was doomed to fail. Jencks went so far as to urge the public schools to change their focus from the long-term effects of schooling to the short-term enjoyment of their students.

The previously listed studies showing that compensatory education has failed, combined with the conclusions of Jencks's and Moynihan's reports, have badly demoralized the professional educational community. One symptom of this demoralization is that the failure of compensatory education has been largely left unexamined and unexplained, except in the terms of the critics who maintain that such programs are doomed to fail.

While I am not so naïve as to dismiss totally the influence of nonschool factors on a child's cognitive development, I believe the demoralization of public-school educators is an inappropriate response to the available research evidence. Four excellent studies flatly contradict the conclusions of the reports cited above. In the first of these studies, David Wiley of the University of Chicago also reanalyzed the Coleman report, and concluded that a 24 percent increase in the number of hours of instruction resulted in a two-thirds increase in reading comprehension achievement, and more than a one-third increase in math achievement.[164] The AIR report cited earlier in the chapter confirmed some of Wiley's findings, but, more importantly, indicated that the academic achievement of students at all socioeconomic levels can be significantly improved by good instruction.[71]

The two most useful studies in this area used essentially the same methodology. They studied extremely effective compensatory-education programs (where educationally deprived students were achieving at or above national norms), in order to isolate instructional factors that led to program success. The more recent of these studies, a 1976 Michigan Department of Education report, cited the following factors as associated with program success: increased classroom time devoted to reading instruction; increased teacher time spent in training and program planning; longer working hours for teachers; increased teacher authority over the program and materials they were using; high teacher morale.[128] The other study, a 1971 report by George Weber of the Council for Basic Education, used the school as the basis of his analysis.[158] He chronicled the cases of four successful inner-city schools attended by very poor black, Mexican-American, and Puerto Rican children. A list of Weber's success factors includes strong administrative leadership: high expectations of pupils by teachers and administrators; good school atmosphere; strong schoolwide emphasis on reading; additional reading personnel; use of phonics; teacher-initiated individualization; careful evaluation of pupil progress.

The most important message of these four studies is that our public schools can successfully teach disadvantaged children to read. Once this point has been established, it is incumbent upon us to examine the failure of compensatory education in its own terms, rather than merely dismissing it as a hopeless bet from the outset. Such an examination has convinced me that the programs have failed not because poor children are hopeless cases, but because the programs are poorly conceived, poorly administered, and poorly taught.

The most obvious fact to anyone who has spent much time investigating compensatory programs in a metropolitan school district is that they are in a state of almost total anarchy. It is not unusual for every school in a district dependent on federal funds to have a number of different compensatory programs in operation. Thus a metropolitan school district of moderate size is likely to have several hundred special programs under way at any one time. These programs are not part of a coordinated effort to attack the educational problems of the district's students; rather, they are a combination of disconnected efforts of individual teachers and school administrators.

If the chaos at the district level is baffling, at the school and classroom level it is tragic. It is quite common for one school to be using several different approaches to beginning reading instruction, perhaps a special phonics-readiness program in kindergarten, one of the new individualized systems in first through third grade, and maybe a basal reader in fourth through sixth. Because teachers are permitted to modify program content to suit their preferences, it is not unusual for several teachers to be using programs that are different from the prescribed programs.

Teachers in these schools are often confused and upset because there is constant pressure on them to change from one program to another, and they are not able to develop proficiency or confidence in any one approach. Furthermore, compensatory programs tend to denigrate the role of the classroom teacher, by building up the importance of teacher-proof materials, paraprofessional aides, and outside specialists. The schools are inundated with adults, each vying with the classroom teacher for authority with the children.

I believe it would be worthwhile to describe the effect of this educational anarchy on a child who is attempting to learn how to read. Recall that a student learning to read must master a sequence of several hundred skills. Among these are such things as the sounds of the letters, a basic sight vocabulary, and an understanding of the sound and meaning of endings as *-ed*, *-s*, and *-ing*. The major publishers of basic reading programs do a generally good job of building these skill components into their programs. However, they do not necessarily follow the same time scheme. To take a real example, the new Ginn 720 series introduces most endings at the first- and second-grade levels.[32] Many older series did not get to this skill until the third grade. If a school changed from an older series to Ginn 720 as a student went into third grade, the child would completely miss the basic introduction to endings.

This example of endings is but one of hundreds of skills that must be learned. If a student changes his basic program at any time in elementary school, and especially in his first four years, there is a very real likelihood he will miss the introduction to many of these skills. If he is a weak student and does not receive skill reinforcement at home by reading with his family, these holes in his education could seriously interfere with his mastery of the reading process.

Other aspects of the transition from one basic reading program to another can create problems. The vocabulary in each series is somewhat different, which could cause trouble for weaker students. While the basic programs of the biggest publishers are conceptually quite similar, there are many new programs on the market using substantially different conceptual frameworks for teaching basic reading skills. A transition to or from one of these programs could create quite severe problems. For example, there are two fundamentally different ways to teach beginning phonics. The mainstream publishers, such as Ginn, Harper and Row, and Houghton Mifflin, use what is called the analytic approach. This approach does not initially teach the sounds of letters in isolation. Instead, the student first learns a number of very basic sight words—*boy, bat, big*—and then learns that when he sees the letter *b* at the beginning of a word, it makes the same sound as in those words. Some of the newer programs, such as Distar, use what is called the synthetic approach, which first teaches the sound of isolated letters and then teaches students how to blend them together to make words. Thus the student is taught the sound of *b*, the sound of *a*, the sound of *t*, and then taught how to blend them together to make the word *bat*. Although the goal of both approaches is the same, the paths are substantially different. This is just one example of major conceptual differences that exist between available reading programs.

A child's difficulties are compounded if he is exposed to three, or four, or five basic reading programs in his first six years. This occurs frequently in school districts that receive a good deal of federal funding for compensatory education. In these districts it is customary for schools to switch programs every two or three years. It is just as common for each school in a district to use a different program. I've investigated the rate of basic program change in metropolitan school districts receiving federal funds for compensatory education. In California, I estimate, the average child will be exposed to three basic reading programs while in elementary school. It is very unlikely that a youngster in one of these schools will stick with the same program throughout his first six grades, or even his first four.

A final factor in the damage caused by program instability probably dwarfs in importance any of the previously discussed factors. When a student changes to a new reading program it is fairly likely that his teacher will be teaching the program for the first time. It is in the nature of reading instruction that the first time most teachers use a new program, they are simply not terribly good with it. When programs change every few years, they do not get very good with any of them.

The indicated chaos is not limited to the reading curriculum. It affects the teaching of math, spelling, writing—indeed, the entire school experience of children who attend schools involved with compensatory education. Many of these children come from unstable homes in which parents do not enforce disciplined behavior, and this kind of educational chaos is devastating in its effect.

There is a feeling of great bitterness on the part of many teachers and administrators toward the federal and state offices of education that manage compensatory education. These teachers and administrators feel that the educational anarchy associated with compenstory education is directly caused by a mass of conflicting, restrictive, and self-defeating guidelines which they must follow. The ostensible reason for these regulations is to ensure that the extra services targeted for educationally disadvantaged youngsters actually reach their target. In fact, many of these guidelines are politically, not educationally, motivated.

The first guideline says that a district cannot spend any of its extra federal or state money to supplant regular district services.[51a] The U.S. Office of Education (USOE) does not want the district simply to add the federal money to its general fund. It wants the district to spend the federal funds to provide extra services to the target students. This regulation prevents districts from hiring full-time classroom teachers in order to reduce class size. The reason given for this rule is that smaller class size is an educational benefit which is being given to all the students in a school, not just the ones whose achievement test scores indicate they qualify for extra services.

The basic unit of elementary and secondary education is the classroom—one teacher working with a group of students. This first guideline ensures that federal money will not be spent to improve the functioning of this basic educational unit, but instead will be spent for auxiliary services. Many inner-city schools are virtual technological laboratories of sophisticated electronic gadgetry that nobody uses. These funded schools are saturated with nonteaching adults. Investment in these secondary services has little relevance to educational process and practically no impact on educational outputs.

The educational rhetoric surrounding the second guideline provides only the thinnest disguise to its baldly political purpose.[51b] This regulation specifies that parents of children served by compensatory programs are to have an active planning, advisory, and participatory role in the compensatory program. School districts must set up a number of local parents' committees associated with the schools receiving federal funds. Before the state office of education will accept a district's proposal regarding allocation of compensatory funds, the district parents' committees must approve the plan.

I have discussed the effect of this regulation with budgetary officers of a number of the nation's largest metropolitan school districts, including San Francisco, Oakland, Detroit, Washington, D.C., and Philadelphia. They inform me that about 50 percent of the compensatory funds allowed to a school are spent to pay the salaries of parents who live in the community. Through the mechanism of the parents' advisory committees, the parents hire themselves as teacher aides, community aides, clerical aides, and hall aides.

Following is the breakdown of the personnel list of one real inner-city school before and after federal funding. The school serves 550 students, and has a compensatory program budget of approximately $225,000 a year, approximately 60 percent of which is used to pay the salaries of the parent aides.

The educators and politicians promoting this guideline claim that parents working in a school will develop positive attitudes toward education. These attitudes will diffuse into the community, positively affecting the environment in which the community's children will develop. Within the school, the aides will take such non-teaching administrative tasks as correcting papers or taking roll out

TABLE 6

PERSONNEL LIST OF ONE INNER-CITY SCHOOL,
BEFORE AND AFTER FEDERAL FUNDING

District Funded Positions	Before	After
Full-time certificated teachers	20	20
Administrator	1	1
Clerical and janitorial	3	3
Professional support staff (*e.g.*, librarian, nurse, psychologist)	2	2
Federally Funded Positions		
Teacher aides (parents)		56
Clerical and other aides (parents)		7
Project coordinator (certificated)		1
Full-time teachers (certificated reading and math specialists)		2
Half-time teachers (certificated)		3
Half-time professional support staff		3
Total Parents	—	63
Total Professional Staff	26	35
Total Adults in School	26	98

of the hands of teachers, thereby leaving the teacher more time with the children. They will also perform some instructional tasks, which will increase the individualization of instruction. Finally, the improved adult-to-student ratio will increase the orderliness of the classroom process.

The major flaw in this rhetoric is that it bears practically no relationship to reality. Many parents hired as teacher aides exhibit the same learning deficits and attitude problems as the students. They often resist and subvert the authority of the classroom teacher. Far from making the educational process more orderly, the saturation of the school with adults has a tendency to produce educational and administrative chaos. Finally, the guideline tends to disrupt parent/school relations. Because the parents' source of institutional power is outside the normal channels of school administration, an adversary relationship develops between them and the traditional holders of school authority, the teachers and administrators.

The Michigan Department of Education study cited earlier in this section demonstrates what school officials have known for years: a school's use of parent aides does not increase the academic achievement of its students, and may contribute to their continued poor academic performance.[128] This report indicates that the most effective compensatory programs make little use of part-time parent aides, and that the least effective programs make extensive use of such aides. As I indicated at the beginning of this section, these guidelines are essentially political in nature, not educational, and it is this political interference more than anything else which has caused the failure of compensatory education. Anybody familiar with big-city politics knows that the real purpose of this guideline, in combination with the first one I discussed, is to turn education money into job money.

Probably the single most damaging guideline is the rule determining which students are eligible for special services in schools provided with federal funds. This rule says that students may not receive special services unless their scores on a standardized achievement test fall below the national average.[51c] This regulation is interpreted by many state departments of education to mean that a student must score in the lowest quarter of students at their grade level in the nation. Other states arbitrarily rule that a student must be at least one year below grade level to qualify. This regulation is heavily enforced, with school districts constantly under the threat of federal or state audit to prove they are providing no services to students who do not meet the criteria for program participation.

The effect of this guideline is to deny eligibility for program participation to many students who could benefit from such participation. A child of above-average ability, who reads slightly below grade level as a result of inadequate educational reinforcement from his family, should not be automatically denied access to the special help that would enable him to realize his educational potential. Some students scoring a year below grade level may be fulfilling their educational potential, while others scoring a year above may not be fulfilling theirs. The decision as to who could most benefit from compensatory instruction should be made at the school level by the professional staff, not at the state or federal offices of education.

It requires an enormous investment of time and resources for a school district to comply with all of these regulations. They must set up special accounting procedures, and compel teachers and administrators to spend a significant amount of time filing paper work which will prove to federal auditors that all regulations have been satisfied. Teachers and administrators intensely resent these intrusions, yet feel powerless to stop them.

I know one elementary-school principal, whose school had recently qualified for compensatory funds, who told me that the reading ability of his students was declining because the formal individualized reading programs required by the California State Department of Education were ineffective with the type of students in his school. He could not urge district officials to turn down the compensatory funds, because both he and they would be liable in the event of a taxpayer's suit.

According to a number of recent newspaper reports,[47] several members of the Richmond, California, school board are desperate to get out from under federal control, yet are almost powerless to take such a step. Their ire was provoked most recently by a federal court order requiring them to reassign about one hundred teachers. The California State Department of Education had previously ordered all districts in the state to assign teachers in such a way that the racial composition of each school's faculty would be as reflective of the racial composition of its student body as possible. After Richmond had carefully reassigned their teachers to comply with this state regulation, the federal government instructed all school districts receiving federal money to assign their teachers so that the racial composition of the teachers at any school would reflect the racial composition of the faculty district-wide. When Richmond moved too slowly to comply with the new regulation, they got hit with a court order threatening an immediate cutoff in federal funds.

The following reported congressional testimony by Wilson Riles, California's superintendent of public instruction, reflects the frustration of our nation's school officials with the contradictory and self-defeating federal compensatory education guidelines discussed above:

> "Recently," Riles said, "a principal asked a federal Title I official if it were permissible to take 10 non-Title I children in a class of 30 on a field trip. The principal said it would cost no more to include the 10 youngsters on the trip planned for the 20 eligible Title I students."
>
> The answer was no, because "regulations" forbid non-Title I children from benefiting from Title I money. The principal asked if the district could pay for the non-Title I children. Again, the answer was no, because this would violate "comparability" requirements.
>
> (The comparability guidelines mandate comparable *local* expenditures for Title I and non-Title I students, thereby preventing districts from giving extra services to non-Title I students.)
>
> The confused and frustrated principal proposed leaving the non-Title I youngsters at home. Once more the answer was no, this time because the action would amount to segregation.
>
> "The principal knew he was licked," Riles said, "so he asked for advice. But the federal official replied that he was not there to provide advice, just to enforce the law."
>
> The principal said he would cancel the trip. But again the reply

was no, because field trips are required to provide cultural enrichment for Title I students.

Not wanting to violate the law, the principal said, "Okay, we'll have the field trip."

The official then asked suspiciously, "How are you going to pay for it?"

"You'll never know," the principal replied with a smile and walked away.

"Our responsibility to help children is too important to play this kind of game," Riles told the subcommittee. "People in the field who are trying to make compensatory education work should not be forced into hypocrisy." [55]

A researcher attempting to investigate compensatory education is immediately struck by the extremely low caliber of local and state program evaluations. A caveat to the conclusion of the Rand report quoted earlier states:

> However, the local evaluation reports on which the surveys are based are often poor and the research designs suspect.[11]

The December 1975 GAO evaluation of Title I actually printed the following conclusion on the cover of the report:

> The Office of Education has not required adequate information on student achievement from State and local educational agencies for measuring the national effect of reading projects funded under the program. The local evaluations made generally have not contained uniform data and often have been incomplete.[10]

It is not accidental that the evaluations are inadequate. School districts usually maintain separate administrative units for administration and evaluation of federally funded compensatory programs. What happens in these administrative units is a classic case of bureaucratic goal displacement.

The administrators realize that standardized achievement tests indicate that their programs are failing. It is not in their self-interest to report failure year after year, nor is it part of human nature even to admit failure to one's own self. The result is that school-district personnel associated with compensatory education develop a strong bias against the measuring instruments demonstrating program failure, i.e., standardized achievement tests. Since they find it convenient to believe the tests biased and inaccurate, they refuse to learn the most fundamental techniques of educational measurement. Local evaluations are hopelessly inadequate, because it is in the self-interest of the local evaluators to make them so.

Administrators and teachers associated with compensatory education will almost universally report that their subjective evaluations are more accurate than the results of standardized tests. In the 1975 GAO report on Title I cited above, project administrators unanimously reported program success in the face of statistics indicating program failure. The basis for the claims? Positive subjective response by project personnel.

A brief personal account may illuminate the issue. A local school administrator recently asked me to make an informal assessment of his school's secondary-level reading program. I spent an afternoon looking at reading scores with the school's reading coordinator. To my dismay, I discovered that over 30 percent of the scores had been eliminated prior to the analysis of the data that had been sent to the school board. Every student whose post-test score was lower than his pre-test score had been eliminated prior to the data analysis. When I confronted the coordinator with this fact, she replied that she personally knew a great many of the students whose test scores had gone down, and she knew they were better readers at the end of the program than at the beginning. Therefore, she had concluded that all of those students showing a drop must have been tested inaccurately.

Lest the reader suspect I am exaggerating the scale or the importance of these inadequate evaluations, three recent reports should be instructive. A. Alan Post, the highly respected budget analyst for the California state legislature, recently published two reports excoriating the evaluations conducted by the California State Department of Education.[6, 46] In these reports he criticized the state evaluations of Title I projects, and he also criticized the state evaluations of Early Childhood Education (ECE), which is the pet project of the California Superintendent of Public Instruction, Wilson Riles.

In its evaluations, the State Department of Education had claimed that both programs were extremely successful. In his analyses, Post concluded that the State Department of Education had used faulty statistical techniques which had inflated program results. He concluded that the evaluations were so inadequate that no conclusions regarding program success or failure could be drawn. Despite Post's analyses, the Department of Education was able to parlay its faulty evaluations into a 32-million-dollar funding increase for ECE in 1976.

The third report was a 1976 Rand educational policy study which confirmed the findings reported above, *i.e.*, an overwhelming proportion of local evaluations are conducted poorly, and the few evaluations which can be analyzed indicate that compensatory education is not working.[96] Two more of the report's findings provide a devastating indictment of Congress and USOE. First, the study found that the only evaluations Congressmen want conducted or reported must show the benefits of compensatory education, because they see compensatory education primarily as a local jobs program designed to win them support from their constituencies. Second, USOE has bowed to Congressional pressure, and no longer attempts to use evaluation as a tool to increase the effectiveness of compensatory programs. Instead, USOE now centers its evaluation efforts on discovering and publicizing exemplary programs, in order to increase political support for compensatory education.

There is a lesson to be learned from this discussion of bureaucratic mismanagement of the evaluation process. The public must learn to analyze the public pronouncements and written documentation of the education establishment with as jaundiced and careful a scrutiny as it applies to the self-serving statements of any other entrenched bureaucracy. Remember, we trusted the evaluations by our generals in Vietnam to our everlasting national shame.

To repeat something I said earlier in the chapter, the basic unit of elementary and secondary education is the classroom—one teacher working with a group of students. Strengthen that unit, and you strengthen the educational process. Weaken that unit, and the educational process deteriorates. The only way to strengthen that unit is to increase the expertise and authority of the classroom teacher. This means recruiting talented, intelligent, and hardworking teachers. It means hiring and supporting school principals who have the ability and courage to perform the following educational leadership functions: establishing a stable, educationally sound curriculum; motivating the teaching staff; firing incompetent teachers; motivating parents to reinforce schoolwork in the home; creating an orderly school environment which supports the teacher in his efforts. It means providing teachers with ongoing training in the theory and technique of basic-skills instruction, and providing them with diagnostic information on their students. It means backing up their basic-skills instruction with motivating materials and programs which they can use at their discretion. It means increasing their power, authority, and prestige within the classroom, the school, and the community.

Compensatory education failed, and will continue to fail, because it did not accept the primacy of the classroom unit, and therefore did not recruit good teachers and principals into inner-city schools, or support the good ones already there. Instead, compensatory education focused on secondary services—parent aides, reading and math specialists, teacher-proof programs—all of which denigrate the role and the authority of the classroom teacher, and prevent the principal from being able to fulfill his leadership role. Compensatory programs exacerbate the very severe problems of classroom control and motivation which are at the heart of the educational problems in our inner cities. As a result, the overwhelming majority of teachers and principals in these schools are demoralized, and function very poorly. Competent personnel flee these schools, or they sink to a level of functional mediocrity, or worse, after but one or two years teaching in them. Underprivileged children, who need good, orderly educational experiences, are subjected to a chaotic curriculum taught by the worst public-school teachers in the country. (See Interview 13.)

The federal and state control of local education which compensatory education brings in its wake is a very destructive force. The politically motivated regulations discussed in this section virtually ensure that compensatory education will become a jobs program rather than an effective educational program. These same regulations contribute to the educational chaos that reigns in many of our large metropolitan school districts. It is a national tragedy that children who desperately need special educational assistance have become the victims of political forces that do not hold their interests to be primary.

STANDARDIZED TESTING

A wide-scale campaign is currently under way to ban the use of all standardized educational tests, including IQ tests, achievement tests, and aptitude tests. If this movement is successful, American schoolchildren will no longer be tested with such tests as the Stanford Achievement Test, the Comprehensive Tests of Basic Skills, the Iowa Tests of Educational Development, or either the SAT or ACT. The recent actions of the states of New York and California in banning all group IQ tests are indicative of the growing strength of this movement, as is the ongoing campaign by the National Education Association (NEA), the nation's largest and most powerful educational organization, for a complete moratorium on the use of standardized educational tests.

The antitesting movement has also found support in a number of recent Supreme Court and lower federal court decisions, and a number of government regulations, restricting the use of educational tests in employment.[134] One of these decisions prevented a Mississippi school district from using a minimum score on the National Teacher Examinations put out by ETS as a criterion in the employment of teachers. Another prevented a New York school district from using a procedure for selecting school principals that relied in part on tests of general intelligence and cultural breadth. A whole series of decisions and regulations prevent private industry from using IQ or educational test scores as criteria for employment.

The antitesting campaign is one of the most acrimonious in

the history of American education. One of the leading voices in this campaign is the *National Elementary Principal*, whose articles on standardized testing read like the polemics of a particularly vicious political campaign. The following quotation from Gerald Zacharias was excerpted from the most recent of the two full issues of the magazine devoted to this movement:

> I feel emotionally toward the testing industry as I would toward any other merchant of death. I feel that way because of what they do to the kids. I'm not saying they murder every child—only 20 percent of them.[85]

A similar style of rhetoric was used by Terry Herndon, executive director of the NEA, in a recent speech to the Commonwealth Club in San Francisco:

> What we object to is accountability to standardized test results. We object to the tests themselves, as I have said. We object to an evaluation system designed to make tanks rather than mold minds.
> . . . But to those of us who resist the imposition of a sterile industrial model on what should be a liberating, exciting and individual experience, the standardized test is like a lock on the mind, a guard at the factory gate.[63]

In my opinion the success of this campaign would jeopardize the education of every American child, by preventing parents from monitoring the educational progress of their children, by encouraging educational experimentation on America's children without the safeguards of proper evaluation procedures, and by insulating the schools from the scrutiny of an informed public. I am well aware that standardized educational tests are imperfect measuring instruments, and that they can be used unwisely and their results misinterpreted. Nonetheless, they are uniquely useful educational tools that make a real contribution to the education of America's young people.

A standardized educational test is a test which has been previously administered to a national sample of students at several grade levels, who have been carefully selected to be representative of the national population of students at each grade level. The scores achieved by these students are called norms. *Percentile* norms tell the test administrator the exact percentage of the initial national sample at each grade level who attained a score equal to or less than each of the possible scores on the test. *Grade-equivalent* norms tell the test administrator the grade placement of the average student who attained each of the possible scores on the test.

Perhaps the best way to develop an understanding of a standardized test is to examine one. The Nelson-Denny Reading Test, published by Houghton Mifflin, is very commonly used with high-school and college students, which is the reason I am familiar with it.[38] The test consists of a series of short paragraphs, each followed by a number of comprehension questions. There are a total of 36 comprehension questions on the test. Assume that I administer the test to a ninth-grade student who answers 16 of them correctly. I then compare his score of 16 with the norms provided by the publisher. The percentile norms tell me that when the publisher administered the test to his initial national sample of ninth-grade students, 71 percent of the students scored 16 or lower. Thus I know that my student is as good or better at reading than 71 percent of the ninth graders in the country. The grade-equivalent norms tell me that the average student in the seventh month of tenth grade scored 16 on the test. Thus, according to the Nelson-Denny Reading Test, my student is reading at a 10.7 grade equivalent.

The reader should carefully note this last point. Many parents, when informed their child reads at a 10.7 grade equivalent, would misinterpret this information to mean that their child reads the way a student is supposed to read after completing seven months of the tenth grade. In fact, it merely signifies he scores as well on a standardized reading test as the *average* student who has completed this amount of schooling.

Despite their indicated limitations, grade-level scores given by standardized tests are extremely useful. A parent who obtains his child's standardized achievement test scores can monitor his educational progress year after year. The parent can tell whether his child's academic achievement is developing at the same rate or at a slower or faster rate than the average child his age in the nation. Parents can also evaluate the performance of their child's school if the school publishes the average standardized achievement test scores of its students each year. The school's average can be compared to school averages across the country by means of special group norms. Similarly, program evaluators can compare the effectiveness of two educational programs by pre- and post-testing the students in each program, and comparing the gain scores.

Despite their utility, there are three powerful forces in education which adamantly oppose the use of standardized educational tests. The most influential of these is the civil-rights movement, which opposes their use for the same reason it opposes ability grouping and restrictive admissions policies. It sees standardized tests as a mechanism that restricts the access of minority persons to the training they need in order to advance in society. As a group, economically disadvantaged minority persons score significantly below average on standardized educational tests. Since these tests are frequently used to regulate access to universities and other institutions and programs which offer the training required for entry to socially prestigious careers, the civil-rights movement has mounted a campaign that urges their total elimination.

The civil-rights movement contends that standardized educational tests are biased against individuals who do not have a middle-class background. It maintains that the vocabulary and content of the tests assume familiarity with a middle-class environment, and thus discriminate against children who have been raised in economically deprived and culturally different environments. It asserts that the middle-class bias of these tests causes them to measure inaccurately the ability and achievement of minority children. One recommendation of the civil-rights movement is for tests written in black dialect whose norms would be developed from a sample of inner-city youngsters.

The second group campaigning for the elimination of these tests is a loose coalition of educational liberals from the ranks of the teaching profession and university departments of education. The quotations at the beginning of this section by Terry Herndon, NEA executive director, reflect the belief of this group that standardized tests compel narrow and rigid educational objectives which are not appropriate for all children. They believe that the curricular rigidity enforced by accountability to standardized test results prevents teachers from encouraging their students to fulfill their unique abilities.

These educators claim that the most important educational outcomes are untestable. They believe that the development of creativity, self-esteem, self-fulfillment, and independence of judgment is far more important than the development of the skills which will generate high scores on standardized tests. They also resist testing because many students find the experience unpleasant and anxiety-producing, and the students who score poorly receive a real blow to their self-esteem. Most of these teachers believe in the goals of open education discussed earlier in this chapter, and see standardized tests as instruments that prevent them from teaching the curriculum they believe is best for their students.

School administrators comprise the third group opposing the use of standardized tests. They claim that these tests are inadequate tools for educational evaluation. They cite the fact that many standardized tests do not diagnose program strengths and weaknesses, but report only one overall score which is rarely helpful in deciding how an educational program should be improved. They also cite evidence that shows that standardized tests are especially unhelpful in measuring the educational improvement of students who are significantly below average in achievement.

Many of these arguments against standardized tests are based on the assumption that there is no common body of academic skill and knowledge that all children should be compelled to learn. The arguments of the educational liberals, with their expressed concern for the unique talents of each child and for the multicultural pluralistic diversity of today's schools, all boil down to this one point. When the civil-rights movement argues for tests in black dialect with local norms, it is saying the same thing.

All I can say to these groups is that I believe they are dead wrong. I contend, and have contended throughout this book, that there *is* a common body of academic skill and knowledge that all children should learn, which includes proficiency in reading, writing, computing, and spelling, and a basic knowledge of history, government, geography, science, and literature. I believe the study I mentioned in the Introduction, which analyzed the level of reading ability required for career entry, and the APL study discussed several times, offer compelling evidence that there is a high correlation between literacy and the ability to function in society. I believe that a core of common knowledge and skill serves the individual in his attempt to achieve personal fulfillment in life, both extrinsically and intrinsically. This common core of knowledge serves our society by creating a bond of experience, values, and knowledge which all Americans can share.

The alternative to this core curriculum of academic skill and knowledge is educational chaos. This chapter's catalog of the major curricular changes of the past dozen years makes it very clear that we are moving away from the concept of a core curriculum. The violent social disruption this country has recently experienced has been reinforced by the failure to institute a common curriculum of shared values and experience.

If the reader agrees that a common curriculum of academic skill and knowledge should be instituted by our schools, many of the arguments against standardized tests disintegrate like snowflakes in a rainstorm. If ours is to become an integrated society, minority children need to learn how to read in standard English. If standardized tests indicate that they do poorly as a group, it is because they lack reading vocabulary, knowledge of phonics, interest in reading, and other components of reading skill. If middle-class children do not have as many of these deficits, it is because a middle-class culture serves the interests of children who live in a modern society better than an economically deprived culture does.

The arguments of the civil-rights movement against standardized tests fall apart on technical grounds as well. A number of studies indicate that black children read material written in black dialect no better than material in standard English.[92] Other studies show that rewriting tests in black English does not significantly change the scores achieved by either black or white children on the test.[66] Finally, several studies show that standardized aptitude tests are even more valid predictors of the academic performance of black youngsters than white youngsters.[30]

In my opinion, the attempt by the civil-rights movement to ban standardized tests does not serve the interests of minority children. The achievement gap between majority and minority students is real, and we need to close the gap, not mask its existence. I, for one, believe the gap can be closed, over time, if the proper social and educational policies are adopted. So long as standardized tests reveal an academic deficit, our society will be obligated to attempt to close the gap. If we alter or ban the tests in order to disguise the deficit, what is to prevent the society from lapsing back into complacency about the educational problems of minority children?

I agree with the educational liberals that accountability to standardized test results prevents teachers from having complete curricular freedom. Where I differ from them is that I believe this is a good thing. I do not believe teachers should have complete curricular freedom, and I believe most parents would agree with me. I am reasonably certain that most parents prefer the educational objectives built into standardized tests to the almost total lack of cognitive objectives embodied in the open-education curriculum. Standardized tests measure students' mastery of the skills and subject matter taught in the most widely accepted textbooks and curriculums used in the country. When a curriculum indicates that it is failing to meet the objectives built into standardized tests by producing a disproportionate number of students with low scores, parents will be in a position to demand curricular changes. If standardized tests are eliminated, how will parents be able to protect their children from untested educational innovations?

During the past dozen years, there have been numerous battles between groups promoting curricular change, and the standardized test publishers. The former have demanded that the publishers change the tests to accommodate the curricular focus they were trying to promote. The battle over the new math was especially intense. If the major test publishers had changed their tests as demanded, it is likely that the weaknesses of the new math would never have reached the public eye. If we eliminate standardized tests as demanded, we eliminate an important educational safeguard.

One additional argument of the groups opposing standardized tests deserves comment. The most frequent proposal of these groups is that standardized tests be completely replaced with criterion-referenced tests. A criterion-referenced test can be used to determine whether a student knows his times tables, or the names of the letters of the alphabet, or how to perform long division, which are kinds of information most standardized tests do not give.

Most educational administrators who oppose standardized testing, and many in the civil-rights movement, have seized upon the mastery aspect of criterion-referenced tests as an educationally sound and politically acceptable alternative to standardized testing. They argue that a standardized test does not tell you *what* a child or group knows, only how well he compares to other children, whereas a score on a criterion-referenced test tells you exactly what the children do and do not know. Thus, these tests can be used as diagnostic instruments for children and for educational programs.

In order to analyze the arguments of the criterion-referenced test proponents, let us assume that criterion-referenced tests have completely replaced standardized tests. Now assume that your child's third-grade class is administered a criterion-referenced test in math, and the teacher discovers that 50 percent of the students do not achieve the mastery level for knowledge of the multiplication tables. What does this tell the teacher about his class? Are they doing well or poorly? If you discover your child did not meet the mastery level, should you be concerned? Unless we know the percentage of third-grade students nationwide who know their times tables, we cannot evaluate teacher, student, or school performance.

Clearly, a criterion-referenced test, unless it has been standardized, is not much good for educational evaluation. And a criterion-referenced test that has been standardized—becomes a standardized test! Indeed, many of the best educational tests available, such as the 1973 versions of the Stanford Achievement Test and the

Iowa Tests of Basic Skills, are criterion-referenced, standardized tests. While it is certainly true that there are standardized tests available with poor diagnostic capabilities, this hardly seems adequate justification for banning all standardized tests. Indeed, the arguments of the criterion-referenced test proponents are basically specious, and should be resisted (or ignored) by America's parents and educational community.

Robert Ebel, one of the nation's leading authorities on educational measurement and testing, sums up the opposition to testing as follows: ". . . the main reason for opposition to tests and testing is the reluctance of educators to be judged and held to account for their stewardship." [42] Recall NEA executive director Terry Herndon's statement given at the beginning of this section: "What we object to is accountability to standardized test results." The American public must not underestimate the desire of educators to avoid accountability. Until very recently, officials of both the NEA and the American Association of School Administrators were denying vehemently the existence of an achievement decline. If the evidence of the various standardized tests analyzed in Chapter One had not been available, they would be denying it still today.

Throughout the bulk of this chapter I attempted to describe the curricular changes that contributed to the achievement decline of the past dozen years. One pattern common to all of these changes was a failure to test and evaluate prior to implementation. The most critical curricular change facing our schools in the next ten years is the elimination of standardized testing, which would permanently fix this pattern in our educational system.

3

AUTHORITY

THE LAST DECADE HAS WITNESSED A DEGENERATION OF PUBLIC EDU-
cation in the United States. The primary goal of teachers in
our inner-city schools is their own physical and emotional survival.
Our burgeoning educational bureaucracy and its coterie of private
contractors use the children in these schools as guinea pigs for their
studies and experiments. Ingraciously, poor children continue to
exhibit the same pattern of learning deficits and behavior problems that existed before they were the object of so much attention.

In the suburbs, public education suffers a subtler type of
decay. Students reject traditional subject matter such as composition,
literature, science, and math, for more "relevant" subjects such as
film literature, world revolutions, and feminism. Teachers cannot
get their students to do schoolwork, so reading and conventional
writing assignments are sharply reduced. Curricular changes are
reflected in a ten-year downward slide in academic skills.

The same decade witnessed a frontal assault on America's

institutions of higher learning. As if the attacks on the universities in the late 1960's by radical student groups were not damaging enough, the 1970's subjected them to the ravages of inflation and governmental attack; the latter in the form of complex racial and sexual quotas for enrollment and hiring. The external attacks were matched by internal decay, as virtually all colleges reduced their requirements for a degree. Academic standards were subverted by rampant grade inflation and reduced readability levels of textbooks used at junior colleges and many four-year schools.

These symptoms of educational decay are manifestations of a deeper malady, the breakdown of authority relations in education. Virtually every significant educational problem of the past decade results directly from the abrogation or subversion of normal educational authority. The authority relationship bonding teacher to student makes the educational process work. A number of societal forces have subverted the normal exercise of educational authority over the past ten years, causing a degeneration of the educational process.

Any discussion of the function of authority in education must take cognizance of the widespread and historical antipathy to authority that permeates American society. Escaping from political, religious, and economic oppression abroad, our immigrant forefathers carried a fear and hatred of authority into the pioneering experience, from whence it became a core part of our American heritage. Our nation was born in rebellion against authority, and opposition to authority runs strong in our history, from 1776 to the Whiskey Rebellion, from President Jackson to the Civil War, from the Populist Movement to the labor movement, from the civil-rights movement to the current widespread hostility toward post-Vietnam and post-Watergate government. Despite this heritage, I am convinced, the only way to solve our educational problems is to reinstitute normal authority relations in the American educational system.

Basic to the educational process is something I will call natural authority. Natural authority is the essential core of the relationship between adults and children, consisting of a nurturing and training function on the part of the adult, and a learning function on the part of the child. The basis of the relationship is the autonomy of the adult, his knowledge and competencies that enable him to survive and function in the world, and the dependence of the child on adults for survival.

When a child comes into the world, he is not equipped for survival. Even after he matures sufficiently to achieve a certain degree of physical independence, he must be trained by the adults in his society to acquire the skills and understanding that will permit him to survive in his environment. It is the biological and cultural responsibility of adults to train the young, and the capacity to discharge this responsibility grants a natural authority to the training agent.

Training agents exercise their natural authority in four fundamental ways. First, they define a body of skill and knowledge whose acquisition will enable a child to survive and function in the world. Second, they obtain the child's participation in learning this body of material. Third, in teaching this skill and knowledge they set performance standards sufficiently high so that achievement to the standard will indicate a functional level of performance. Fourth, in the teaching process they require a sufficient amount of practice so the standards will be met. Since an enormous range of behaviors are possible to any child, the training agent must channel the child's energy to those behaviors that have survival value in his world. The exercise of natural authority by the training agent as described above is the basis for the educational process in all human societies.

Even in advanced animal species, the training function is essential for the proper development of the young. Arctic wolves teach their young how to spot weak or aged caribou so they will not waste their energy attacking the strong ones. Baboons teach their young how to watch for large carnivores and alert the tribe if one is spotted. Chimpanzees teach their young how to catch termites with a piece of straw.

We can see the same process at work in primitive human societies. The training function of natural authority is evident in the behavior of the Tasaday father as he teaches his child to identify edible species of root in a venture into the forest. The Polynesian boy learns how to fish by helping his father with the day's catch. The Navaho girl learns an important survival skill by helping her mother weave a rug. Education is an evolutionary vehicle for advanced species realizing their survival potential. The adult with mature survival skills exercises his natural authority by teaching the young how to survive in the world.

The same process of survival training is the basis for education in the modern world. Reading, writing, and computational skills are as essential to a person in modern American society as root-gathering ability is in Tasaday society. The fact that the skills are more complex and take longer to acquire does not alter the core of the process or the basic mechanism for its realization. If it is not clear to a child why he must learn grammar or long division, educational authority should communicate its utility and the consequences of not acquiring it, *but above all insist it be learned.* Educational authority abrogates its responsibility when it permits children to choose not to acquire the basic skills and knowledge necessary to survive and function in modern society.

This model of natural authority as the core relationship in education clashes violently with the contemporary concept that teachers and students should have a democratic relationship. The misapplication of the democratic ideal to parenting and teaching is the single most destructive force in the education of America's youth. Democracy assumes a capacity for choice based on independence and responsibility, which is developed as an individual experiences the consequences of his life choices. The dependent state of childhood, in which young people are sheltered from the world and the consequences of their actions in it, is a state of development in which this kind of responsibility and independence does not normally exist.

It is current educational policy to give children a great deal of choice over what, how, and even whether they study. In every school in the country, students determine how much science, math, history, and composition they will take. The basis for these choices is the paradigm of democracy applied to education: the consent of the governed becomes the consent of the children.

Educators avoid their primary responsibility by giving curricular control to students. Society's training agents must define an essential body of skill and knowledge for their students, and motivate or compel them to learn it. The issue of freedom of choice for students is specious. The only freedom for students that educators should be concerned about is the freedom to function in the world which comes as a result of an adequate education. Upon graduation from high school, how free is the young person who freely chose not to study any math, science, history, or composition? Freedom and democracy are highly charged words which have proper reference to adult behavior. Their use in educational discussion serves primarily to camouflage the dissolution of adult authority and responsibility.

Parents delegate to educators the task of transmitting an essential body of skill and knowledge to their children. They do not hire educators to offer their children a choice between this core learning and superficial entertainment. Certain choices should simply not be offered to children. A parent should not offer his two-year-old a choice between vegetables and candy. An educator should not offer a sixteen-year-old a choice between English composition and film literature. Permitting these kinds of choices to children is an abrogation of adult responsibility. In this society, it is the function of educators to train young people to become autonomously functioning adults. Autonomy is not something that can be given. Autonomy must be acquired.

Another plank of contemporary educational policy is to lower or eliminate objective standards for performance. The rationale behind this policy is that imposition of standards creates the possibility of failure and ranks children in their own and in others' eyes. Current policy holds that fear of failure interferes with real learning, and that failure itself reduces self-esteem. The process of ranking is also supposed to reduce the self-esteem of low-ranked individuals, and furthermore it is held to violate the ideal of equality between individuals. Manifestations of this policy include grade inflation, the NCTE policy on dialect, reduced readability levels of textbooks, and the extreme open-admissions policies recently established at many universities.

The responsibility of educational authority to impose standards is integral to the process of education. The standard imposed by nature on the wolf cub or young baboon is survival. The standard imposed by nature on the primitive child is also survival, but this standard is mediated by the adults in the child's society. They train him to a performance standard whose achievement indicates a survival level of functioning.

In our complex society, it is the function of educational authority to act in nature's place by imposing standards. Because of the affluence, technology, and organizational complexity of modern society, many educators have lost sight of their basic function, which is to transmit survival skills and knowledge to youth. The first-grade teacher teaching the alphabet, the high-school teacher teaching American history, the college professor teaching engineering are all training their students to survive and function in the world.

Nature's standard is harsh. The primitive parent ameliorates the harshness as he teaches his child to survive in the world. As gentle as he may be while teaching, he will not drop the standard of skill required, for he understands that to do so would jeopardize the life of his child. Contemporary educators who reduce or eliminate standards out of concern for a child's self-esteem risk damaging the child far more seriously when they send him into the world poorly prepared to survive and function. The stories of Peter Doe and the valedictorian of Western High School demonstrate the pernicious effects of such a policy.

Modern egalitarianism is a perversion of the ideal of equal opportunity, which holds that all individuals should be given the opportunity to achieve to the limits of their abilities. Imposition of standards helps children achieve to the limits of their abilities by encouraging them to mobilize their energy and intelligence toward a concrete target. The student who writes well is superior to one who writes poorly. If the school does not acknowledge this superiority of rank, then it fails to reward the acquisition of a socially important skill, and thus evades its responsibility to train young people to survive and function in the world.

Another tenet of modern educational policy holds that demanding work from students is an old-fashioned and outmoded way to educate children. The work ethic is held to be a relic of a previous era, to be replaced with the concept of self-directed play. The educational process is a discovery process, according to this tenet, the basic model being the child as scientist making basic discoveries about the world, with his natural curiosity the motivation for him to study things that interest him. So he needs no discipline, and he certainly does not need anybody to force him to work.

The essential flaw in the above argument is that it focuses accurately on half of the educational process, and denies the other half. It is true that children possess a natural curiosity about the world which motivates them to study things that interest them. But how do they know what interests them unless they are exposed to the most important creations of human imagination and effort? Because they have short attention spans, are easily distracted, and have little sense of delayed gratification, most children will not choose tasks that require continued effort over a long period of time, and which will not have significant rewards for weeks, months, or even years. It is the teacher's job to channel the child's effort in socially and personally productive ways. By imposing sustained demands, the teacher helps the child acquire difficult but rewarding skills and knowledge. The child's success reinforces his will to learn and excel.

Teacher demands are essential for other reasons. By demanding work of children, educational authority represents the reality of life and teaches students attitudes about work which will permit them to function in the world. By producing the work their teachers demand, children learn how to channel their energy. They learn how to work.

People need to work in order to maintain their physical and emotional health. I am defining work to be the goal-directed expenditure of physical and mental energy. Each individual has a unique energy economy which creates distress if violated. It is well known that if a person works too hard, his physical and psychological systems become exhausted. What is not so widely known is what happens when an energy economy is violated in the direction of too little work.

What frequently happens is that the individual's energy becomes destructive, manifesting itself in forms as varied as neurotic problems, physical illness, and hostility. If a child does not learn how to work in his first eighteen years, he will tend to have problems regulating his own energy economy. If he has not learned to channel his energy in socially productive ways, his adjustments to his own energy imbalance are likely to be self-destructive or socially destructive. Our country's mass of disaffected, confused, and hostile young people is a stark witness to what happens when children do not learn how to work.

A great deal of the error and confusion in contemporary educational theory and practice results from the failure to differentiate the two primary child-rearing functions. Adults have the responsibility of nurturing their children to maintain their physical and emotional health, and of training them to survive and function in the world. Nurturing is the feeding, the protecting, the loving, the accepting, the respecting, the responding to the child's needs. A nurturant environment, and especially a nurturant mother, create healthy and vigorous children. Two primary expressions of this health are the child's curiosity and his high energy level. The nurturing process creates children eager and ready to learn. The training process channels their energy and curiosity along pathways that will be personally and socially rewarding.

In failing to differentiate between these two processes, educators have saddled our educational system with many of the nurturing responsibilities. They eliminate or reduce standards out of concern that failure to meet high standards will cause a child not to feel accepted or appreciated. They reduce work demands in the hope that their students will feel happy and loved. They provide democratic choices to their students in order to communicate an attitude of respect and acceptance.

After the primary grades, the educational process should be primarily a training process. Teachers should be positive and responsive, but they must not permit an overly friendly relationship with their students to sabotage the educational process. By allowing the nurturing functions to dominate the training functions, post-primary-school teachers and administrators sacrifice a great deal of their authority, and in so doing undermine the education of their students.

One of the most fascinating pieces of educational research of the past decade bears directly on the issues raised in the preceding pages. Dr. Sanford Dornbusch of Stanford University directed an investigation into academic achievement and standards, and student attitudes and work habits in San Francisco public high schools.[53] He compared the work habits, attitudes, and educational experiences of different groups of students, in an attempt to discover why some groups perform better academically than others.

He developed two measures for work habits and attitudes. The first was a purely subjective measure which indicated how hard a student believed he was working. The second was an objective measure which indicated how hard the student was really working. The second measure took into account how much homework the student did, how many classes he cut, and how he behaved in the classroom—paying attention, daydreaming, and bringing required materials to class.

Dornbusch found that the lowest-achieving students were putting out the least amount of effort, but assessed themselves as putting out the most effort. Fifty-four percent of the lowest-scoring math students believed they were working quite hard. The objective measure showed that, in fact, only 18 percent of these students actually worked hard. In contrast, only 37 percent of the highest-scoring students believed they were working hard, when the objective measure showed that, in fact, 63 percent of these students were actually working quite hard.

I am certain that it surprises no one that hard work is highly correlated with high achievement, and lack of effort with low achievement. The fascinating finding is how deluded the poorest students are when it comes to assessing their own effort. How can they possibly feel they are working hard when the data show they do very little homework and cut a large number of classes? This question is extremely important, especially to low-achieving students. They will not improve their academic performance until they start working much harder, yet they have no reason to work harder because they already believe they are working hard.

Dornbusch discovered that the teachers were applying a differential pattern of response to their students: high standards, heavy work demands, and some positive feedback to the good students; low standards, negligible work demands, and *much more positive feedback* to the poor students. Approximately half of the students reported that they would not be assigned a low grade if they did poor work or did not try. Dornbusch's data indicated that a minimal amount of work, as long as it was not associated with cutting classes, would not be reflected in a low grade. Approximately 60 percent of the lowest-achieving students reported that the difficulty level of their work was usually or always just right, compared to only 20 percent of the top students, and a higher percentage of the top students reported that the assigned work was too difficult. The devastating finding was that despite the fact that they were puttng out practically no effort to improve their academic standing, 48 percent of the lowest-achieving students reported usually or always receiving academic praise, compared to only 30 percent for the top group.

The following graphs from Dornbusch's study reflect the pattern of real effort, self-assessment of effort, and academic praise from teachers, for students grouped according to math achievement scores. Analogous graphs for students grouped for verbal achievement scores show the same pattern.

What we see in Dornbusch's study is the breakdown of authority in the educational system he examined. Educational authority is responsible for establishing standards sufficiently high so that

Graph 4

PERCENTAGE OF STUDENTS SCORING HIGH
ON REAL EFFORT AND SELF-ASSESSMENT
OF EFFORT AT DIFFERENT LEVELS
OF TENTH GRADE MATH ACHIEVEMENT

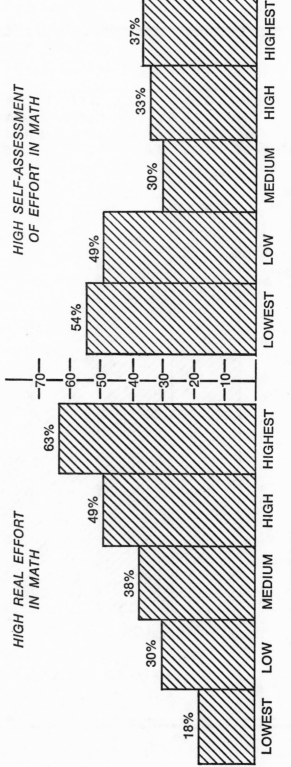

HIGH REAL EFFORT
IN MATH

HIGH SELF-ASSESSMENT
OF EFFORT IN MATH

63% 49% 38% 30% 18%

54% 49% 30% 33% 37%

—70
—60
—50
—40
—30
—20
—10

LOWEST LOW MEDIUM HIGH HIGHEST

MATH ACHIEVEMENT

Graph 5

PERCENTAGE OF ALL STUDENTS REPORTING THAT THEY USUALLY OR ALWAYS RECEIVED ACADEMIC PRAISE BY HIGH-SCHOOL MATH ACHIEVEMENT SCORES

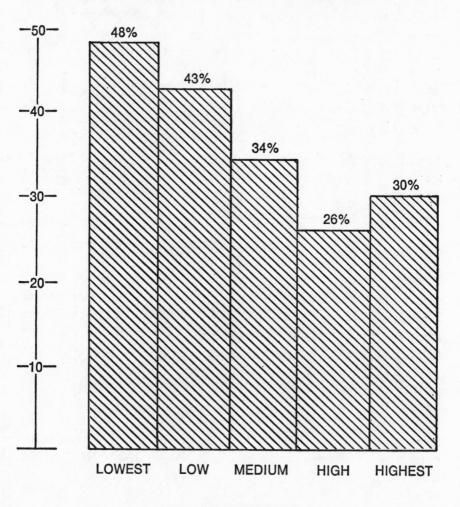

MATH ACHIEVEMENT

students will develop functional levels of skill. In the schools Dornbusch analyzed, standards were reduced or eliminated for large numbers of students. Educational authority is responsible for placing sufficient work demands on students so they will develop functional levels of skill and knowledge, and habits and attitudes about work which will permit them to function in the world. This responsibility, too, was evaded for large numbers of students. Finally, educational authority is responsible to communicate honestly to students whether or not they are working hard enough to acquire an adequate education. Graph 5 is a devastating indicator of the abrogation of this responsibility also, and indeed of the extent of the degeneration of educational authority in America today.

Dr. Dornbusch was especially disturbed because a disproportionate number of the low-achieving students were minority students. He was concerned that the low standards and insufficient work demands placed on low-achieving minority students, combined with the excessive positive feedback, would delude them into believing they were working sufficiently hard and doing adequate work, and would thus serve as a mechanism to ensure their continued failure in the public school system.

It is reasonable to wonder why educators are renouncing their authority and thus their responsibility to their students. Earlier I referred to several contributing factors including the permissive ideology of many young teachers and the demoralization of many older teachers. At least part of the blame for the attitude of the young teachers must rest with the teacher-training programs at our colleges and universities. The educational standards applied to teacher candidates are lower than in most other fields, so those with responsibility to impose standards have had little experience meeting high standards themselves. Probably more important, the permissive ideology of Holt, Kohl, and company exerts a strong influence in our teacher-training institutions. It is not entirely fair to blame a young teacher for adopting the attitudes he was exposed to in his training program.

The demoralization of the older teachers is especially sad because many of them have the skill and underlying attitude to do an adequate job. They are demoralized because the system has let them down. A classroom teacher can exercise his authority only if he is backed up by his students' parents and the school administration, and also by the community and larger society. Today we find each of these groups actively subverting the teacher's authority.

A teacher attempting to maintain high standards for schoolwork and classroom behavior will quickly discover that administrators will sabotage his efforts if those efforts are creating any significant student resistance. Administrators adopt policies that will maintain a calm and pacific school environment. They will unhesitatingly adopt a policy that panders to student laziness if they believe it will reduce school conflict, even if it also reduces the amount of real learning taking place. The policy that permits a student to choose his subjects and teachers is a good example of this kind of administrative decision. The policy that permits students to drop a class many weeks into the semester without penalty is another.

While part of the administrator's problem is simply a failure of nerve, some of his behavior can be explained by the political conditions in his community and the larger society. There is no doubt that communities are more concerned with the peaceful demeanor of a school than with the real learning that may or may not be taking place. Administrators have to respond to that reality if they hope to keep their jobs. Administrators are also subject to intense pressure from various community groups for changes in educational policy. They risk school disruption, job loss, and even violence if they resist those pressures.

The group on whom teachers count most for support is the parents of their students. In hundreds of conversations with teachers and school officials over the past several years, I have been told that parents are not backing up the schools the way they have in the past. They are not reinforcing the teacher by making sure their children do their schoolwork every day. They are not nearly as concerned about their children cutting classes or using drugs. Some parents actively subvert the teacher's authority by denigrating the teacher or the school to their children, or siding with a child in a dispute with the school.

Teachers and school officials are virtually unanimous in reporting a wide-scale and severe deterioration in the attitude of their students. They insist that they cannot maintain standards of previous years against the wholesale resistance and negativity of their current crop of students. They report that students are contemptuous, lazy, manipulative, and superficially sophisticated but actually far more ignorant of basic subjects than in years past.

A great deal of the deterioration in student attitudes can be explained by the recent history and pattern of parent-child interaction in American society. The generation of adults that became parents after World War II had been through some of the hardest times in American history, including our longest economic depression and a frightening and murderous war. Most had experienced real hardship and suffering and had been exposed to extremes of human misery totally foreign to today's common experience. They were a hardworking and productive generation, and when the G.I. bill gave them the opportunity to go to college, their academic achievement surpassed that of non-G.I.-bill students in every field.[57] Today, they are the managers of American society. Their self-disciplined productivity was largely fueled by a desire to escape from the suffering in their past.

This group of adults moved out of the cities into the suburbs to create a life which they hoped would shelter their children from the types of life experiences that had caused them so much pain. Because they had been raised by rigid and authoritarian parents, they were aware of the pain this type of rearing could cause children. In their desire to shelter their children from all possible sources of suffering, they were very susceptible to the influence of child-rearing specialists such as Dr. Benjamin Spock, who advocated an extremely permissive style of child rearing.

A self-disciplined, responsible, and hardworking generation proceeded to raise an undisciplined, irresponsible, lazy, and self-centered generation. Parents who spent their lives attempting to provide decently for their families were rewarded with contempt and hostility from the objects of their concern and love. Patty Hearst's public rejection of her parents was a symbolic manifestation of the feeling of an entire generation for its parents. How did this happen?

Young children need to be provided with copious quantities of love and attention so that they may properly develop. In their earliest years, however, children are extremely egocentric. They are barely cognizant that the world does not revolve around them. When they want something, whether that something is their mother's breast or their parent's attention, they demand it by yelling their heads off. The result of the child-rearing advice of the 1940's and 1950's was that many parents, especially mothers, felt guilty if they did not immediately respond to their children's demands. They failed to differentiate adequately between their children's expressions of fundamental biological and emotional needs, and their egocentric, manipulative tendencies. By giving in to the demands of their children, these parents failed to establish the standards for behavior and responsibility that are essential to healthy social and psychological development. As a result, many children learned to manipulate their parents to obtain material possessions, such as toys, clothes, stereos, or cars, to avoid household chores and other family responsibilities, and to circumvent parental restrictions and limits on behavior.

A child's parents are his primary training agents, and although they can delegate some of the training function to his teachers, they bear primary responsibility for raising him in such a way that he can survive and function in the world. They deny this responsibility if they raise him in a fantasy world, in which all his desires are fulfilled without his having to work, and in which he is sheltered from reality and the consequences of his actions in it. Today's dropouts, living on food stamps and welfare, are one of the end products of this process. They are still successfully manipulating their social environment to obtain what they want without having to work for it.

As a result of the abrogation of parental authority, the postwar generation of children tended to be demanding and manipulative. Their ability to overcome the will of their parents resulted in an unrealistic sense of ego power and self-importance. As they grew to maturity in the 1960's and 1970's, they developed a contempt and hostility for adults that was based on their inflated sense of power and their experience of the weakness of authority. Children intuitively know that the reason they can manipulate their parents is the latter's confusion, guilt, and lack of perception. Indeed, their sense of the weakness of the authority figures in their own lives is based on an intuitive understanding that they have no right to wield power over adults, and that they need adults to be sufficiently authoritative so they can develop properly.

Dr. Diana Baumrind, a noted expert on child rearing, studied the effects of different types of child-rearing practices, diffentiating parental behavior into the categories of permissive, authoritarian, and authoritative.[15] According to Baumrind, the *permissive* parent attempts to behave in an accepting and affirmative manner toward his child. He consults with the child about policy decisions, and makes few demands for household responsibility or orderly behavior. He does not try to control or regulate his child's behavior, does not use punishment, and discourages conformity to externally established standards. The *authoritarian* parent, in contrast, attempts to direct the behavior of his child to accord with a set standard of conduct, usually an absolute standard. He favors obedience as a virtue, and punishment as a tool for its accomplishment. He does not encourage verbal give-and-take, believing his child should accept his word for what is right. The *authoritative* parent also attempts to direct his child's behavior, but in a rational, issue-oriented manner. He encourages verbal give-and-take, and explains the reasoning behind his policies. He values both autonomy and disciplined conformity. He affirms his child's present qualities, but believes it is the parent's responsibility to set standards for future conduct, and direct the development of the child. He does not hesitate to exert control when he disagrees with his child, but he also does not hem his child in with restrictions.

Baumrind's research indicates that the permissive child-rearing pattern was developed out of a fear that the exercise of parental control had damaging effects on children. Specifically, advocates of permissive child-rearing practices warned that close parental supervision, high parental demands, and all forms of punishment would result either in alienated and hostile children, or in children who were passive and dependent. Contradicting these claims, Baumrind found that the parents of the most mature and independent children exercised the firmest control over their behavior. Permissive child-rearing advocates also claimed that parents who exercised firm control over their children had authoritarian personalities. Contradicting this claim also, Baumrind found that while authoritarian parents certainly exercised control, authoritative parents exerted even stronger control, yet manifested none of the characteristics of the authoritarian personality syndrome. (Psychoanalyst Erich Fromm has used the term "authoritarian personality syndrome" to characterize a person who defended his own weak and insecure ego by attempting to control other people's behavior.) The authoritative parents "were open and receptive although highly authoritative in their requirements for compliance."

The implications of Baumrind's research for adolescent development are particularly pertinent to this chapter. In the following passage, she describes the kinds of life experiences adolescents need in order to mature properly.[16]

> Youth is the appropriate time for the individual to adjust to the fact that options are finite. One's actions bring about predictable alterations in future options. During childhood, parents protect children from the natural consequences of their actions by functioning as buffers and preventing premature foreclosure of opportunities for later action. . . . Adults who continue to protect the youth in this way or to reward into late adolescence his egoistic, antisocial, irrational side prolong unduly his period of childhood omnipotence.

> Unconditional approval or excessive indulgence by adults delays the young person's realization that *personal freedom is a consequence of competence.* [Emphasis added.]

> Adolescence is the time of life for the individual to come to terms

with the reality principle. The universal experiences of loneliness, fear of failure, and insufficiency must be faced; they cannot be blocked indefinitely with drugs, sex, or, for that matter, obsessive involvement in work. The adolescent must learn (if he ever is going to learn) how to tolerate delay, control rage and sexual desire, sublimate, think rationally, act responsibly, endure suffering, adjust to that which cannot be altered and serve the community. Because young persons today believe that they have or should have more options than they do, it is more difficult for them than it should be to endure situational and social imperfections. They feel as though conditions which they do not like are intolerable. They demand meaning, as though one generation can deliver meaning to another on a silver platter.

The unfortunate lessons the postwar generation learned in infancy and early childhood were reinforced in late childhood and adolescence as a result of American economic, technological, and demographic expansion. Poverty prevents a society from pandering to the whims of its spoiled children. Affluence does not. A pioneer family needed the help of its children in order to survive. The post-World War II family did not. They wanted to protect their children from all possible suffering. Their affluence permitted them to do so far too successfully.

American economic and technological development reduced the opportunities for adult-child contact. The pioneer child identified with the adult roles in his world, because he was continuously engaged in survival-level work with adults. The postwar economic expansion created jobs that precluded adult-child contact, and thus child identification with adult roles. The problem of reduced adult-child contact was compounded by the increase in mothers working outside the home, up from 9 percent in 1940 to 46 percent by 1974.[60] The postwar baby boom reduced the basic population ratio of adults to children. The confluence of these factors produced a predictable result. Dr. Urie Bronfenbrenner of Cornell University reports a forty-year decline in the amount of time American children spend with their parents.[24] The time they are not spending with their parents, they are spending with their peers or with television.

At every age and grade level, children today show a greater dependence on their peers than they did just a decade ago. Bronfenbrenner cites research showing primarily negative effects of increased peer influence. Young people who are highly peer-dependent tend to have a negative view of themselves, their friends, and their future. Compared to youngsters who make a greater identification with their parents, these children tend to be less responsible and to get in trouble more often. They generally report that their parents are less affectionate and less firm in discipline.

Television has equally pernicious effects on children. Its most obvious effect is the time it subtracts from other activities. Over 95 percent of the homes in the United States have a television, and over 30 percent have two or more.[22] The average television is turned on for six hours a day, up from five hours a day in 1960. The average American child, upon graduation from high school, will have spent approximately 15,000 hours watching television, compared to 13,000 hours in school. The average child watches three to four hours of television each day.

Consider what a child misses during the 15,000 hours he spends in front of the TV screen. He is not working in the garage with his father, or in the garden with his mother. He is not doing homework, or reading, or collecting stamps. He is not cleaning his room, washing the supper dishes, or cutting the lawn. He is not listening to a discussion about community politics among his parents and their friends. He is not playing baseball, or going fishing, or painting pictures. Exactly what does television offer that is so valuable that it can replace all of these activities?

Television offers an enormously powerful, hypnotic form of visual entertainment. The characters and behaviors exhibited in many television programs represent extremes of neurotic and socially pathological behavior equaled only in prisons and mental institutions. Children passively absorb these behaviors as life options for themselves. A number of recent studies suggest that violent television shows directly induce violent behavior in children.[13, 48, 157] More significant for education, perhaps, is that television actors and commentators use a purposefully simplified vocabulary and concept level so they may reach the widest possible audience. Even with serious subjects the program goal is maximum entertainment, which is realized through a sequential pattern of highly entertaining vignettes. With programs budgeted at $4,000 per minute, and commercials budgeted at $100,000 a minute, television can afford to create thoroughly entertaining programs.

Television's effect on children is to create an expectation that learning should be easy, passive, and entertaining. They judge their teachers by the entertainment standards of television. Undoubtedly part of the shift in public education from teaching to entertainment, from Miss Grundy to Johnny Carson, can be explained as the response of the teaching profession to the changed expectations of its audience. Children fail to develop the essential intellectual skill of being able to take a logically connected series of propositions to their culminating conclusion, since the only logic connecting the sequence of vignettes on a TV show is the logic of maximum value of entertainment. They do not learn how actively to apply themselves to a task, because television promotes almost complete passivity. Most damaging is the sense of knowledge and sophistication which young people acquire from extensive exposure to a medium which attempts to convince its audience that its programs have depth and significance, when in truth most information children acquire from television is so superficial and discontinuous as to have little value.

The postwar generation suffered from parental permissiveness compounded by parental neglect, within an environment which permitted them to retain the delusions this kind of upbringing engendered. The delusion of tremendous ego strength which came from their ability to manipulate their parents was reinforced by the delusion of knowledge and sophistication supplied by television. American society's postwar affluence did not force a sense of economic reality or survival into the consciousness of these children. Our society's complexity tended to replace parental influence with peer influence at adolescence, which removed one more factor that might have helped bring these children into greater contact with reality. The only significant point that requires clarification is how they were able to subvert educational authority into abrogating its responsibilities of determining curriculums and imposing standards and work demands.

The basic technique was developed in infancy, when this generation found that it could manipulate its parents by playing on their guilt, insecurity, and ignorance. They carried this basic methodology with them into the schools. They learned to manipulate their teachers and the school administrators by attacking them at points of personal vulnerability, or at points where the teacher-administrator relationship was vulnerable. Young teachers were vulnerable to manipulation because they were sympathetic to their students, and inexperienced at classroom control. School officials were vulnerable because they were afraid of the personal consequences of school disruption. Many older teachers were vulnerable because they were afraid of the personal consequences of not having enough students sign up for their classes.

Students are also very talented at spotting points of institutional vulnerability. These are most frequently issues about which adults are confused and divided in opinion. The issue of a relevant curriculum, whether this means black studies, feminist literature, or ecology, is an example of an issue where students can use a powerful group of adults to subvert educational authority. Other issues that students can use in the same way include student evaluation of teachers, the elimination of punitive disciplinary methods, changes in grading policies, and the various student freedoms such as the freedom to choose courses, the freedom to choose teachers, and the freedom to dress any way one wants.

It is really quite tragic that the schools and the society pander to student resistance to educational authority. After all, the reason students are in school is to learn, not to teach educators how to run our school system. Their behavior is a direct attempt to subvert educational authority, and, when successful, it is enormously destructive to the students involved. A group of students who con a school into accepting film literature in place of English composition may feel quite successful about their victory over the school administration, but how successful are they going to feel a few years later when they cannot get a job because they cannot write a simple English sentence?

The fact that seems to slip by many educators in these confrontations with students is that the students do not really want to win. They want and need adults to exercise authority by imposing limits and holding firm to demands. Their constant testing is really a search for adults strong enough to allow them to be children, which is evidenced by the fact that the only teachers they respect are the ones they cannot manipulate.

The various political, community, and professional organizations that support student resistance to educational authority, and in so doing legitimate that resistance in students' own eyes as well as others, do young people real and lasting damage. In the previous chapter I referred to the policy statement on composition by the National Council of Teachers of English that attempted to legitimate the reduction of writing standards to the level of street talk. This organization does not help young people with policies such as this.

Another organization playing a similar role is the Children's Defense Fund. This group is currently exerting significant legal and community pressure on the schools, in an attempt to stop them from suspending students.[130] They believe that by suspending students, schools are denying them their right to an education. Needless to say, they fail to recognize that disruptive students interfere with the educational process, and that suspension is a tool with which administrators can safeguard the education of students who are eager to learn. The movement against suspensions has been quite successful, as indicated by a recent Supreme Court decision forcing schools to initiate quasi-legal due-process proceedings before they suspend a student.[59] In communities in which the Children's Defense Fund or similar organizations operate, school administrators are very hesitant to suspend a student for fear of legal action. Such fears are heightened by an even more destructive decision, which held that a school principal could be forced to pay financial damages if a suspended student could demonstrate an unjustified suspension.[169]

A plethora of local organizations have set up counter-culture institutions, whose primary effect is to reinforce the antisocial tendencies of many young people. By providing young people with free health clinics, runaway centers, and counter-culture high schools, these organizations subvert the attempts of responsible adults to instill a sense of values, discipline, and responsibility in the younger generation. These counter-culture institutions attempt to convince young people and the society at large that irresponsibility, hedonism, and laziness comprise an acceptable, alternative value system, which is superior in many respects to the uptight values of the older generation. The existence of these alternatives makes it more difficult for school authorities and parents to direct the development of the younger generation.

As if the subversion of the schools by various political organizations was not sufficiently damaging, the last few years have witnessed a series of legal decisions undermining educational authority. The legal decisions mentioned above, the U.S. District Court decision mentioned in the section on ability grouping, and the Supreme Court and lower federal court decisions mentioned in the section on standardized testing are only a few of the recent court rulings that interfere with the operation of the public schools.

In the same category as the decisions just listed, the Supreme Court's *Lau v. Nichols* decision forced the nation's schools to adopt bilingual educational programs. The ostensible purpose of bilingual education is to help non-English-speaking children make the transition to an English-speaking culture and school environment. The recklessness of the Supreme Court in educational matters is demonstrated by the fact that when this decision was handed down, no research existed that demonstrated that bilingual educational programs were, in fact, effective in accomplishing this goal.[170]

Several years after the Lau decision was reached, a USOE study of the nation's bilingual educational programs established the following points: bilingual education adds about 35 percent to the cost of education; children in these programs make less progress in English-language development than comparable children not enrolled in such programs; over 85 percent of the nation's bilingual-education project directors keep students in these programs after they can function successfully in English; less than one-third of the students in these programs are of limited English-speaking ability.[49] It is an inescapable implication of this study that bilingual education has become another educational boondoggle, where children are used as counters by educational bureaucrats to keep the money flowing and the petty empires growing.

As damaging as any of the decisions mentioned above was the California Supreme Court's Serrano decision, which declared the local property tax to be an unconstitutional method of financing public education because it resulted in unequal public-school expenditures for rich and poor children.[133] By forcing state financing and greatly increased state control on California's schools, this decision drastically undermines the ability of local citizens and their school boards to determine educational policy, and will, I predict, have an extremely chaotic and destructive impact on California's public schools.

Perhaps exemplifying legal interference in public education have been the Supreme Court and lower federal court decisions forcing school districts to adopt mandatory busing policies. These decisions were based on arguments of social scientists who hypothesized that such programs would improve the academic achievement of minority students, and reduce the racial prejudices of all the students involved. At the time of the initial busing decisions, there was no hard evidence supporting these hypothesized effects. Today we know that busing produces no significant effects in the academic achievement of minority or white students. A few studies show small improvements in the achievement of students in busing programs, a few studies show declines, while most show no educationally significant change that can be attributed to busing.[9, 101] These same studies, unfortunately, also show that busing programs tend to increase the racial prejudices of the students involved. There is also evidence that in certain situations busing actually fosters racially segregated housing patterns, by causing the flight of middle-class, mostly white people to areas not affected by the busing policy.[160] (White flight, as it has been called, is not a universal effect of busing, and it is properly called middle-class flight, since there are widespread reports of black families moving to escape deteriorating public schools, or placing their children in private schools.)

Discussions of judicial interference in school affairs would not be complete without mention of *Tinker v. the Des Moines Community School District*.[149] In this decision the Supreme Court laid the groundwork for the recent series of decisions regarding school discipline, including the due-process decision discussed above, which have had the effect of limiting the ability of our public-school officials to maintain safe, orderly schools, whose environments promote disciplined academic learning. In 1965, several Des Moines high-school students, including John Tinker, were suspended after refusing to remove the black armbands they were wearing to protest the Vietnam War. Their principal stated that he suspended the students after several warnings because he was concerned that the wearing of the armbands could initiate a disruption of the educational process. The Supreme Court ruled that by suspending the students, the school had violated their right to free speech.

The question, of course, is whether the principal had the right to make the decision, not whether he had made the right decision. My opinion of his judgment, or anybody else's opinion including the Supreme Court's, should be an irrelevant issue. The only real issue in this case is whether a school administrator has the authority to run his school to the best of his ability without fear of judicial reversal of day-to-day administrative decisions. Until Tinker, school administrators had that authority.

The damage done to American education by this ruling was summed up by Supreme Court Justice Hugo Black in his dissent to the opinion:

> The Court's holding in this case ushers in what I deem to be an entirely new era in which the power to control pupils by the elected officials of state supported schools in the United States is in ultimate effect transferred to the Supreme Court.
>
> . . . I repeat that if the time has come when pupils of state supported schools can defy and flaunt orders of school officials to keep

their minds on their own school work, it is the beginning of a new era of permissiveness fostered by the judiciary.

. . . School discipline, like parental discipline, is an integral and important part of training our children to be good citizens—to be better citizens. Here a very small number of students have crisply and summarily refused to obey a school order designed to give pupils who want to learn the opportunity to do so. One does not need to be a prophet or the son of a prophet to know that after the Court's holding today some students in Iowa schools and indeed in all schools will be ready, able, and willing to defy their teachers on practically all orders.

. . . it is nothing but wishful thinking to imagine that young immature students will not soon believe it is their right to control the schools rather than the right of the States that collect the taxes. . . . This case, therefore, wholly without constitutional reasons in my judgement, subjects all the public schools in the country to the whims and caprices of their loudest-mouthed, but maybe not their brightest, students. I, for one, am not fully persuaded that school pupils are wise enough, even with the Court's expert help from Washington, to run the 23,390 public school systems in 50 States. I wish, therefore, wholly to disclaim any purpose on my part, to hold that the Federal Constitution compels the teachers, parents, and elected school officials to surrender control of the American public school system to public school students. I dissent.

Paralleling the recent court decisions have been a plethora of bureaucratic regulations undermining educational authority. Earlier I mentioned the morass of state and federal guidelines that ensure the continued failure of compensatory education. Almost as pernicious at the university level are a multiplying mass of regulations emanating from the Veterans Administration, the Civil Service Commission, and the Departments of Health, Education, and Welfare (HEW), Labor, Justice, and Agriculture, regarding pensions, taxes, student and occupational health and safety, veterans' benefits, affirmative action, privacy of student records, the rights of human subjects in government-financed research, and the rights of the handicapped. Compliance with these regulations cost American universities approximately two billion dollars in 1976, which equals the total amount of voluntary donations the institutions received during the same year, and is ten to twenty times greater than compliance costs just ten years ago.[93]

The various government agencies involved are competing for bureaucratic power. On November 23, 1976, the Civil Service Commission and the Departments of Labor and Justice published their regulations outlining the procedures they wanted universities and colleges (and other employers) to follow in preventing employment discrimination. On November 24, the Equal Employment Opportunity Commission published its own guidelines, because it disagreed with the November 23 ones. The Rehabilitation Act of 1973, as amended in 1974, is one paragraph long, and deals with the rights of handicapped persons. The HEW regulations for carrying it out are voluminous, an expansion which was partially achieved by bureaucratically extending the definition of a handicapped person from the physically handicapped to drug addicts, alcoholics, and homosexuals. The HEW regulations, in turn, must compete with a different and sometimes inconsistent set of regulations on the handicapped put out by the Department of Labor. (These regulations include a provision that a contractor who does more than $2,500 worth of business a year with the federal government must have an affirmative-action hiring program for drug addicts and alcoholics.[156]) Each set of these overlapping regulations requires America's educational institutions to fill out immense amounts of duplicative paper work. In the 1974–1975 school year, Harvard estimated that 60,000 hours of its faculty's time were devoted to complying with federal regulations.[167]

The most damaging effect of bureaucratic overregulation is not the subtraction of money and faculty time from the educational process, although both are considerable, but rather the reduction in the autonomy and authority of America's educational institutions. It is axiomatic in management science that to burden an organization with secondary functions is to reduce its ability to accomplish its primary function, but that is exactly what we have done in American education. Government regulations, like court decisions, are merely mechanisms by which the society ensures that our educational institutions carry out certain specific secondary functions. The problem of overregulation is really part of a larger problem: American society has decided to burden its educational system with a wide variety of tasks other than education.

In addition to the secondary functions embodied in the regulations discussed above, American society assigns its educational system the following tasks: eradicating racial prejudice in the younger generation; eradicating sexism in the younger generation; providing jobs for community people; reaffirming ethnic values, culture, and language to members of ethnic groups; equalizing percentages of minority persons and women hired to teach and enrolled as students at all levels of our educational system; providing jobs for educational bureaucrats and specialists; involving community people in academic planning, administration, and teaching; making sure the twelve years a child spends in school are fun and enjoyable; safeguarding the self-esteem of the younger generation. A creative reader could extend this list indefinitely.

The primary function of our educational system is to transmit to our young people the skills and understanding that will help them survive and function in the world. Each of the secondary functions we assign our schools limits the authority of educators to run their schools and classes in the way they judge to accomplish most effectively their primary goal. To limit that authority is to undermine education itself, and do inestimable damage to children.

Of all the secondary functions American society assigns its educational system, the most significant is that of keeping children in school as long as possible. If nothing else, we have developed the most expensive babysitting mechanism in the history of civilization. According to the FBI, approximately 45 percent of the serious crimes committed in this country are committed by individuals under eighteen years of age.[3] Society apparently hopes that if we keep children in school, they will not be out on the streets robbing people. Police departments are adamant in their insistence to high schools, "No matter how academically unmotivated your students might be, keep them busy in class doing something." Labor unions are equally insistent on the same point. They want to keep cheap labor off the market as long as possible. Mothers unanimously endorse the concept of keeping sixteen- and seventeen-year-olds out of the house as much as possible. Thus, the child-care function of our educational system has virtually unanimous societal support. It is interesting to note that European countries do not burden their high schools with a child-care function. The average graduate of a European high school has attained the level of writing skill, breadth of reading background, and knowledge of math and science of the average American college junior or senior.

The burden of this child-care function to our high schools is nearly insurmountable. We burden our teachers with a significant number of students who are totally resistant to their authority, and tell them that short of overt violence, they are to accommodate themselves to the presence of these students in their classes. It does not require an educational expert to see that if a teacher cannot exercise authority over a subgroup of students within his class, his authority over his whole class will be diminished. As a result, he is considerably less effective than he could be, even with his receptive students.

Burdening our schools with turned-off kids leads directly to school violence and crime. A 1975 study on school vandalism and violence by the Senate Subcommittee on Juvenile Delinquency reports sharp increases in all categories of violent crime and vandalism in the nation's schools.[117] Over the period 1970 to 1973, violent assaults on teachers increased over 75 percent, and violent assaults on students over 85 percent. An earlier study by the same subcommittee showed a 612 percent increase in assaults on teachers between 1964 and 1968. Murder, rape, robbery, burglary, and drug and alcohol offenses committed on school grounds each averaged an approximate 35 percent increase over the three years of the report. The study reports that 75,000 teachers are injured badly enough each year to require medical attention. A figure of 500 million dollars is quoted as a conservative estimate of the cost of vandalism to the public schools each year. This figure is equal to their total yearly expenditure for textbooks. These figures are undoubtedly underestimates, because school personnel have an unstated policy of covering up as many incidents as possible. The subcommittee cited a report on the New York City schools that indicated that the rate of unreported incidents ranged from 30 to 60 percent.

Symptomatic of the breakdown of the socialization process discussed earlier in the chapter is the frightening increase in gang activity in the schools. The New York City Police Department reports that juvenile gang activity is four times as violent today as in the 1950's, largely because of the increased availability of high-quality guns.[126] In just five major cities, New York, Los Angeles, Chicago, Philadelphia, and San Francisco, there were 525 gang-related murders between 1972 and 1974.[102] In the first four months of the 1972–1973 school year, there were sixty reported gun episodes in the Los Angeles public schools alone, many of them gang-related.[117] Gangs no longer restrict their violent attacks to each other. They are increasingly involved in robberies, burglaries, assaults, and extortion against non-gang-member students, and even teachers.

Walter B. Miller of Harvard's Center for Criminal Justice reports that gangs are moving the center of their operation from the street into the schools.[102] Gangs actually claim territorial control of certain areas within a school, such as the cafeteria or gym, and extort use fees from students for the right to use these areas without being assaulted. In New York City it is reported that some schools have made deals with gangs, permitting them to operate within the school in return for a pledge of nonviolence. A New York state legislature study reports that in certain New York City high schools, students sell guns, narcotics, and the services of both male and female prostitutes with the full knowledge of teachers who take no action for fear of retaliation.[117]

According to Dr. Robert Poindexter, Executive Deputy Superintendent of Philadelphia's public schools, gang activity in the City of Brotherly Love is so severe that many students are too frightened to attend school. Official district programs bus children across gang-controlled areas, and other district programs provide safe corridors through gang-controlled neighborhoods.

Gang activity in Los Angeles high schools is increasingly violent. One of the large L.A. juvenile gangs is called the Crips, short for the Cripples, a name derived from the gang's trademark of maiming or crippling its victims. The Crips have two auxiliary units: the Cripettes, composed of girl members, and the Junior Crips, made up of elementary-school members. In Miller's recent work a Los Angeles youth worker is quoted as saying, "The problem is out of hand. . . . We've had three years of violence and killing in the schools with no real action by the authorities. . . . *All* the schools in the inner city have large gang populations."

A 1977 *Newsweek* story on our inner-city schools reported the case of a young student who came to class with a loaded .22-caliber pistol.[29] After disarming the student, his teacher took him to the school principal, who refused to take any action against the youngster, even permitting him to return to class the following day. When the school's teachers took the case to family court, their complaint was dismissed because the principal had not informed the student of his constitutional rights. I am personally acquainted with a junior-high-school teacher who has been the object of three premeditated, but unsuccessful, armed assaults during the past five years. Upon each occasion his principal has refused to prosecute or suspend the student involved. These incidents underscore what is perhaps the most destructive element of this entire trend—in numerous schools and school districts around the country, the primary administrative response to student crime and violence is cover-up. The lesson this nation's juvenile delinquents are learning in school is that there will be no repercussions for violent antisocial behavior.

If gang violence in the school is largely restricted to urban centers, drug usage is epidemic in almost all school settings. Use of all drugs—heroin, Quaaludes, L.S.D., amphetamines, cocaine, marijuana, alcohol, and others—is sharply rising. At the conclusion of the student interviews in Part II I indicate my shock and dismay at the number of students I talked to who got stoned every day during school hours. In the metropolitan high schools I visited, I estimate that 40 percent of the students take some form of drug several days a week during school hours, and at least 80 percent use drugs regularly. Analogous percentages for the suburban high schools I visited would be about half of these figures. The Los Angeles Police

Department informed the Senate Subcommittee that "80 percent of the students with whom police agents came in contact while posing as students and attending classes were using drugs of some kind."

The epidemic of drug-taking is not restricted to older children. Use of drugs is extremely widespread in junior high schools and in the last few years has infiltrated the upper-elementary grades. Drug-taking fills a need in young people for a kind of gratification they are not learning to obtain through the discharge of energy in hard work. One of the functions of the educational process is to teach young people how to work and how to regulate their own energy economy, by putting rigorous work demands on them. Because of the exceedingly light work demands of today's schools, young people do not experience the natural gratification that comes from the discharge of energy in hard work. Drugs permit the internal discharge of an individual's unexpressed energy, creating an artificial kind of euphoria or gratification. If their energy was expressed in schoolwork, athletics, or planned activities with peers and adults, children would not find the drug experience nearly so attractive.

The most valuable legacy we have as Americans is our liberty. The most powerful force protecting this liberty is the strength of the authority inherent in our various political, social, and economic institutions. The destruction of institutional authority in American society, whether the authority of the family, church, political party, or school, leaves a vacuum which is almost certain to be filled by the centralized authoritarian power of government. In one of the most important books of our time, *The Twilight of Authority*, sociologist and historian Dr. Robert Nisbet discusses the historical parallels between contemporary American society and certain previous periods of Western civilization.[112] He calls this a "twilight period," characterized by decreasing authority in societal institutions, a loss of faith in intellectual attempts to solve problems and a concomitant turning to mysticism and subjectivism, and a declining faith in the society, its institutions, and its future. He believes that unless there is a regeneration of authority relations within our social institutions, we will see a continuing deterioration of the social order into chaos and violence, which will be followed almost certainly by political totalitarianism. He writes:

> Periodically in Western history twilight ages make their appearance. Processes of decline and erosion of institutions are more evident than those of genesis and development. Something like a vacuum obtains in the moral order for large numbers of people. Human loyalties, uprooted from accustomed soil, can be seen tumbling across the landscape with no scheme of larger purpose to fix them. Individualism reveals itself less as achievement and enterprise than as egoism and mere performance. Retreat from the major to the minor, from the noble to the trivial, the communal to the personal, and from the objective to the subjective is commonplace. There is a widely expressed sense of degradation of values and of corruption of culture. The sense of estrangement from community is strong.
>
> Accompanying the decline of institutions and the decay of values in such ages is the cultivation of power that becomes increasingly military, or paramilitary, in shape. Such power exists in almost exact proportion to the decline of traditional social and moral authority. . . . The centralization and, increasingly, individualization of power is matched in the social and cultural spheres by a combined hedonism and egalitarianism, each in its way a reflection of the destructive impact of power on the hierarchy that is native to the social bond.
>
> . . . So, I believe, is the twentieth century in the West a twilight age. . . . It is hard to think of any other useful perspective in which to set the combined phenomena of sense of cultural decay, erosion of institutions, progressive inflation of values in all spheres, economic included, and constantly increasing centralization—and militarization —of power. If there were no other indicator, the impact of war and of the military on the West, especially since about 1940, would be sufficient—that and the cognate spread of the kind of social equalitarianism which is bred less by the moral value of equality than by centralized power's leveling effects upon the natural hierarchies of all social institutions.

We damage authority relations in education at our own risk. Subjected to an educational system sapped of its authority, our children will not develop the skills and knowledge necessary to func-

tion autonomously in modern society. Because democracy presup-
poses a degree of autonomy in its citizens, the stripping of authority
from our educational system jeopardizes our democratic way of life.
Paradoxically, our most potent protector against authoritarianism is
authority.

4

EDUCATIONAL

LEADERSHIP

THE OBJECT OF THE FIRST THREE CHAPTERS OF THIS BOOK WAS TO analyze some of the problems affecting American education. This chapter will propose some possible solutions to those problems. Before doing so, I will briefly restate my conception of the educational problems facing us.

Our problem is a nationwide deterioration in basic academic skills and knowledge. Students do not read, write, or compute as well as they did ten years ago. Nor do they know as much about history, science, or literature. The deterioration starts at about fourth grade and worsens steadily throughout junior and senior high school. The decline in academic skills is not restricted to poor, inner-city, or minority students. Middle or upper socioeconomic status does not protect a student against the decline. Nor is the deterioration restricted to average- or below-average-ability students. Above-average and even exceptional intelligence is not protecting students against the decline.

As Chapter Two indicated, the decline in basic academic skills is directly attributable to the curricular degeneration of the past dozen years. It does not require much educational expertise to realize that if writing assignments are stripped from the curriculum, students will not learn to write. Over the past dozen years, there has been a widespread movement in education away from traditional schoolwork. Not only are teachers assigning less reading, writing, and homework of all kinds, but students are avoiding rigorous subjects such as math, history, and science, in favor of less scholarly courses on such topics as science fiction, feminism, and world revolutions.

The curricular deterioration is a direct result of the degeneration of authority relations in education. Educational authority has been under attack since the mid-1960's from community organizations, from the courts, from government agencies, from liberal educators in the universities and professional associations, and from students. It requires tough educational authority to impose a rigorous curriculum on students and make it stick. Once school authorities buckle under to pressure and tell teachers to relax their grading standards and work demands, course work and curriculum start to degenerate. The wholesale subversion and abrogation of educational authority since 1965 has led directly to the widespread deterioration in the academic curriculum and the nationwide decline in basic academic skills.

Our educational system is a sick 130-billion-dollar-a-year social institution. The achievement decline, the curricular degeneration, the grade inflation, the literacy hoax—these are symptoms of educational decay. Because our public schools are such an important socializing force in the lives of America's young people, their continued deterioration is extremely dangerous for our society, and enormously damaging to our children.

The first step in the solution of our educational problems is a societal reaffirmation of traditional educational goals and the necessity for strong educational authority. If I read their mood correctly, the great majority of the American people still believe quite strongly in the traditional educational goals outlined in the Introduction—the overriding importance of teaching all American children the primary academic skills, reading, writing, and computing, and the enormous individual and social value inherent in instruction in math, science, history, and literature. Unfortunately, there is not the same degree of public recognition of the necessity of strong educational authority. Herein lies the great educational dilemma of our time. A social institution, like an individual, cannot fulfill its responsibilities unless it is given sufficient authority. The American people must realize that the public schools will not be able to fulfill their traditional purpose unless they are given a great deal of authority and autonomy.

Successful educational systems, such as American parochial schools (whose students attain much higher levels of academic achievement than comparable public-school students, at less than half the cost [14, 45]), Russian schools, and most European schools, are characterized not by high per-pupil annual expenditures, but by traditional educational goals and societal acceptance of school authority. As long as teachers hesitate to assign reading and writing assignments because they do not receive the administrative and parental support they need, as long as principals feel they cannot expel repeatedly disruptive and violent students because community organizations and the courts will not allow such expulsions to stand, as long as students feel it is perfectly acceptable to take as little English, math, science, and history as possible because nobody authoritatively tells them otherwise, our educational problems will remain unsolved.

In order to effect the profound ideological change this first step calls for, public opinion must be influenced on a wide scale. The most effective way to influence public opinion on this issue would be for representatives of America's educational community to affirm publicly the necessity of strong educational authority. An example of the type of public pronouncement I believe is necessary was the publication of "A 1976 Declaration of Independence" by the presidents of the four major private universities in Washington, D.C.[1] The declaration catalogs the numerous ways in which governmental and judicial intervention in university affairs has subverted the authority of these institutions and damaged their ability to provide a high-quality education to their students. The declaration goes on to state that the four universities intend to resist further government interference that saps the ability of the universities to meet their primary responsibilities.

A similar public position was taken in 1977 by the presidents of fourteen of the nation's leading medical schools, including Stanford, Johns Hopkins, University of Chicago, Yale, and the University of California. These institutions announced that they would refuse federal financial assistance rather than comply with federal regulations that forced them to lower their admissions standards.[98] Analogous public positions have been taken during the past few years by Brigham Young University in Utah, Hillsdale College in Michigan, and several other universities and local school districts.[47, 17] These public declarations should be joined to equally strong pronouncements from additional representatives of America's educational community, and such declarations should be supported by civic and community organizations. Representatives of the intellectual community, especially, could make a valuable contribution by publicly affirming the individual and social value of intellectual training and scholarship, and the concomitant necessity of educational authority and institutional autonomy. School boards, the PTA, and teachers' unions should be in the forefront of the effort to influence the American public on this issue.

It is extremely important that parents who believe in the necessity of strong educational authority make their beliefs publicly known. It is essential that such parents voice their support of school authority (and authorities!), academic standards, and work demands in PTA meetings at school-board meetings, and at conferences with individual teachers and school administrators. A public-relations effort by America's educational leaders, combined with the individual efforts of thousands of parents, could mobilize public and scholarly opinion in defense of the authority and autonomy of our educational institutions.

This public-relations offensive should be joined to a legislative and legal offensive designed to reduce judicial and bureaucratic interference in educational policy decisions. This offensive should include legal action directed against any community or political organization, or government agency, whose actions threaten the normal functioning of an educational institution. It should include a united and intensive lobbying effort by all of the various components of the powerful education lobby to influence state legislatures and the Congress to restrict the ability of the state and federal educational bureaucracies to intervene in local educational affairs.

Toward accomplishing these goals, I endorse a series of recommendations made by Louis Bender for the American Association of Higher Education.[17] These include a Magna Carta for Higher Education, which would affirm the fundamental principles of academic freedom and institutional autonomy and authority, and would be submitted to Congress for enactment. They also include a number of regulation reforms submitted by ex-HEW Secretary David Mathews, and a proposal for the establishment of an independent institute that would analyze the effects of legislation and government regulations on the nation's colleges and universities. I believe each of these proposals has an appropriate analogue at the public-school level, which should also be implemented.

Anybody who is familiar with the legal history of the United States recognizes that our courts are greatly influenced by public opinion and especially by a consensus of personal opinion among members of the academic community. If public opinion and scholarly opinion reaffirm the necessity of strong educational authority, it will not be long before the courts accept the legal argument that there is a constitutional basis for educational authority and autonomy. Until quite recently there was a widely accepted judicial principle of restraint in educational matters; indeed, the recent interventionist attitude of the federal courts on this issue is actually an historical anomaly. If we are able to achieve a major shift in public and scholarly opinion in defense of the authority and autonomy of our educational institutions, I would predict a similar, albeit delayed, shift in legal opinion.

A societal reaffirmation of traditional educational goals and the necessity of strong educational authority is a necessary but not a sufficient condition for the solution of our educational problems. Even if we are able to accomplish this enormously important but difficult first step, we will still face the reconstruction of a badly deteriorated educational system, where teachers are saddled with a chaotic and inadequate curriculum, where they feel compelled to reduce performance standards and work demands, and where the only psychology many of them have learned equates authority with authoritarianism and confuses training with nurturing. The second step in the solution of our educational problems is to reestablish normal authority relations at every level of our educational system. A reader who rereads Chapter Two after completing Chapter Three will find that virtually every instance of curricular deterioration results directly from the subversion or abrogation of educational authority. Whether the issue is open education, grade inflation, or the reduction in the volume of assigned reading and writing, the curricular weakness can be remedied only by reestablishing educational authority.

In the remainder of this chapter, I propose a systematic approach to the reconstruction of our educational system. I would caution the reader that my approach is only meaningful in the context in which it is offered—as a general guideline for our schools to follow, and as part of the *second* step in a two-step solution to our educational dilemma. The first step, the societal reaffirmation of traditional educational goals and the necessity for strong educational authority, is a prerequisite to any meaningful solution of our educational problems.

If one were to ask most parents of school-age children how to improve our public schools, the answer would be simple and forthright: Get better teachers. If one were to ask the same question of America's most competent educators, the answer would be just as unhesitating, but different: Get better principals. Indeed, both answers are correct, and will form the basis for the recommendations in the balance of this chapter.

As I stated in Chapter Two, the basic unit of elementary and secondary education is the classroom—one teacher working with a group of students. In order for children to learn successfully, their teacher must fulfill three basic teaching functions.

First, a teacher must have his class under control. Most students must be on task most of the time. A teacher must have both the character and the teaching skills to get his students to do what he wants them to do while they are in his class. Without control, a teacher cannot teach.

The teacher's second responsibility is to assign meaningful tasks in a meaningful curriculum. A child who completes his assignments should master an essential body of skill and knowledge which will help him to survive and function in the world. The teacher must understand the goals and methods of the curriculum, *i.e.*, how sequential completion of a series of tasks will result in real and valuable learning. He must plan his assignments to achieve the curricular goals with the unique group of students he is teaching.

The reader will note that by adequately meeting these two basic responsibilities, a teacher exercises his educational authority in the four ways outlined in Chapter Three. He defines an essential body of skill and knowledge (meaningful tasks in a meaningful curriculum), and he gets his students to learn the material he assigns by establishing standards and requiring practice (control). A traditional curriculum can be defined as one in which teachers are obliged to fulfill only these two basic functions. American public education up to the 1920's, and continental European education and American parochial education up to the present, can be defined as traditional in this sense.

The modern American curriculum legitimately assigns its teachers a third basic function, one which I endorse, but which must always be subordinate to the first two. Teachers should primarily use positive forms of motivation with their students. Classrooms should be lively, happy places. Students' art work should fill the walls. Teachers must not be punitive or abusive; they must be firm, direct, and in control, but they should also like and love children, and respond to them with praise and other expressions of positive emotion. The reader will note that this third function defines the teacher's nurturing responsibility, which, as Chapter Three indicated, must be subordinate to his training functions.

The abuse of progressive education that we have seen in the past dozen years, and to a certain extent since the 1920's, comes, in my judgment, not because teachers were expected to fulfill this third basic function, but because the hierarchical ordering of the three functions was neglected. Students must be under control and assigned meaningful tasks before the fulfillment of the third function makes any educational sense. Teachers who confuse the ordering of these three functions, or who deny either of the first two, rescind their educational authority and their primary educational responsibilities. However, a teacher who can successfully meet all three responsibilities is, in my estimation, a better teacher than one who meets only the first two.

How many of our public-school teachers are adequately discharging their responsibilities as defined above? My personal estimate is about half. My judgment is that from 5 to 10 percent of our public-school teachers are superb, another 15 to 20 percent are good, 25 percent are adequate but should be better, 30 to 40 percent are inadequate but trainable, and 10 to 20 percent are so bad they should not be teaching under any circumstances. These are not bad odds for gambling, but they are not good if you have children in the public schools. My estimates are based on personal observation of the public schools, and conversations with numerous parents and school officials during my eight years as the director of my private reading school in California. These estimates have been reinforced in conversations with a number of extremely competent and experienced educators, who consult widely in public schools around the country, and who are directly involved in university programs of teacher training.

A reader who has had little direct experience with the public schools might wonder exactly what I mean when I say that a teacher is not adequately discharging his responsibilities. Several years ago I worked as a consultant in an inner-city school, ostensibly training fifth- and sixth-grade teachers to teach reading. One of the sixth-grade teachers was hopelessly ineffective in that environment. His class was so noisy that it was impossible for students to concentrate on their schoolwork. Many of the students ran wild, fighting, swearing, throwing spitballs at each other and at him, virtually ignoring his efforts to teach them. One day in the late spring, expressing their intense frustration at having wasted a year of their lives, a number of the students ganged together and beat up this man right in the middle of class. This teacher had a basic problem in classroom control.

Another teacher in the same school had a different problem. She had total control of her class, but unfortunately she had them spending from three to four hours a day engaged in round-robin oral reading. The students who read poorly or could not read at all were completely ignored. She permitted no distracting noise in her room, but she did permit her students to sleep in class. Indeed, every time I walked by her room there were several students sleeping in their chairs. Year-end achievement testing the previous June had shown that her students had made no measurable improvement in reading or math during the entire academic year. While this woman had excellent classroom control, she did not assign educationally meaningful tasks.

I have visited classrooms in middle-class, suburban schools which also were largely out of control. One kindergaten teacher I observed simply could not control her five-year-olds. I have a vivid memory of her standing in the midst of thirty milling children, admonishing them, "I'm going to start counting, and when I get to ten, I want to hear a pin drop." She finally stopped counting at twenty-five, having accomplished nothing more than a further diminution in her own authority.

I observed innumerable high-school classes where the teacher was giving an excellent lecture to two or three students, while another ten or fifteen talked to each other, applied their makeup, or caught up on the sleep they had missed the night before. I have been in dozens of classrooms in both inner-city and suburban schools where the walls were totally barren, reflecting a classroom environment equally barren of enthusiasm for life or learning. (For dozens of firsthand reports of adequate and inadequate teachers, see the interviews in Part II, especially Interview 13.)

There are three primary reasons for the high degree of teacher incompetence in our public schools. First, the teacher-training programs established at most universities and colleges are inadequate, which has the twin effect of producing poorly prepared teachers and denying teachers a source of high-quality training which they could use throughout their professional careers. Second, the overwhelming majority of school principals and educational administrators and supervisors do a very bad job of providing their teachers with training and supervision in classroom management and curriculum development. Finally, the breakdown in educational authority over the past fifteen years has demoralized many potentially competent teachers, and caused them to become ineffective, and causes most top-notch male teachers to get out of teaching within three to ten years. While this analysis is partly based on discussions with educators who are deeply involved in teacher training, and on dozens of interviews with public-school teachers, it is also based on an excellent study of teacher education in American universities and colleges which was conductd by James Koerner, formerly executive director of the Council for Basic Education (CBE).[80]

How do we get better teachers into our public schools? I have heard numerous proposals for accomplishing this end, ranging from the American Federation of Teachers and National Education Association proposal that we sharply escalate teacher salaries, to the CBE proposals that we abolish tenure and institute merit pay. In the study mentioned above, James Koerner recommends that teacher training be largely taken out of the hands of the education faculties at our large universities and teachers' colleges and put into the hands of the liberal-arts faculties. Although I am somewhat sympathetic to all of these ideas, I am not confident that any of them would significantly improve the caliber of the nation's teachers.

I am confident, however, that if we sharply upgrade the caliber of our nation's school principals, they will act to significantly and rapidly improve the quality of our nation's teachers. Although it is rarely acknowledged, it is axiomatic in American public education that where you find a functioning school, you find an excellent principal. A highly competent principal provides expert and authoritative leadership to his teaching staff, which has the net effect of reinforcing the efforts and confidence of the good teachers, maximizing the performance of the marginal teachers, and causing the incompetent, untrainable, and lazy teachers to quit. Indeed, the authoritative principal-teacher relationship is as central to the effective operation of our schools as the authoritative teacher-student relationship.

A mediocre principal does not back up his good teachers. He fails to provide the curricular direction and continuous training and supervision that his marginal teachers need in order to become functional. He will not establish the level of professional demands or apply the necessary pressure that will cause his incompetent teachers to quit. A mediocre principal simply does not fulfill the authoritative leadership functions that are central to the effective operation of a school. (Note the studies by Weber [158] and Silberman,[135] both of which acknowledge the primacy of the principal in a functioning school. See also Interviews 8, 13, and 14.)

The essential educational function of a school principal is to ensure that all of his teachers are teaching well. Most principals are so preoccupied with the day-to-day management of a frequently chaotic institution that they lose sight of their primary task. They spend exorbitant amounts of time developing a budget, ordering books and equipment, meeting with parents, disciplining children, dealing with the custodial and clerical staffs, engaging in public-relations efforts with various civic and community groups, and frequently performing important district-office functions as well. More often than not they fail to fulfill their three essential leadership functions: providing curricular direction; training and motivating teachers; evaluating and firing teachers.

An excellent principal will establish a stable, educationally sound curriculum. While he may delegate some aspects of the curriculum-development function to a highly competent teacher or group of teachers, he will nonetheless take full responsibility for the final decisions regarding what and how the students in his school will be taught.

At the elementary-school level, the principal's most important curriculum-development function is to establish a continuous, six-year program of basic-skills instruction. In many schools, the principal does not even know what reading programs his teachers are using, nor does he know enough about the theory and method of reading instruction to provide curricular direction in this area. I strongly recommend that school districts choose any of the available basal reading series put out by a major publisher and make a commitment to stick with this series for a minimum of ten years. Every elementary school in the district should use the same program. The district should institute mandatory and extensive training for its principals, teachers, and reading experts in the proper use of the program it chooses.

Through careful diagnostic testing of its students each year, the district should determine the strengths and weaknesses of the program it is using. When testing uncovers a program weakness, by determining, for instance, that many students are deficient in syllabication skills, or comprehension, or rate, or interest in reading, a committee of teachers and reading experts should develop or find supplementary materials that will improve the skills of students in those specific areas. Over a period of years, the district should develop a comprehensive, stable reading program, which all teachers will master, and all students will experience. It should be the responsibility of the school principal to ensure that the program is effectively taught by all of the teachers in his school.

At the secondary level, the principal's primary leadership function in the area of curriculum is to establish a policy that all students will take an academic core curriculum. As indicated earlier, there has been a drastic reduction in the amount of academic course work taken by the average high-school student during the past fifteen years. This trend will continue as long as high-school principals abrogate their leadership responsibilities in this area. It is a terribly destructive practice to permit young people to study only the courses they believe they are interested in. While there is nothing wrong with permitting them to choose one or two courses out of six, high-schools principals should establish the policy that *each student will take a core curriculum chosen for him by his high-school counselor.*

It is an act of caring, commitment, and concern for our young people to ensure that their education is structured so that they will learn what they need in order to function in modern society, and fulfill themselves as human beings. Adolescents in modern American society desperately need guidance in many areas, and guidance in schoolwork is certainly one thing the school should provide them. Counselors should impose a heavy academic load on students as a matter of course. College-bound students should be assigned four years of English, math, science, and social studies. Vocationally oriented students, or students who think they are vocationally oriented, should also be assigned an appropriate, and relevant, academic core curriculum, which includes four years of English and several years each of math, science, and social studies. Classes should be grouped by ability, but teachers in all classes should impose high standards and heavy work demands.

The high-school principal's leadership responsibilities extend into two additional areas of the curriculum where a policy vacuum has proved to be very destructive to the educational development of America's secondary students. The first is basic-skills instruction. The reading crisis in American education is that such a high percentage of our high-school graduates do not like to read and lack the advanced comprehension skills required to read the specialized types of materials used in technical areas. At my reading institutes in California, I have developed programs specifically designed to teach advanced comprehension skills and a love of reading, because most of the several thousand secondary and college students we teach each year have had inadequate instruction in both areas. High-school principals must direct their teaching staffs to find or develop such programs, and institute them as part of the subject area curriculums. Analogous problems in writing and math must also be addressed. School districts might take a lesson from Pasadena's secondary schools, which have instituted a comprehensive program of basic skills instruction in the junior-high-school and high-school English curriculum.[127] The district provides its teachers with suggested lesson plans and materials to accomplish a set of targeted proficiencies in each of the twelve semesters of English.

The other area of the curriculum which requires the principal's leadership is values education. In this country's first 185 years of existence, values education was an integral part of the public schooling process. Indeed, moral and religious education was the rock upon which public education was founded. During the past fifteen years, our schools have responded to the national climate of self-doubt and self-hatred by largely eliminating any kind of moral education from the school curriculum. In so doing, they have shirked the basic responsibility of providing children with the emotional support and guidance they need for healthy psychological and social development. Young people need the security and stability of a basic set of societal values and ideals. They are damaged when they are raised in the emotional vacuum of a value-free environment.

The field of values education is one of the most controversial in public education today. According to George Gallup, 84 percent of parents with children in the public schools want to see some form of moral instruction in the schools (12 percent were opposed, 4 percent registered no opinion).[28] Unfortunately, the questions, What values? Whose values? and How? have proved to be major stumbling blocks in translating parents' desires into the classroom. While most parents and educators (and I) believe there is a core of common values all children should be taught, a number of liberal educators believe it is extremely important to discover and affirm the unique values of America's cultural, racial, and ethnic minorities. Traditional educators who favor values education tend to support the method of direct instruction in moral behavior and values, combined with the teaching of values in the subject-area curriculums.[28] Most liberal and psychologically oriented educators who favor values education opt for a system called "Values Clarification," which is a method of instruction designed to help children develop and clarify their own values, under the nondirective guidance of the teacher.[69]

The role of the secondary-school principal in the area of values education is to make sure it happens at his school. If the principal fails to provide leadership in this field, values education will continue to be left out of the curriculum. Under his direction, the teaching staff should develop a program that will meet the needs of the school's students and the community it serves. If there are hard decisions to be made regarding what and how values are to be taught, the principal should make them.

The principal's second primary educational leadership function is to ensure that all of his teachers receive the training and supervision they need. Virtually every study of teacher training in this country has found that once a teacher enters the classroom, he receives virtually no further organized training or supervision. As a result, many (perhaps most) teachers feel isolated and demoralized, and fail to develop adequately their teaching skills. A good principal will see to it that a competent teacher-trainer works with every teacher on his staff, developing the teachers' skills in classroom management, basic-skills instruction, and subject-area teaching.

At the elementary-school level, an excellent principal will perform a great deal of the teacher training himself, by personally going into each of his teacher's classrooms on a regular basis. He will work especially closely with his marginal teachers, providing the daily supervision which they need. He will motivate his superior teachers by regularly observing their classes, and complimenting them on the good job they are doing. (A reader unfamiliar with the normal operation of an elementary school should note that the average principal observes each of his teachers' classes only once or twice a year, for approximately fifteen minutes each observation. Of all the complaints I hear from elementary-school teachers, this is the most common.)

Because of the large size of most high-school teaching staffs, and the large number of subjects which they teach, a high-school principal must delegate a great deal of the teacher-training function to his department chairmen. However, as department chairmen are part of the teaching staff, not the school administration, they cannot realistically be expected to maintain an authoritative relationship with their colleagues. Thus, the principal must consistently and authoritatively back their actions and policies, and must not neglect his leadership responsibility in the area of teacher training and motivation. While he will spend less time in the classroom than his elementary-school counterpart, he must still be intimately involved in the teacher-training process. He must know the strengths and weaknesses of each of the teachers on his staff, and must take the time to provide personal supervision to those who need it, and perceptive compliments to those who deserve them. His job is to motivate all of his teachers, the good as well as the marginal.

The principal must also support the authority of his teachers in conflict situations. Most teachers tell me that their principals lack the courage and integrity to back them up in serious disputes that they cannot handle alone. I met several extremely competent and dedicated teachers who had been falsely accused of being sex perverts or racists, whose principals refused to support them publicly for fear of alienating powerful segments of school or community opinion. Dedicated teachers, who put their energy and heart into teaching, become terribly demoralized when their principals abrogate their authority and responsibility so blatantly, and destructively.

Finally, a competent and conscientious principal will force his incompetent and untrainable teachers to quit, or he will fire them. I have heard repeatedly from the top school principals and educational consultants I know that if a principal has established an authoritative and helping relationship with his teaching staff, and the school is functioning well, a bad teacher can be forced out with a minimum of effort. If a principal has the courage to confront an incompetent teacher with his poor performance, most will respond by resigning or transferring to another school.

A bad teacher on a good staff feels extremely uncomfortable. He is aware of his inadequacies, and once confronted he will usually quit without making a fuss. Needless to say, it is unfair to provoke such a confrontation until a principal has spent a considerable amount of effort attempting to provide the teacher with training and supervision. But once a principal decides that he has an incompetent and untrainable teacher on his staff, he must find the courage to force the teacher's removal from his school, even if this provokes a tenure battle in the courts, or a confrontation with the teachers' union. An obvious corollary to this point is that a principal who authorizes tenure for an incompetent teacher, and most principals are notorious for doing just that, is likewise setting aside his responsibility and authority.

I hope I have demonstrated that the previously stated problem of obtaining better teachers for our schools can be translated into what I believe is the more manageable problem of obtaining better principals. Principals are school-district employees who serve at the request of and can be replaced by the district superintendent. Except in very few school districts, principals do not have tenure as administrators (virtually all have tenure as teachers). Just as a principal is responsible for the quality of his teachers, a superintendent is responsible for the quality of his principals.

The relationship between a superintendent and his principals virtually parallels the relationship between a principal and his teachers. It is the responsibility of the superintendent to ensure that all of his schools have good principals. To accomplish this goal, he must provide his principals with educational goals for their schools, and training programs which will teach them the skills they need to fulfill the leadership functions discussed above. He must force his incompetent and untrainable principals to resign or retire, or he must fire them. Unfortunately, most superintendents become so preoccupied with the political and paper-pushing aspects of their jobs that they spend an insufficient amount of time motivating and training their principals. Few superintendents have the integrity to fire an incompetent principal who has been at the same school for a number of years.

The only way I know for a community to obtain good principals is to elect a school board that will hire an extremely competent superintendent, and then instruct him to institute a program designed to improve the caliber of the district's present principals, fire its incompetent ones, and hire only superior ones in the future. The superintendent will have to order his priorities so that the development of his personnel becomes the most important. He must recognize that his primary function is not to administer, but to *lead*. He must be a strong motivator, and must not flinch from placing exacting demands on his key personnel.

The superintendent should spend a significant amount of his time in the schools, motivating, training, and evaluating his personnel. He should oversee the development of training programs designed to increase the expertise of his principals, by personally hiring outside consultants, or recruiting highly competent district personnel who can conduct such training programs. He should develop a system of evalution, to judge the performance or ability of his principals in the following areas: the academic achievement of students (taking socioeconomic status into account); teacher morale and staff cohesion; teacher training; knowledge of and expertise in curriculum; human-relations skills; organizational ability. He should compare his own evaluations to those of others he is using in a training capacity, and he should communicate to his principals the results of the evaluations. Throughout all of this activity, the school board must be prepared to back the superintendent as conflict develops over his new policies and his personnel changes.

I am familiar with a fairly large suburban school district in California, comprised primarily of middle-class and working-class families, which is acting to improve its schools in a manner virtually identical to the way I have recommended. A number of concerned and capable citizens, including a very competent professional educator, were elected to the school board of this district after an active but nonhysterical campaign. Their principle campaign pledge was that they would improve the academic achievement of the district's students, which had fallen precipitously over the previous dozen years as a result of the kind of curricular degeneration described in Chapter Two.

The new board's first step was to hire a new superintendent. They chose a very able man who had previously straightened out two badly deteriorated districts. He demanded, and was given, carte blanche in hiring and firing district-office administrators and the principals of the district's forty schools. The board promised to back him legally and in the community if disputes arose over his policy changes.

Six months after assuming his position, the new superintendent announced that 15 percent of the district's schools would be closed the following year, as a result of declining enrollment and a shift in the city's pattern of residential development. He appointed a commission of private citizens and educators to evaluate all of the schools in the district. The appointment of this commission defused some, but not all, of the criticism of the announced school closings. Because he was able to pressure several principals to take early retirement, the net effect of this move was to eliminate *25 percent* of the district's principals. As promised, the board provided public relations and legal support when two of the fired principals sued the district for their jobs, with the support of several neighborhood groups who did not want to see their local schools shut down. The superintendent was able successfully to use the evaluations of the citizens' commission to justify both the closings and the firings.

At this writing, the superintendent is halfway through his third step. He has instituted a training program for the remaining principals, which is designed to give them the skills they need to fulfill the leadership functions described earlier. The training program includes formal classes in curriculum development, reading theory and method, and teacher evaluation. He is personally spending half his working hours in the district's schools, training and evaluating the principals. The outside consultants he is using have all been instructed to evaluate the performance of each of the principals. At the end of his second year, the superintendent intends to replace a number of his remaining principals with several of the district's competent and ambitious young administrators. By the end of his second year, the superintendent will have fired at least a third of his principals, and retrained the rest.

He has instituted other policy changes as well. He has banned blue jeans and all other forms of casual attire among the district's teachers. He requires that every room and every hallway in each of the district's schools be decorated with students' art work. Each week he visits several teachers' classrooms and is quick to offer praise or constructive criticism based on what he has observed. He spends time in the teachers' lounges at each of the schools in the district, listening to teachers' complaints, attempting to motivate them to achieve his vision of what their school could be. He is a cheerleader, a drill sergeant, a psychologist, a planner, attempting to mold his district into a cohesive, functioning, educational vehicle.

This story has two messages. The first is that dynamic, effective educational leadership is one key to sharply upgrading the quality of our schools. I have seen principals make an impact on their schools the same way this superintendent is making an impact on his district. Schools are people. People respond to leadership. We need people in leadership positions in our schools, principals and superintendents, who are motivators, who make good things happen. Such people exist—they need to be found, developed, and supported.

The second message of this example is that concerned citizens can act effectively through local school boards to improve their schools. The school board in this story deserves the lion's share of the credit for the improvements being made in the district's schools. The board recruited this superintendent, and if he had not been effective they would have found one who was. Yet throughout the country we find deteriorating schools, ineffective educational leadership, frustrated parents, and very little concerted citizen effort to improve the schools by changing the makeup or the policies of local school boards. Clearly, most people do not believe that school boards can make a difference. Why not?

Two very thorough analyses of the recent research on school boards and school-board elections largely answer this question.[81, 109] As a general rule, school-board elections attract a very low voter turnout, primarily because the campaigns are almost totally devoid of any real issues. These studies indicate that a widespread feeling exists among candidates and the public alike that to raise disputed policy issues during a school-board election is to inject politics into the schools, and that such behavior automatically labels a candidate as irresponsible and unfit for office. Thus, more than half of all school-board candidates report that the positions and policies they favor are essentially the same as those of the other candidates.

The studies also found that over a third of all school-board members were either appointed or ran for election unopposed. Many, perhaps most, school-board members were encouraged to run by school-district personnel or other board members, or by members of school-affiliated organizations such as the PTA. While many parents are interested and willing to become involved in their children's education, this willingness does not extend beyond participation in activities at the local school. Few parents understand what a school board does, and even fewer are willing to get involved in its operation.

The most devastating finding of both studies was that school boards virtually never set district policy in substantive areas, such as personnel evaluation and training, curriculum, or discipline. Instead, they rubber-stamp the decisions and policies of the superintendent and his staff. Indeed, the overwhelming majority of school-board members view their primary policy role as interpreting and explaining the superintendent's policies to the community.

School-board members play such a passive role because they lack the knowledge, information, and confidence that are required to make independent judgments. They are usually not professional educators or statisticians, so they find it difficult to follow the jargon-laden arguments supporting the various policies in dispute, and impossible to evaluate the data upon which decisions must be based. They do not have an independent source of information about the operation or effectiveness of the district's schools, as all of their information is supplied by the superintendent or his subordinates.

School boards are virtually defenseless when this situation is abused. I met a statistician who worked in the evaluation department of a large southern California school district. He reported to me that he had been instructed to help prepare an analysis of his district's test scores for the school board, which would show an increase in the academic achievement of the district's pupils over the previous year, when in fact the data could not support such an analysis. I encountered a similar situation in a very small, northern California school district, whose superintendent manipulated the year-end testing of his district's students in order to raise their scores, and impress the school board with the good job he was doing. Recall also the examples of fraudulent evaluation discussed in Chapter Two, one of which had the effect of completely misleading the local school board about the effectiveness of the district's secondary-level remedial reading program.

These stories underscore my belief that school boards need an independent source of information. I therefore endorse a recommendation of the National Committee for Citizens in Education (NCCE) that school boards hire full-time professional staffs that will work independently of the superintendent and the school-district administration.[109] This staff should provide the school board with the following kinds of information:

(1) Achievement Test Data: The staff should prepare an historical record of academic achievement in the district, at each grade level, and for each teacher and principal. This record should include data on any changes that may have occurred in the socioeconomic status or ability levels of the district's students. This demographic information should be used to develop an historical projection of expected levels of academic achievement. A comparison of the expected levels of achievement with actual levels of achievement would provide the board with a rough estimate of the effectiveness of the district's programs, teachers, and administrators.

(2) Personnel: The staff should be charged with ensuring frequent and adequate evaluation of district personnel, including teachers, principals, and district office staff. The staff should be responsible for assembling the evaluation data for presentation to the board, but the evaluations should be conducted by supervisory personnel, *i.e.*, principals should evaluate teachers, etc.

(3) Curriculum: The staff should develop a coherent explanation and analysis of the district's educational program, which includes discussion of basic-skills instruction at all levels, and all course offerings. This presentation should be made from the perspective of the direct and implied curricular recommendations made throughout this book.

(4) Discipline: The staff should develop a critical outline of the district's disciplinary policies and procedures.

(5) Administration: The staff should present an analysis of the district's personnel evaluation and development program, its achievement testing program, and each of its primary administrative functions.

(6) Budget: The staff should develop an historical analysis of the per-pupil cost of educating the district's students, in constant dollars (adjusted for inflation). The staff should work with the board and other consultants to develop the board's collective-bargaining position, and should analyze the proposals that are made during negotiations with teachers' unions and other employee representatives.

(7) Policy: School boards should use their professional staffs to analyze and project the effects of contemplated policy changes, such as changes in promotional policy, tenure, merit pay, replacement of junior-high schools with middle schools, school closings as an adjustment for reduced enrollment, etc.

Use of such a professional staff should greatly enhance the knowledge and competence of local school boards, in much the same way that the operation of the Office of the Legislative Analyst has helped make the California legislature one of the most effective and respected state legislatures in the country. Clearly, access to the type of information proposed above should help school boards discharge their traditional budgetary responsibilities, including the task of collective bargaining. More importantly, school boards will be able to act much more freely in substantive policy areas, especially personnel, curriculum, and discipline.

The professional staff will be able to translate the district's educational-policy options into terms easily managed by a lay school board. Such a staff would not automatically shrink, as most superintendents do, from the recommendations in this section regarding educational leadership, or the implied recommendations in Chapter Two regarding curriculum. School boards would have an independent basis for judging the competence of district personnel, and the effectiveness of its educational programs. The competence and confidence of school boards would be sufficiently strengthened so that they could participate in educational and personnel policy-making on an equal basis with the superintendent and his staff.

Once school boards start participating more actively in policy-making activities, the public should take a much more active interest in school-board politics. Few communities attempt to act through their local school boards to improve their schools because of the widespread feeling that school boards lack the competence to deserve a significant influence in decisions regarding important educational issues. Once a community recognizes that its school board has a sufficient information base to act competently and independently, it should see the school board as a potential vehicle for improving the local schools. I would anticipate that school-board elections in such a community would soon be characterized by lively voter interest and active debate about disputed educational issues.

During the past fifteen years, the governance of American public education has largely passed out of the hands of local communities. The first move in this direction actually occurred during the first quarter of this century, when a reform movement aimed at reducing political influence and corruption in the public schools professionalized the field of education. During this period a significant degree of local control was surrendered to school administrators, their professional associations, and the schools of education where they received their training. The trend toward reduced local control accelerated sharply during the past fifteen years, as a result of the explosive growth in the size and power of teachers' unions and state and federal educational bureaucracies.

As Chapter Two discussed, the government's educational bureaucrats have achieved tremendous influence in the areas of staffing, busing, testing, grouping, and curriculum, especially in metropolitan centers. The influence of teachers' unions was initially restricted to personnel and budget, but the past few years have witnessed a burgeoning movement to negotiate educational policy along with salary and employment benefits. Thus teachers' contracts now frequently display clauses regarding school-district policy in the following areas:

class size; educational testing; extracurricular activities; programs for the educationally handicapped; procedures for transferring teachers to achieve racial balance; the use of teacher's aides. This tremendous expansion in the influence of teachers' unions and government bureaucracies has come at the expense of both school administrators and local school boards.

The NCCE proposal for independent staffs for local school boards returns to local communities a measure of influence and authority in school governance, without distorting normal channels of educational authority. While each of the groups listed above can make a positive contribution to school control, only the local community is exclusively concerned with the interests of its children. Each of the other major forces is preoccupied with the protection and aggrandizement of its own influence. The current situation, in which local communities and school boards make little real contribution to curricular and personnel policies, is dangerous for our children because it exposes them to many teachers and educational programs that were selected for the wrong reasons.

I am not arguing for a return to total local control of our nation's schools. After all, such a situation has not existed in American education for the better part of this century, nor could it exist in modern American society. I am arguing for a return to a balance in school governance which gives the local community, through its school board, a significant influence in the major educational decisions that affect the community's children. I urge school boards to adopt the NCCE proposal, and I urge parents to become involved in school-board affairs. Local communities, acting through their elected school boards, can act effectively to improve our nation's schools.

Once a school board has established an effective policy-making partnership with the superintendent, it will be in a position to take policy initiatives that will redound to the educational benefit of the district's students. I will recommend three more programs a school board could implement, in addition to the changes suggested above, as examples of the kind of actions a school board could take to affect a district's educational policies and programs.

School boards should establish a district policy that upon completion of twelfth grade, all students will be administered a school-leaving exam. Currently, a number of school districts and state offices of education are developing such proficiency exams, partially in response to state legislation requiring their use.[136] School boards should mandate the use of such tests as a way to reestablish educational standards and strengthen authority relations in the schools.

A high-school leaving exam should test students in all basic-skill areas, including reading, writing, and computing, and in basic subject areas, including English, social studies, science, and math. The test should be scored with a simple 0, 1, 2, 3 system. A score of 1 would indicate basic competency to handle societally necessary tasks such as reading a want ad or filling out a simple job application. A score of 0 would indicate functional incompetency. A score of 2 on any of the subtests would indicate high-school level mastery of subject matter. A score of 3 on any subtest would indicate a degree of mastery equivalent to a term or more of college. To receive an overall score of 2 on the test, which would establish the basic standard of skill and knowledge expected of students after twelve years of schooling, a student would have to score a 2 or 3 on all of the subtests. A student's performance on this exam should be indicated on his high-school diploma.

Use of such a proficiency test would have several significant benefits. Students, parents, educators, and the community at large could evaluate student and school performance against the imposed standard of this exam. It would provide a reality test against which the effects of the curriculum and especially curricular reform would have to be measured. A diploma embodying these proficiency standards would guarantee basic literacy to a student's potential employer, or college.

Colleges could use the exam as a college entrance exam. A college using the test would not permit entrance to any freshman-level course in a particular subject until a student had achieved a score of 2 on the mastery-level subtest for the subject area and a score of 2 on the mastery-level subtests for the basic academic skills.

Colleges that wished to continue policies of open admissions could still do so, by instituting a series of prefreshman courses. They would require an exam score of 1 for entry into the prefreshman classes, and would permit students to spend as many semesters in these classes as proved necessary.

In his comparative study of the effects of different teaching styles, discussed in Chapter Two, Neville Bennett discovered that those schools that administered the English grade-school leaving exam known as the 11+ significantly outscored the schools that did not use the exam. This effect was produced whether the teaching style was open, mixed, or traditional, and the subject in which the effect was most pronounced was reading. Bennett inferred that the curriculum will be oriented toward basic skills if teachers and administrators know that their students will be tested in basic skills at the completion of their education. If my recommendation for a high-school leaving exam were adopted, I would predict a similar effect.

A second area where a school board could make a positive impact on district policy is the field of parent training. As indicated earlier, a number of studies have demonstrated that parents can exert an enormously beneficial influence on the educational development of their children. Unfortunately, many parents lack the skills or confidence to provide their youngsters with the necessary educational stimulation, support, and training. I recommend that school boards take the initiative in this area, by instructing the district's schools to develop a series of classes for parents, designed to teach them the skills that will enable them to help their children fulfill their educational and intellectual potential. These classes would also be excellent vehicles for accomplishing the first step in my proposed solution to our educational problems—the societal reaffirmation of traditional educational goals and the necessity of strong educational authority. Following is a list of the kinds of courses that might be offered.

1. How to work with preschool children.
Classes should be offered in nutrition, educational prepa-

ration, discipline, verbal stimulation, arts and crafts—indeed, all of the areas in which our society leaves many new parents virtually unprepared. The classes should provide examples of materials and games that parents could make for their children, and should also provide a reading list of available books on child rearing. Associated with these classes could be some provision for periodic medical and educational diagnostic services for all of the preschool children in a community.

(I offer this proposal as an alternative to an American Federation of Teachers proposal for a 40-billion-dollar-a-year program of preschool education, to be offered through the public schools.[121, 125] Considering the research on preschool education cited in Chapter Two, I believe my proposal makes considerably more sense.)

2. *How to instill a love of reading in children.*

a. Establishing family traditions of reading together, including reading out loud to and with children, and playing word games.

b. Recommended books for children of different ages and interests.

c. Use of the community library with children of different ages.

3. *How to help children with writing and arithmetic.*

a. Helping children write letters, messages, plays, and stories.

b. Family games and activities that use arithmetic, including "going to market" and keeping a personal or family budget.

4. *How to help children with homework.*

a. Helping children develop good study habits by teaching them to organize their time and by helping them to set up specific homework and study times.

b. Teaching children how to outline their reading and writing.

c. Ensuring that a child is doing a proper amount of homework at each grade level.

d. Regulation of TV viewing.

5. How to interpret standardized achievement test scores, and other educational test information.

6. How to guide a child's choice of classes at the high-school level (conducted by high-school guidance counselors).

7. How to motivate young people to make a commitment to their own education. This course should include discussion on how to help young people integrate their education with their career aspirations.

8. Values training in the home: including guidelines for discipline, family discussion, parental demands, and children's rights and responsibilities at different age levels. This course should be taught by a licensed clinical psychologist, probably the school psychologist, with support from school staff and representatives of responsible community organizations.

A third area where school boards can make a significant impact on school-district policy is in the development of highly structured, academically oriented alternative public schools. A number of school districts around the country have opened such schools, which have been variously labeled 3R, fundamental, structured, basic, and traditional. The academic achievement of students in these schools is reported to be excellent, and according to one report, black students in 3R schools are scoring above district and national norms for both black and white students.[155] Parents who live in these districts have the option of sending their children to a regular neighborhood school or to a 3R school. In many of the districts where this alternative is available, there are waiting lists of several thousand students to fill the few hundred available spots.

These 3R schools embody a number of the principles, goals, and suggestions I have made in this book. I believe the reader will recognize some of the key points from the following published description of Palo Alto's Hoover Structured School:

Classroom activities will be teacher initiated, directed, and supervised.

Parent participation in the classroom is not permitted at Hoover because it often leads to erosion of the teacher's authority.

In all grades except kindergarten, homework is given an average of four nights a week.

The Metropolitan Achievement Test is administered to students each spring to determine their progress over the past year.

The principal will exert strong leadership in order to establish unity of purpose among teachers, students, and parents.

In addition to quarterly report cards and (mandatory) parent-teacher conferences, *weekly* written reports on achievement, effort, and behavior are sent home for parents' signature.

A majority of the school day will be devoted to the teaching of reading, writing, spelling, language, and arithmetic.[68]

The most significant aspect of the development of these 3R schools is that they have developed within public-school districts as an alternative type of public school. In a few cases these schools have opened after a conservative majority was elected to the school board,[155] but more often they have been authorized by school boards that were responding to the request of an organized group of parents within the district.[40, 124] The following school districts had opened at least one 3R school by the fall of 1976: Charlotte-Mecklenburg, North Carolina; Jefferson County and Aurora, Colorado; Cincinnati and Columbus, Ohio; Houston, Texas; Dade County, Broward County, and Pinellas County, Florida; Jefferson County, Kentucky; Andover and Cambridge, Massachusetts; Philadelphia, Pennsylvania (17 schools); St. Louis, Missouri; Grand Rapids and Flint, Michigan; and Cupertino, Lagunitas, Pasadena, Palo Alto, Santa Ana, and Monterey Peninsula, California.[159]

Some 3R schools tend to make exorbitant claims in favor of their educational programs. Thus we find synthetic phonics touted by the John Marshall Fundamental School (Pasadena Unified School District) as the solution to the nation's reading problem.[155] It is not. If taught properly, it is an acceptable way to teach beginning reading. Despite the rhetoric, these schools are, in fact, professionally and humanely managed. I have visited several 3R schools, and my own observation is that their teachers are both competent and kind, although somewhat firmer than most. Where there is organized parental interest in this kind of education, I urge school boards to establish optional 3R schools.

The first step in the solution of our nation's educational problems is to reestablish normal authority relations between the larger society and our educational institutions. This will require a societal reaffirmation of traditional educational goals and the necessity of strong educational authority. Each of the branches of government at both the state and federal levels must acknowledge that if our schools are to meet their institutional responsibilities, they must be allowed to maintain their institutional autonomy, and authority.

The second step in the solution of our educational problems is to reestablish normal authority relations in the schools themselves. This will require that our school people fulfill their educational leadership functions. Teachers must control their classes, assign meaningful tasks in a meaningful curriculum, and positively motivate their students. Principals must meet their leadership responsibilities in the areas of curricular direction, teacher training and motivation, and teacher evaluation and firing. Superintendents must establish educational goals for their schools, hire competent principals, and provide them with the training and support they need to discharge their responsibilities. School boards should hire independent, professional staffs so they will have a sufficient information base to participate competently in educational policy-making. They should implement the curricular and personnel policies recommended throughout this book. Parents should get actively involved in school-board affairs, and communities should use their school boards to improve the local schools.

The recommendations in this chapter are designed to strengthen every link in the chain of educational authority: parent/student; parent/school board; school board/superintendent; superintendent/principal; principal/teacher; teacher/student. Wherever you, the reader, find yourself in this chain, I urge you to do your part to help America's students receive the education they need, and deserve.

PART

II

INTERVIEWS

FROM

THE FRONT

DURING THE COURSE OF THE RESEARCH FOR THIS BOOK, I INTER-viewed over two hundred individuals who were actively involved in public education. They ranged from a world-renowned authority on reading and evaluation to a high-school drug peddler. Most were ordinary students, teachers, and school administrators who were willing to share their perspective on contemporary public education with me. A great deal of the material presented in Chapters Two and Three was based on these interviews.

In order to preserve accurately the views of these teachers and students, I tape-recorded and transcribed most of the interviews. In this section of the book, I present a number of these transcripts. I have done so because I want to show you, the reader, the reality of our public schools today. I want to present the flesh-and-blood people behind the statistics, the analyses, and the conclusions of previous chapters. There is a sense of immediacy and reality to these interviews that is lost as soon as I start talking *about* them, or *about* education. I have presented these interviews to give you an opportunity to participate intimately in my investigation of our public schools.

Almost two-thirds of the interviews presented here were conducted in a number of California public high schools in the winter of the school year 1975–1976. The schools represent a cross section of the public high schools in California, ranging from racially mixed city schools to suburban high schools serving upper-middle-class communities.

The interviews are divided into two sections, high-school students in Section One, and teachers, administrators, and evaluation experts in Section Two. I did very little editing in these interviews. I cut out some repetitive material, and eliminated some of the *uhs, ums, likes, you know what I means,* and other inarticulate place holders that occasionally made the transcripts difficult to read. I also changed some verb tenses and made a few other grammatical and syntactical corrections in order to make the transcripts read more smoothly. Names have been changed.

1

STUDENTS

My usual procedure for meeting students was simple and direct. Most of the teachers whom I was interviewing invited me to observe their classes. At the end of a class period the teacher would introduce me to his class with a few words about the book I was writing. I would tell the class a little bit about some aspect of the research I was involved in and then ask if there were two or three students who would like to be interviewed. Initially, I chose students for the interviews who were actively participating in the classroom activities. Later on, I chose some students who were not participating, but whose raised hands indicated they were willing if not eager to tell me their feelings about school.

The six interviews in this section represent the full range of the views expressed and cover all of the important issues raised in the student interviews I conducted. The students in the first four interviews attend racially mixed city high schools. The students in the fifth interview attend a suburban high school which serves an integrated, upper-middle-class professional community. The girl in the final interview attends a private academic preparatory school.

INTERVIEW 1

The boy in the first interview was a neighbor of an instructor for my San Francisco Institute. She is one of many people to be captured by Steve's charm, friendliness, and problems. Steve's biggest problem is that he barely knows how to read. I believe most of his behavior is a compensation for this fact. He looks to be at least five years older than his sixteen years, a tall, long-haired, good-looking boy whose social skills are about as well developed as his academic skills are undeveloped. Like many students, Steve works part time. His job allows him to combine a major interest of his, one could almost say a habit, with an opportunity for pecuniary reward. Since he knew I was interested in the subject, that is where he started off the interview.

STEVE: I used to be really into drugs, you know. Doing acid every day and going to school and just sitting in the courtyard and tripping out.

C: How long did this go on?

STEVE: Half a year. This was fall of last year.

C: What happened last semester?

STEVE: Okay, midterm I go into an alternative school. I got a lot more interested in school when I was in that program. I didn't get so much static and bullshit. I used to always, like I'd get kicked out of classes. Like I had a test; I asked a kid in front of me, "Hey, like I don't understand what this test is about." The teacher turns around and says, "I don't want to hear you talking." She's got a really high-pitched voice and really loud. I didn't want to hear her voice, just like she didn't want to hear mine. I says, "Well, I don't see how the rest of the class can study when I'm whispering to one person in front of me and you're screaming at me across the class. The whole class has to listen to you. Nobody heard me but the person in front of me." And she just, well, you know, she started screaming at me, saying, "You want to get out of class, leave." I said, "Fine." I got up and I walked out.

I was really fucking up, so I decided I'd better get into something. I got into the alternative program, and then I began to get my shit together. I started cutting down on the acid until I got to the point where I wouldn't do it except for every now and then. I even cut back a little on my dealing. I used to deal a lot of dope that went through there, like I'd come to school with a big paper bag.

C: How many ounces?

STEVE: I'd usually bring a pound to school, already bagged up into ounces.

C: How many pounds did you deal a month?

STEVE: Oh, I don't know, there was one point where I went in partners with a friend and we had an average of two and a half pounds a week, which is really good.

C: Just to students at your high school?

STEVE: Yeah.

C: Was it just students or was it teachers, too?

STEVE: No, not the teachers. There are teachers that get loaded, though. There's—

C: Don't give me any names.

STEVE: I know one person that works at _____ that is into dealing cocaine, but he doesn't deal with the students. Then there's two of my present teachers. I know one smokes, but he doesn't smoke with the kids or around the kids. He tries not to let them know.

C: How about harder drugs, is there anything harder than grass going around among the students?

STEVE: Always, always.

C: Smack?

STEVE: The smack is mainly around blacks. It's mainly snorted, though, because a lot of people don't like needles. They think that if they snort it, then they can't get hooked.

C: Is that true?

STEVE: Ummm, not really.

C: What percentage of the students are into heavier stuff? Coke, smack, acid, pills?

STEVE: One hundred percent of the grass smokers.

C: You mean everybody who's doing grass is also doing something else?

STEVE: It depends what's around. There's always acid around. Like how many kids are getting stoned or whatever, it depends. If there's a lot of grass around and it's a low price like one hundred dollars a pound, then it's nonstop dope smoking. No one goes to class, everyone is either across the street, at the park, or they're hanging out on the stairs. The blacks somehow seem to have some right that they can walk through the halls and smoke dope and not have anyone hassle them. Probably the reason is that they travel in crowds, you know.

C: Is there a lot of acid being used here?

STEVE: There's always acid.

C: You're not making any of this stuff up?

STEVE: No, this is all true.

C: What percentage of the kids are stoned on something during school hours besides grass, on any given day?

STEVE: I'd guess between a quarter and a third of the grass smokers at the school, which are over seventy-five percent of the students.

C: When you were smoking a lot of dope during school hours, didn't that pretty well blow your concentration?

STEVE: I used to get so stoned that I'd just fall asleep in class, you know, if I went to class.

C: How often would you cut?

STEVE: Every day, at least two classes, if not the entire day.

C: What kind of grades were you getting in all these classes? Were you flunking them all?

STEVE: Well, I was taking six classes and I got kicked out of four, I think. I stayed in music because I was into music. But there was a lot of times where I'd be really loaded and not give a shit and sit around and laugh my ass off in class and really blow it, you know.

C: How much grass are you smoking now?

STEVE: Depends. A few months ago when the bucks were really rolling in, I was smoking about an ounce of Colombian every two or three days. Like I rarely smoke rag anymore.

C: Rarely smoke what?

STEVE: Rag, regular. It doesn't get me off unless I smoke, you know, four joints of it, and by that time it gets me tired and burned out, and I just fall asleep.

C: How much grass do you smoke? In an average week, say.

STEVE: I'd say about two ounces a week. [*Ed. note*: At two ounces a week Steve would be stoned 90 percent of the time.]

C: Is that by yourself or with friends?

STEVE: Well, it's rare that anybody I know sits around and smokes to themself, unless it's, you know, a before-going-to-sleep joint, you know. I mean, everybody needs one of those. Really puts your lights out.

C: Your school has a pretty good racial mixture. Are all groups as heavily into drugs as you've indicated?

STEVE: There's not that many Orientals. Like I'm talking in a stereotype, but Orientals always seem to really be superintelligent, really into school.

C: How about the white kids?

STEVE: If they're not drinking hard liquor then they're smoking dope or on pills. But one way or the other the majority is always loaded.

C: Your answer to my question about smack seemed pretty knowledgeable. Have you ever taken it?

STEVE: No, but there's a lot of it around. I know people who do it.

C: Is there much violence associated with drug dealing here?

STEVE: Oh, yeah. You've got to watch out the wrong people don't know you're dealing, or they'll jump you and steal your dope. A lot of kids will sell fake dope to raise some bread, then there'll be a fight. I've been jumped by black kids every year I've been in school, from seventh grade on.

C: Is most of the fighting associated with drugs?

STEVE: I'd say no. I'd say about a third is racial, about a third is drugs, and the last third is just normal fights. The only problem is the weapons. I don't know anybody who doesn't carry a knife. A few have guns. A friend of mine really freaked me out the other day. He's Chinese. We were down at the park, and some black dudes were hassling us pretty bad; they were from school. I thought for sure we'd have a fight. Then this guy, he's really a nice guy, I was pretty shocked, he pulls out a gun and shot down at the ground by this big black dude's foot. Told them he was going to blow their fucking heads off. They ran. Really freaked me. I would never pack a rod.

C: My God! How about reading, what are the reading habits of the students here? Does anybody read?

STEVE: Nobody's got the habit, I'll tell you.

C: Give me a percent.

STEVE: Twenty-five percent. Like the twenty-five percent of non-grass-smokers, they are the ones that do a lot of reading, but they do it because it's been forced down their throat. But I don't think they have enough good books, also. The schools I've gone to, they'd give us a book, we'd read it, and it would be a lot of long and drawn-out bullshit. Not the kind of stuff that anybody's into. Like *Huckleberry Finn* gets a little old, you know.

C: What are your own reading habits, how much time do you spend reading every day?

STEVE: I don't.

C: Not at all?

STEVE: I can read, but I don't.

C: What are you taking in school?

STEVE: I'm taking driver's education. I'm repeating communication workshop, which is an alternative class which did me wonders. It really did me wonders. It's a kind of psychology class. It talks about communication with you and the people around you. Then there's like civics.

C: What?

STEVE: Civics. They talk about the country and the way it's being run and all that. I don't really want to know what's going on with our government. All I know is prices are going up and people are getting impeached and people are shooting Presidents. I don't know what the hell it's all for and I don't want to know. You know, I want to just get my shit together and leave this country. I want to go somewhere else, like Canada. Canada's supposed to be nice. And if I ever have kids, I want them to grow up anyplace but the United States, because it isn't what it's supposed to be, especially for learning, you know. Like if I send my kids to a school, it is not going to be a public school, definitely not, because I hope my kid will be a little bit smarter than me, you know.

C: How about writing? Do you do any writing in school? Compositions, paragraphs, essays?

STEVE: In certain English classes, but most of the English classes I've been in nobody ever did it. Even in junior high school.

C: What kind of writing have you been assigned here?

STEVE: We had to keep a journal. Every day we'd have a certain length of time to write in our journals. We could write personal things, we could write abstract things, and if we were really not in the mood for writing, we'd sit there and draw pictures of our feelings or whatever.

C: What kind of reading assignments do you get?

STEVE: Well, the reading that was assigned to me I didn't do, you know. Or if I did I'd just read bits and parts.

You know, I'd like to warn kids not to goof off and get behind. You'll end up cutting class because you don't understand it. Teachers won't help you, and it's really weird because you go into a class, you don't understand it, you're embarrassed to tell the teacher you don't understand it, because you're afraid that the teacher's going to laugh at you, because it's happened for so many years. Teachers will just laugh at you if you don't know it and they'll say, "Man, why didn't you learn this a long time ago?" Or they'll say, "Where have you been for the past twelve years?" You know. Like they'll get on your case about it.

I really wish school could be better. I wish there was a way that in the future all the rest of the students don't turn out like

I'm turning out, and don't turn out like the majority of the students.

C: What kind of job do you want to get when you get out of high school?

STEVE: It doesn't really matter. Like, I mean, I'd really like to enjoy whatever I'm doing. One thing I enjoy doing is like working with people. I thought a lot about being a social worker, some type of counselor, or working with kids. Like working in, like maybe a youth center that is centered around drugs. Like there's a lot of kids that are really fucked up on drugs, really spaced out, you know, and like nobody can help them but themselves, but they need a little guiding, you know. So I'd like to get my shit together with any kind of job. I'd enjoy like maybe making certain types of ice cream. Experimenting with different types of food or cooking. I've got an ex-old lady who really wants me back. She's got a father that's supposed to die within a year. He has got thirteen houses and thirty acres of land.

C: Your idea is to marry this girl? Then you wouldn't have to work?

STEVE: I was thinking about it, but we broke up just the other day and I don't know if I want her back. My other ex-old lady has got a father who has owned about four or five different companies. One way or the other, I know I'm going to get by.

INTERVIEW 2

The three students in the next interview are all academically motivated juniors. Barbara is a rather pretty and rather conventional young lady. She is somewhat above average in ability, not brilliant, but a fairly hardworking student. She comes from the large San Francisco Italian community. Randy is an engaging youngster, very intelligent, rebellious against the establishment in an open, friendly kind of way. He's a tall, dark, good-looking boy, who always seems to be wearing a big grin. Ivan is a brilliant, disciplined student with a barely repressed bitterness about the inadequacies of his school. He is tall and blond, and is ranked number two on the school's tennis team. I started out the interview by trying to find out if the school was challenging these students to their potential.

C: How many of your teachers make pretty heavy demands on you?

RANDY: I don't have any teachers who make demands.

BARBARA: There's one teacher who makes outrageous demands; she has about three people in each of her classes, because every semester there's a mass exodus from her classes. That's Miss M_____. She teaches English.

IVAN: This school is so easy, I'm getting out.

RANDY: It's so easy to bullshit your way through this school. The students get used to it. When they find a class is too hard, they just get out of it. They can always pick up the credit here or there washing the teachers' cars.

IVAN: Oh, yeah, two credits there.

RANDY: The valedictorian took the easiest classes. It's unbelievable. A four-point average, he's smart, you know, but the classes that he took aren't really anything.

BARBARA: Jewelry, six honors.

RANDY: You can get five units' credit for being a library monitor, which is nothing. Or five units to answer phones in the office. Which they don't do too efficiently.

BARBARA: Or run messages from the office. You'll get the same credits for that as you do in a normal class.

RANDY: But in most classes you don't learn anything. Like film lit. He gives you an assignment sheet and says analyze such and such a movie. It's almost like fill in the words. One page of it will be a little ditto sheet where he'll analyze the whole thing for you. You have to fill in about ten key words.

C: What in the world is film lit?

RANDY: Film literature. It qualifies for English credit. You watch movies and analyze them.

C: How many kids take film lit instead of regular English?

RANDY: Everybody.

C: What would you do if you were a teacher? You're saying some classes are really absurd because they don't make you work, but if they do make you work then all the students are going to drop out of their classes.

BARBARA: There's a group of people that just like to stay out in the courtyard and smoke dope and hang around and be popular. Then there's the others who want to be in class. There's two different groups to deal with.

C: Are you three more the academic type?

RANDY: Yeah, we're probably the only ones in history.

BARBARA: You saw us raise our hands in the class. We're the only ones that have been answering questions.

IVAN: This is our class.

BARBARA: We used to do a thing called a weekly news where the teacher would ask for volunteers.

RANDY: We would be the only volunteers. We did it about three times each.

IVAN: After that he just got fed up, and he said we're not doing the news anymore; nobody else wants to do it.

C: Out of how many students?

RANDY: There's supposed to be thirty people in the class, and you just saw the average attendance, about ten or twelve.

C: You're kidding me. Where are the rest of the students?

RANDY: They're either in bed or outside or just, you know, wandering the halls. Just anywhere but in class. I heard from my cousin in Kentucky that they put all the smart students in one class. Is that true?

C: Yeah. How would you feel about going to school with that kind of system?

RANDY: I'd rather have a class where the teacher could teach more of what he knows. Most of the students don't care anyway so the teacher might as well just dig down and teach them what he wants.

C: As a matter of fact, there's a theory that you three are supposed to be the spark plugs. You're put into the classes with all the average kids. You're supposed to motivate those kids, ask questions, get everybody interested.

IVAN: It doesn't work. The other students say, "Let them do it all."

BARBARA: I'd rather be in a class where I'm not the only one giving feedback to the teacher, where we could get some pretty good discussions going. Not just you back and forth with the teacher, but you to the teacher, you to the student sitting next to you.

IVAN: And the student back to you.

RANDY: The idea would be fine if it worked, but it doesn't.

C: Are you in any classes with primarily smart and motivated kids?

IVAN: Most of my electives are with the brighter kids, but the ones that you have to take, like history, English, biology, those are the slow ones.

C: Is that frustrating for you?

IVAN: That's why I'm getting out of this school. Take French, for instance. I'm in second-year French and I have never had to study in the class and I always get A's on the tests. He'll bring up a point at the beginning of class and he'll just go over it for forty minutes until everyone gets it. I've gone to University High and sat in on a French class and everyone participated—everyone asked questions and talked and they were ahead of us, and that was first-year French. They had a harder book, they were farther along in it than we were, all of them spoke it pretty well and some of the kids in my class here can't speak it at all.

C: What makes the three of you so different from the other twenty-five in the class?

IVAN: I want to learn something. I don't just want to go to school to sit in class passing time.

BARBARA: I want a good grade so that I can get into college.

IVAN: If I was grading myself, I'd give myself a D in every one of my classes. Don't think I'm proud of it. But you know what I get? All B's and A's.

RANDY: The class I work the least in is the class that I never fail to to get an A in, German. I can do my homework in a couple minutes before class.

BARBARA: The big problem is a lack of respect for the teachers. They say do a paper by next week, but you know that if you don't do it for three weeks, the teacher will still accept it, since only about four people will hand it in at all

IVAN: In every class there are students who sit in the back of the room and just emit hostility. They answer back haughtily, and the tone of their voice really gets the teacher upset. They come almost every day and never work or do very poor work.

BARBARA: In the private schools they're harder on the students than in public schools. I didn't have any time for playing ball. I was always studying. Here the teachers want to please the students.

IVAN: I don't feel challenged by any of the work assigned in this school. All of it's very easy. That's why I'm getting out.

C: Where are you going to transfer to?

IVAN: University High. It's a private school, two years old. Supposed to be the best in the city.

C: How much does it cost?

IVAN: I'm getting financial assistance, but it's supposed to be twenty-six hundred dollars or something.

C: A year! For high school! Unbelievable. How many solids are you taking?

IVAN: Six. History, chemistry, advanced algebra, two lit classes, French, and P.E.

RANDY: I'm taking German, advanced algebra, history, chemistry, and English. Five solids. Plus dance production, that's P.E. I think next semester I'm going to have seven classes, I'm going to throw in a guitar class.

C: Are you learning to write here?

BARBARA: I don't put my writing skills to use in most of my reports. I do for my English term report.

C: Why not?

IVAN: It's not required. You just need to put down the facts.

BARBARA: You pull some facts out of a book and string them all together.

IVAN: You do whatever you want. Just put them down in your own words; you don't even have to worry about how you're constructing. Then the conclusion and whatever. If you turn it in, and it makes some sense, you're guaranteed an A or B. So few of the students do anything, that makes it super easy for us.

RANDY: I don't think any of those other students are really dumb;

they're not really stupid, they're just lazy. Whenever we got a good dialogue going, there was really a hostile feeling inside the room.

BARBARA: There's a tension.

RANDY: They resented our enjoying class or just getting something out of it. They were sitting back hating every minute of it and hating us every minute too.

C: So how do you solve that?

IVAN: We don't pay attention to them and they ignore us. There's about ten students in there who I've never said a word to for six months. They're the ones that came every day and didn't hand in any work.

RANDY: Yeah, my math teacher was talking about this one student who flunked the class. He came up to her and said, "Well, couldn't you at least give me a D, I was there every day?" And she said, "No! You didn't do any work." Most teachers don't do that. In my English class the teacher announced that if you attended you were guaranteed a D.

IVAN: I had a family-life class, which is sort of sex education and drug education rolled into one, where the teacher said that to get a C in the class you had to write two book reports and pass the the midterm and the final. To get a B or an A you had to do an extra book report. I got a B and a C on the book reports, and a couple of A's on the tests. I got a C on a very sloppily done extra-credit assignment, and I was the only person that got an A in all three of his classes. Not one other person even turned in that extra-credit thing. And that class you can't even graduate from high school without passing it.

C: How about drugs? How prevalent is marijuana in this school?

RANDY: Oh, God!

BARBARA AND IVAN: Everybody.

RANDY: Over eighty percent of the kids turn on.

C: How many people here smoke once or twice a week or more, during school hours?

IVAN: At least fifty percent. Probably more.

C: Do you agree?

BARBARA AND RANDY: At least.

RANDY: There's a little place right across the street behind some trees. Kids smoke there all day.

BARBARA: A lot of students are drinking too. I mean during school. You can see the bottles lying around.

RANDY: It's really weird too; you can be walking down the hall, and all of a sudden you smell the devil weed.

BARBARA: A couple of people in the library—nobody cares if they do it.

C: Are the students who smoke a lot of grass more likely to be turned off to school?

BARBARA: Yeah, definitely.

IVAN: If they smoke at school, you know they don't care.

BARBARA: They don't know where they're going; they're insecure.

RANDY: You come on the bus in the mornings on the way to school, all of a sudden you catch a whiff coming in from the back.

C: How much violence is there in this school? Not stories .you've heard, but things that have actually affected you personally?

RANDY: It depends. You can pretty well avoid it, I think.

BARBARA: As long as you don't use the restrooms.

EVERYBODY: Yeah!

C: What do you mean?

IVAN: Well, a friend of mine doesn't bring any money to school anymore. He's kind of skinny, not too athletic-looking. His first two or three months here he got jumped three times in the restroom. Another friend, they jumped him, stole his tape recorder, smashed his glasses into his face—he was cut up pretty bad.

BARBARA: These girls stole my purse when I was in the restroom. There's always boys in there. I never go in there.

RANDY: There's certain areas you just don't go into. Third-floor stairs, lower courtyard. You're just looking for trouble if you do.

C: Is this just student against student or do teachers get involved too?

IVAN: Mostly students. But some black dude beat up two teachers a few weeks ago. This guy stopped me on the back stairs the other day. Asked me if I wanted to buy a gun.

RANDY: Actually, things really aren't that bad this year. I think you can pretty well avoid any trouble.

C: Is that true?

BARBARA AND IVAN: Yeah.

INTERVIEW 3

The two students in the next interview are quite different from those in the previous one. Georgia is a very cute little black girl, with a mischievous grin always present. Joey is pure working-class Italian, a big strong man of a boy, one semester away from his high-school diploma; he hopes never to see the inside of a classroom again. During the time I spent observing their class, Georgia spent most of her time applying lipstick and fiddling with her compact. Joey was called on a number of times to answer questions put by the teacher; he accepted in a rather good-natured manner the fact that his answers were usually wrong. I did not actually choose these two, but when it became clear I wanted to interview a couple of students, Joey simply stood up, walked over to Georgia, and said, "Come on," and then the two of them walked over to the door where they waited for me. Since I got the strong feeling they had never before exchanged so much as a word, my guess in retrospect is that Joey had been waiting all semester for a chance to cross the racial and cultural barriers separating him from Georgia, and I had merely provided a fortuitous opportunity. I started the interview by asking what courses they were taking that semester.

GEORGIA: I'm taking biology, typing, business math, P.E., history, and English.

JOEY: I'm just taking enough credits to graduate. History, English, and weight training—that's P.E. I'm working after school too.

GEORGIA: Yeah, I'm a student teacher for fourth graders. I get ten credits. It's just like taking two classes.

C: How do you feel about your education here?

JOEY: It's been the shits. They've been experimenting, and we just got stuck with it. The teachers, it seems like they don't care.

Like I haven't learned nothing, I don't think, since the ninth or tenth grade.

GEORGIA: Yeah, me too. Teachers, they just don't care.

C: Could you give me specific examples of what you're talking about?

JOEY: Like they assign work and they say it's going to be due at a certain time and you can't turn it in late, but half the class wouldn't turn it in. Then, "I'll give you a couple more days," and then "I'll give you to next week." They just let them slide until they turn in a half-assed paper and then give them a C for it, and it ain't even worth that, really.

GEORGIA: I came to California in eighth grade. I'm from Miami.

C: Compare the schools out here with the schools in Miami.

GEORGIA: Well, you know how it was. Whites are here, blacks are there. I went to all-black schools, and they were strict. I mean they really care about you, you know. Like if we didn't go to class they call your mother, then Mom would get on your butt. I went to class, and I learned a lot too. I like their system there.

C: Why do you feel you learned more?

GEORGIA: Because in the seventh grade down there, if I didn't do my homework, my teacher she'd talk to me and say, "Georgia, why didn't you do your homework?" and also talk to my mother. Like here in the eighth grade if I didn't do my homework, nobody even noticed.

JOEY: They don't care. They just let students just flake off. A student might come to class the first day of the term, and that's it. Every day the teacher marks him absent, and pretty soon he's got about thirty absences. They make no attempt to call the parents or the student. They don't attempt to save the guy.

C: Have you found any teachers out here who are like the teachers in Miami, who you would say are more concerned?

GEORGIA: Nobody.

C: Not even one?

GEORGIA: Not even one. Like here, take Mr. B____. He's a nice guy, but—

JOEY: He just tells you everything, he gives you the answers.

GEORGIA: I mean, you could get up and walk out of his classroom and don't come back, he won't even ask you why. If you don't do the work, he ain't going to say one word to you.

Joey: He says, "I want to prepare you for college; this is the way it's going to be when you go to college; you're going to be all on your own."

C: How many students smoke dope?

JOEY: I'd say forty percent get loaded every day.

GEORGIA: Really, forty percent.

JOEY: Every day.

C: Every day?

GEORGIA & JOEY: Every day.

C: During school hours?

JOEY: During school hours.

C: I've heard that from so many students but I find it so hard to believe. How can they study if they're stoned?

JOEY: Don't ask me; I can't do it. It's got to be either after school or Friday night or something like that.

GEORGIA: One time I went to class I was so high, I was so messed up. The teacher knew, so he just told me to rest my head on the desk; he was so nice. I can't get too loaded at school anymore because I can't concentrate.

C: What percentage of the students don't ever turn on during school?

JOEY: I'd say a good ten to fifteen percent.

GEORGIA: About ten percent.

C: How about the Chinese kids?

Joey: I don't know nothing about them. I don't associate with any of them.

GEORGIA: Me neither.

JOEY: I don't know if I should tell you this, but we've got hired people that dress up just like students, and they're real nice people. I mean, they're not going to bust you for weed or anything; I mean, I've even seen them get loaded here before, but

they are people with weapons. Every three weeks they arrest someone who's carrying a gun.

C: You mean these are undercover cops?

JOEY: Yeah. They try and check out the restrooms, to keep kids
from killing each other.

GEORGIA: Only there's only one woman, so they deal in the girls'
restrooms instead.

C: What if they caught somebody dealing in the restrooms?

JOEY: Well, it depends on who it is. Like if it's a stranger in the
school, they would take him to the principal. But if it was me,
they'd just talk to me, tell me not to get caught again.

GEORGIA: The lady, if she sees us smoking pot or whatever, she just
tells us to put it out, no hassle.

C: Doesn't sound like they do much. Are they necessary, do you
think?

JOEY: I think they're good. They don't do no harm, and I think
maybe it's safer. My friend got shot in the stomach last year.
Right here on campus.

C: Are there a lot of people on this campus who carry guns?

JOEY: Well, like I said, they get one every three weeks. And my
friend who got shot, he says a lot of people do.

C: What's the situation at this school regarding attendance? I've
heard that a lot of students are cutting.

JOEY: Yeah, I agree. That's probably one of the reasons why I
flunked history twice.

C: What percentage cut?

JOEY: It depends, like if there's a three-day weekend coming up,
then seventy-five percent of the class would cut. Like if it was
Friday and Lincoln's Birthday was on Monday.

GEORGIA: And some people would just settle for a five-day weekend
if four isn't enough.

C: What about your reading habits? Do you like to read for pleasure? What kind of books do you read?

GEORGIA: I've been reading a lot—*Sounder, Black Boy,* and a lot of
black books. I'll go in my room and shut my door and turn on

the TV and the music playing too and the book at the same time and just read away.

C: You read and watch TV and listen to the stereo all at the same time?

GEORGIA: No, the TV just be on always; that's a habit. The TV be on and the music just be low and I still read. It's just a habit I got.

C: How much time do you spend reading every day?

GEORGIA: Maybe about thirty minutes a day.

C: How would you improve the school if you were the principal?

JOEY: I wouldn't let the teachers act like they was teaching college. I think everyone here is still in a young stage, and they think that the teachers don't care, so they don't care.

GEORGIA: Yeah, that's right.

JOEY: So I think if the teachers toughen up, I mean every single one of them, maybe it would increase the students' ability a little more.

INTERVIEW 4

The two girls in the next interview presented a stark visual contrast to one another. Cynthia is very white and very plump. Alicia is very black and so thin that her features seem almost chiseled. Cynthia is the better student of the two. She's a B student and will probably be going to college. Alicia will probably learn a marketable skill in a junior college or professional school. Neither girl smiled much during the interview. Mostly the two girls talked about the things holding them back in school. I started the interview by asking them what they thought of their education so far.

CYNTHIA: I was wondering about the books that we have. They're dated like 'sixty-nine and 'sixty-seven. I want to know, do they ever change the books every certain amount of years?

C: Oh, yeah, you just have old books because they haven't bought new ones.

CYNTHIA: You see, I think that the problem is that the kids aren't getting larger words; we're just at elementary reading in history books.

C: Which book do you have?

CYNTHIA: Bragdon and McCutchen, *History of a Free People.* To me it's like elementary reading.

C: That particular book?

CYNTHIA: Yes, others I have seen too. I think they should start changing some of the words. They're really easy words to read. I think we're not given the chance to really expand our vocabulary and get down to learning how to read right.

ALICIA: Like all through my entire education right up to where I'm now, I always have problems reading. When I was young and in elementary school, it was like they just passed you by how old you are. In junior high you just skipping through, barely reading this, barely doing your homework if you want to, but she just passed me through the grades anyway. All right, you're up in high school now. What am I going to do? Oh, I've got to take time to start learning how to read. Mom, what's this word? She tells you the word, you get it, you understand it and remember it just for a little while; after that, it's completely gone. What's you going to do? Some kids, they don't even think of that. When they be coming up elementary, if they didn't really get it then, they just can't see themselves going back over and trying to learn. They're ashamed, really. Like my brother, his main problem is he cannot read.

C: How old is he?

ALICIA: He's seventeen and he cannot read. Elementary, he reads that low. He knows everything that's going on around him, but when it comes down to him getting into a book or reading it, that's where he goes down and he's ashamed of it. He doesn't want to let everybody know that he can't read. When he was coming up, nobody forced him to really get down and learn how to read. He was bad, and now he's got to the age that he sees that he needs to know how to read to know what to do. He feels he's old enough; he should know how, but he's too ashamed to go back to it. This is the average problem of all the black kids now is that their reading is not as well as others.

C: How about you?

ALICIA: Mine, I can read pretty well. I didn't learn how to read very well when I was in elementary school.

C: How do you compare to the other black kids in this school?

ALICIA: Right about average now. My problem is I can read, but if somebody was to ask me what I just read, I wouldn't be able to tell them. My problem is understanding what I read.

C: Are your parents pushing you to do your homework, keep up with your schoolwork?

CYNTHIA: Mine are. I think it's really hard when you get older to be pushed around. You're getting your own ideas then, and you don't want to be picked on. At least when you're younger, if you have parents who push you to read, you buckle down and do it.

C: As far as a general trend, are most parents pushing their kids to do their homework, or are they getting away from that?

ALICIA AND CYNTHIA: They're getting away from that.

ALICIA: Do they make the kids do their homework? No! They say "Go outside and play," or "Get out of the house."

C: So you're saying that the parents aren't forcing the kids to buckle down.

ALICIA: Some kids' mas and pas outside having a good time on the street; you come home, you're inside for a little while; the next minute you're out in the street doing this, doing that, come back in, watch TV. You're taking it day by day, really.

CYNTHIA: The problem is we're getting freer and the school system isn't. That's why I'm glad to have the English classes and math classes in college where they can really start from scratch all over again and teach what you were supposed to learn as you went through school.

C: You resent the fact that they're trying to force you to learn certain things, and yet you're glad that in college they're going to teach you all that stuff over again?

CYNTHIA: Right, you were forced to learn it, and you didn't learn it, because you want to rebel, because you don't like the way the system is being thrown at you.

ALICIA: It's like when you're in college you don't have to, but when you're not forced, you feel more better with it. You're trying to accomplish something. You try to do your best in college or anything you're not forced to.

C: Even if it's the same stuff?

ALICIA: Even if it's the same stuff: When you're forced to do it, you don't care if you learn anything or not.

C: Why not learn the basic skills in high school in the first place? Then you don't have to worry about them in college. You can study something else.

CYNTHIA: Because I don't feel like doing some of the stupid things we have to do now, but I'm still glad later in college I can learn them.

C: Did you resist your parents when you were younger if they said you don't get to go out until you've done your homework?

CYNTHIA: Not when you're younger; it's just when you get older.

ALICIA: Kids are growing up faster than they should be. They think they know everything.

C: Why do they think they know everything?

ALICIA: Like in some families, home is not too good. When the mother and father separate and the mother is out working all the time and she comes home and she's tired and she don't really care—"Kids, get off my back. I'm tired right now; I want to get some rest." They're out in the street learning the wrong things, and they think they know it all. By the time they get in high school, can't nobody tell them anything, because their mind is so far gone on what's happening out there instead of what's happening in here.

CYNTHIA: Like now, I mean I'm fighting myself, but I hate school, fighting that I have to go to school to get where I want to go.

C: Why do you hate school?

CYNTHIA: I just don't like having to start from the bottom to get to where I want to go. Like if I want to become a teacher, I'd have to start from the bottom and climb up all these stairs to get up where I want to be. That sort of scares you a little, because if you've already gone through twelve years of school, then you're faced with another six years of schooling. You keep thinking about getting around all that schooling. You want to take the shortcut.

INTERVIEW 5

Any of the youngsters in the next interview could live next door. Andrew is black, middle class, success-motivated, above average in ability. Dan is a slightly sour, somewhat unattractive chubby kid. He is also extremely bright, which would take him further if he didn't also happen to be extremely lazy. Maria is a strong-minded girl with conventional attitudes, who is somewhat above average in ability. They attend a suburban high school which serves an integrated, upper-middle-class professional community. I started off the interview by asking how hard they had to work in school.

ANDREW: I have only two classes I have to work in. In biology we had to have all our work in at a certain time or we'd get an F for the work even if we had part of it in. So we'd do it on time. Like in English, you know he'll accept late papers so why do them on time?

MARIA: That's the way it is in my English class, he doesn't push us to do the homework. I mean, he just got out of college like maybe four years ago or something, so he's pretty much with it, you know. He feels if you don't do the homework, you're hurting yourself, not him, so he doesn't care. It was the same last year. The only things that I had that were hard were English and geometry.

ANDREW: We have a choice to pick our classes and our teachers. Some students pick the easy classes. But if you want to learn, you can pick the hard classes.

C: How do you know who's easy and who's hard?

ANDREW: It's all around. Talk to students; your counselor will tell you.

C: What do you think about this system where you can choose easy teachers if you want to?

DAN: It's a good system, because if you really want to learn, if you're going to go on to college, well, you can pick the best teachers. And kids who don't want to go on to college, you know, just want to start working right after high school, they pick easy teachers, get it over with.

C: Do you think students should have the right not to have to learn if they don't want to?

DAN: Yeah, it's part of their rights.

MARIA: But it's for their own good; they should learn it.

ANDREW: It's not just for their own good—it's for society's good.

MARIA: I've seen some girls who have P.E., and then sewing, and then food, then typing. What are they learning from that? Nothing. Another thing this school gots that really puts you down is the schedule. I have some friends that get out at around ten-thirty and then they don't have a class until two-thirty. Some days your first class might be at eleven.

ANDREW: It makes it easy for a student, you know, who even though he doesn't want to cut, he'll go do something, then he doesn't want to come back to school later on.

MARIA: I think the reason students are getting turned off so much is, before it wasn't just the teacher-student relationship. The schools really involved the home, and the home set up a disciplinary type of situation. Now if you cut a class, your parents will never even find out about it. The administration, I think that's the whole problem in this school.

ANDREW: That's not true, some of them do care.

MARIA: There are so few of them that care it isn't funny. They should only allow a couple classes to be elective classes. They should make the students take the main courses. There's such a lack of discipline. Students don't have responsibility. I don't think they're mature enough to handle all the freedom the schools give them.

DAN: Well, it's true, but the individual is the one who does it to himself or herself. It's really their choice to hurt themselves or help themselves.

C: At what age does it become their choice?

DAN: Fourteen.

MARIA: Parents are a lot looser, you know. Times have changed. The parents can still not want them to do something, but they'll go right ahead and do it anyway. Usually the parents try not to find out.

ANDREW: More and more's been learned about like smoking dope, you know. Parents are learning more and more about things that are going on, so when they learn what their kids have done, they aren't as hard about it.

MARIA: I'll give an example with my friend. She cut one time in junior high and she caught hell. Now the thing in her family is, if you cut, let me know and we'll talk about it.

ANDREW: College isn't as important anymore, really. You can get a job without going to college and get decent pay. People say, "I don't want to go and spend four years in college, because when I get out it's going to be so hard to find a job. I might as well just start looking now, you know, maybe I'll get one right away."

DAN: Yeah, but I'm still going to go to college.

C: How much reading do you do for pleasure?

ANDREW: Well, if I've got a good book, I'll read it.

DAN: About half an hour a night.

MARIA: When I have time. I'm pretty busy.

C: Is reading something that you do for pleasure?

MARIA: When I have time.

C: There's always time if you want time.

ANDREW: Oh, I've always hated to read. Ever since I was younger I couldn't stand it. I don't know why and I still really don't like to read.

DAN: I like to read, but I can't read fast and it gets boring.

MARIA: Kind of mad at us that we don't read, huh?

C: Yeah, I am.

INTERVIEW 6

This last interview stands in sharp contrast to the previous five. Caroline attends a private girls' school with a very strong academic reputation. She is a tall, thin girl, a rosebud anxious to bloom. She is in the eighth grade.

C: How much reading do you do outside of schoolwork?

CAROLINE: Well, I read at least two hours a day and I read most of the time.

C: How many books do you think you read?

CAROLINE: I don't know; last time I counted I read thirty in one month.

C: That's quite a lot of reading.

CAROLINE: Yeah, we usually try and go to the library every two weeks and get about ten books. My sister and I. If I get out books that I really like a lot, then when I get home, I'll start reading right away. I can read about two books in a day or something. I'll finish them in about a week.

C: How many hours per night do you read for schoolwork?

CAROLINE: Well, not too much, because generally I read for about forty-five minutes for history. I just read the whole chapter at once. That's for a whole week; I do it in one night. And in English she assigns us generally short books with ten pages a night, and it takes me about fifteen minutes or less depending on the book.

C: Are you interested in the kind of reading that you're doing for school?

CAROLINE: No, because it's always about adolescents who find themselves, and it's really boring.

C: How do you feel about school in general?

CAROLINE: It's pretty good; some of the teachers are a little bit wacky. Some of it's a little bit boring.

C: What do you find boring about school?

CAROLINE: Well, sometimes they keep on going over the same thing, over and over for the benefit of the slow students, and everybody else sits there yawning.

C: How many solids are you taking in school?

CAROLINE: Five—English, math, Spanish, science, and history.

S: Are there any classes you especially like or dislike?

CAROLINE: In social studies our teacher never teaches us anything. He just assigns busy work. I don't think he's supposed to be a social-studies teacher; he's supposed to be an art teacher. He just assigns us these units and he's never taught us anything. Today we saw this movie on Daniel Webster. He was a Senator from Massachusetts that Henry Clay wanted to support the Compromise of 1850. Our teacher said that he also wrote the dictionary, but that's about one hundred years before and Noah Webster wrote the dictionary. You'd think he'd read the book. He's a little weird.

C. How many hours a week do you spend on homework other than reading, like math and science?

CAROLINE: Well, at home I usually spend about forty-five minutes a day—it isn't too much. It depends on what day it is. On Mondays I never have any homework, because I have three study halls on Mondays.

C: Three study halls?

CAROLINE: Yeah, they're having a little problem with the schedule.

C: What are your educational goals?

CAROLINE: Well, I want to be a writer.

C: Have you started? Have you written anything?

CAROLINE: Yeah, I want to get this story published in a magazine and my mother typed it up for me, but I haven't found any magazine that publishes things like that.

C: What do you think is the purpose of education?

CAROLIINE: Well, do you mean for me? Because then I could explain it better. I want to go to college and get a job. Even if you don't go to college, so that you can just get along in the world, read the signs, talk with people and you don't have to sit there and talk about dumb things. For writing, if you read a lot, that gives you more ideas about stories and what they're like. I think you have to have an education so that you can write, punctuate, and all that kind of stuff.

I found certain common elements in these interviews to be highly disturbing. The thing that shook me up the most was the amount of drug-taking and drinking during school hours. I was aware that a large percentage of young people smoke marijuana and drink, but I was completely unprepared to find that so many smoke or drink during the school day. I estimate that 40 percent of the students in the metropolitan high schools I visited get stoned regularly during school hours, and over half of these almost every day. In suburban schools the figure is probably 20 percent. How do you teach somebody who is so loaded he falls asleep on you?

I was also quite shocked by the extent of the cutting. Most of the classes I observed in city high schools had between ten and fifteen students present. I would estimate the absenteeism rate in the schools with flexible scheduling to be over 40 percent, and in the other city schools to be between 20 and 30 percent.

The extent of the violence did not surprise me. Almost every student I talked to had had some personal exposure to violence in the schools. City schools simply are not terribly safe places. However, the general feeling seems to be that if you are reasonably careful, you can avoid trouble. Most students do not seem to be walking around in fear, although they do take reasonable precautions, such as avoiding the restrooms and other known trouble spots whenever possible.

I was surprised by the intensity of the bitterness of the motivated and academically talented students. They feel terribly cheated by their teachers and schools. Bright students need and deserve to be in classes with other bright students, and to be taught by teachers whose demands challenge them to work to their potential. Current policies are killing the academic motivation and damaging the spirits of our brightest youngsters and in many cases simply driving them out of the public schools.

Finally, I was pleased by the response of the students to their teachers. When I was in school, no matter how far we might push a teacher, we all secretly wanted him to maintain his standards and authority. The wholesale abrogation of authority and standards in today's schools had created some doubt in my mind. Maybe young people had changed. Perhaps there was something more pathological happening than just the normal adolescent testing of limits. But no, the students with whom I talked sounded just as I would have sounded in high school. They have contempt for the teachers who have dropped their standards and work demands, and respect for the ones who have not.

2

TEACHERS

The eight interviews in this section reflect the content of the more than one hundred interviews I conducted with teachers, administrators, and reading and evaluation experts. The teachers I interviewed are among the best social studies, English, and math teachers in California. I was introduced to them through my contacts in the educational community, who knew I was looking for experienced, talented, and perceptive teachers from whom I hoped to extract an overview of the past fifteen years of American educational history. The reading and evaluation experts are noted authorities in their fields, whom I have known professionally for a number of years.

INTERVIEW 7

The first conversation is with a man who has been mainly teaching history but also some English and remedial reading for seventeen years in San Francisco high schools. He teaches in a racially and socioeconomically mixed high school, which sends 30 to 50 percent of its students on to some kind of college. I had been informed that he was an exceptionally knowledgeable, competent, and dedicated teacher, a judgment I confirmed in several talks with him, and also on the several occasions in which I had the opportunity to observe his classes. In appearance he is a handsome, vital, and athletic-looking man of about forty-five, with graying hair and an irrepressible twinkle in his eye. My first question was whether teachers were assigning less reading today than ten or fifteen years ago.

TEACHER: In my classes I assign almost no reading homework.
C: Did you ten or fifteen years ago?
TEACHER: Sure. I would say read Chapter Four and be ready for a quiz, or do the questions at the end of the chapter, or come in

ready for discussion. Generally speaking, the majority of students did. Today, I can no longer say this to a class because it would be a bomb.

C: What do you mean, a bomb?

T: A bomb, by that I mean that some would cut if I told them to read a chapter and then expected them to come in. Others would not be able to read the chapter, or would have an excuse. A few would read the chapter, those who are motivated, and they would carry the discussion.

C: You're assigning less material because of your feeling that they won't do it?

T: It's not a feeling, it's an experience. I've tried. My demands are less rigorous than they were. No more term papers, more discussion, more oral work, more committee work, more group work, more rapping, less reading, quite a bit less writing.

C: But why?

T: Because any assignment that depends on reading or a library visit or getting reference books is a failure out of hand for fifty to seventy-five percent of the people in that classroom. It requires an extra effort that they will not do. Not that they can't, but they won't try. I can report to you from my own standpoint that this is why I have changed my standards.

You should listen in when teachers BS together. They can't assign chapters anymore and they have to give questions to look up. This seems to be the main assignment in school today. You give kids questions and keep them busy by having them look up answers to the questions or filling in blanks.

C: I still don't see why you have to drop the volume of reading you assign. Why don't you just say, "I'm going to assign some reading, and if you don't do the reading, you're going to flunk?"

T: You couldn't get away with that politically. The community would come down on the principal, the principal would come down on you. Students won't read, and it's almost like you have to seduce them to get any work out of them. There are times I want to get up at large faculty meetings of one hundred and thirty people and give a dramatic statement, just get up on a table and say, "We should flunk the hell out of these damn kids until they know that they've got to put in some work." But you can't do that. You wouldn't last a semester.

We should quit telling students lies. Only the biology department here demands competence before giving a passing grade. There has been a lot of pressure on that department to quit giving so many F's. The principal made a thing out of this, but the science department won't budge, and sixty percent of the students are failing biology because they aren't doing the work. In my heart of hearts I'm pleased with this. I only wish that I had the guts to do it myself.

C: Are you working with the same type of student you did fifteen years ago?

T: Yeah, I've always worked with very mixed groups. You know, Paul, there's been an awful lot of crap shoveled onto teachers. What is remarkable in this school, which is the only world that I know, is how many teachers, tired-looking in their fifties, have been through the mill and never taught at a "good" school. They're working so hard with so much heart, with so much sincerity and devotion to the cause, and they're tired and they're still trying. I can take you up and down the hall and show you those people working hard. Henry Enrico comes to me with tears in his eyes. "What's the matter?" "They're not listening." And he's beautiful, he goes to Guatemala and visits the Maya ruins, he brings slides, he brings stories, he makes drawings, and the students are falling asleep on him because they were up for the late, late movie. They're bored. They want to get out in the yard where the action is, or back to the tube. How can he hope to compete with the excitement, the quick punch line, the easy comprehension of a few words, the street talk that the kids encounter in the media? He can't—none of us can.

C: How about the younger teachers?

T: The younger teachers are a peculiar breed. Some of them want students to write a lot of journals and bring in any old book. There's never an opportunity for a discussion on one book that everyone reads in common, and I think that's vital. I find some young teachers are really crappy. The assumption is that the young teacher comes in fresh, burning, ready to go, full of dreams and hopes. But some of them are terrible. They're too loose. Some of them want to dig the kids and be like the kids, and they can't be. I know I sound old-fashioned, but there has to be a structure in the classroom. The teacher can be relaxed but never too relaxed. Some young teachers are beautiful. Some of them are lousy. What is remarkable to me, as I age and bald and gray and wrinkle up here almost audibly, is how many of the older teachers are still working so damn hard. What keeps them together? I had a heart attack a year and a half ago in the room across the hall. What made me, a very lively, hyperactive guy, have a heart attack? Everyone agrees that my motor is running. You have a lot of adults who are under a lot of strain. They're trying, they're pressing, like I press. I press in class to get this across, try not to cut down some kid, "Come on, get into it. What's the matter, smile, be happy." You know, I used to know men who retired after forty years as teachers. They were still vigorous, enthusiastic, proud, strong personalities. Now you see them after seven, fifteen, twenty years. Tired, cynical, listless. It's a crime. The damned kids make mincemeat out of them.

C: You teach reading. Why won't these kids read?

T: One thing is the type of reading programs we're giving kids in junior and senior high school. All these handy-dandy new programs, built-in cassettes, viewers, and earphones, and learning carrels. I've become highly critical and wary of the reading-gimmick salesman. Anytime there's an electric piece of equipment involved, I'm very touchy. I'm already on the defensive, and I've a lot of consumer resistance. I've served on a variety of committees in the junior and high-school division looking at materials and listening very carefully to salesmen. I usually come away very disenchanted with the things they want to sell. If it has to be plugged into the wall, I find myself with a closed mind.

I feel the same way about writing. A lot of the writing that students are doing in schools is not writing at all—it's a lot of baloney. It's filling in blanks. We've given kids an awful lot of workbooks in the last fifteen years, because there's been a shower of federal money for self-contained programs. A lot of these materials do not involve writing at all. They involve putting a word in a blank.

Another reason for the reading problems is that the school libraries haven't done the job. I've had terrible fights with librarians on this score.

C: I was in your library today and the lights were all turned off.

T: Yeah, well you picked that up right away. That's true in a lot of schools. They're trying to save electricity. I think that librarians should go into classrooms and roll the books right in. To peddle books. Convince the kids such and such a book is fantastic.

C: You mean give them a sales pitch?

T: Absolutely! They won't do it because too many of the prim little women don't want to really circulate those beautiful books they keep buying. They don't want kids' grubby hands on them. Twenty years ago the libraries were filled with kids taking books home. They took piles of books home.

C: What do you think about the fragmentation in the history curriculum? Current events, or contemporary revolutions instead of world history.

T: How do you feel about those courses?

C: How do I feel? I feel like it's really tragic, because I think history is much more exciting than—

T: You're a real conservative. Terrible. You're an educational reactionary. It's good you're not in the department here—they'd wipe you out. But I agree with you. I'm appalled that students can pass through this school and not have a confrontation with the old-fashioned civics. Kids can get through this school without studying the Bill of Rights or the U.S. Constitution. They know nothing about the City of San Francisco and how municipal government operates. Nor do they have the slightest idea what state government is.

First week of ·school, I test them. What are your First Amendment rights? They don't know. How is the Constitution organized? All government in America organized? It's so simple—

three branches. They don't know. What caused and who won the Civil War? They don't know! I'm scared to death. I'm busy trying to teach the Constitution. There it is hanging from the wall. There's the Declaration. They don't know a goddam thing about it and it terrifies me.

INTERVIEW 8

In my work with the Institute of Reading Development, I set up reading programs at a number of California colleges. The man in the next interview was the dean of instruction at a California community college when I first met him. He is a big man, an impressive man, impressive in the depth of his humanity, in the extent of his commitment to his work, to his college, to his community. It was with great shock that I discovered he had been fired as dean and was back teaching, after an ugly, scarring battle between two different factions of his faculty and the board of trustees. The main charge against him was that he was making unreasonable and unprofessional demands on the faculty, and therefore causing a deterioration in the morale of the college. He was further accused of supporting the president of the college, whose contract was bought up at the same time that he was fired, for basically the same reasons. I asked him about the charges.

C: What exactly were you demanding?

DEAN: In each course I wanted them to indicate the texts and the reading schedule, what the basic objectives of the course were to be, what the demands on the students were to be, and how they were going to grade the students.

C: You also demanded to see their tests for each course, didn't you?

D: Yes. When I first came I found that the tests primarily were of an objective nature, true-false, multiple choice. What is multiple choice doing as the main type of question in a literature course, or history? I insisted that every test contain subjective questions, to be answered with essays.

C: What other demands did you place on them that got you in trouble?

D: They were to rewrite or to reorganize and update their course outlines at least once every two years. I insisted that in any general-education course every student would do some real writing and research. The student would have to do a term paper, a book review, something in the nature of a major writing assignment. When I came here, in a lot of courses there was no writing at all.

I also tried to get them to hold to some kind of standards in grading. If a student flunked he was supposed to get a N.P., nonpass. It didn't count against his grade-point average, but three N.P.'s and he was on probation. We had faculty who would not give students N.P.'s. They wanted to remain friends with the students. They just didn't have the guts to say, "Hey, pal, you didn't make it." I looked at the grade-change slips of students who were conning faculty into changing their grade. Fifteen hundred grade changes in one quarter in a student body that only has about twelve hundred and fifty day students. When I saw that, I almost passed out. So with these kinds of policies, and faculty taking it upon themselves to be nice guys instead of teaching to standards, yes, my standards and policies weren't too popular.

C: Do you think it's necessary for a dean of instruction to supervise that carefully?

D: Absolutely not. If you have a professional set of division chairmen or department chairmen, they should be doing this. If two or three people are teaching in the same course area, they collectively should be reviewing material and updating it and strengthening it in a professional context. I found myself in a situation where the president before me hired a faculty as cheap as he could find. When I first came here, our students were transferring with a minus-.85 transfer ratio to State. That meant that a student who went out of here with a 2.0 grade-point average got a 1.15 grade-point average the next year at a state university. So, yes, I did many things that I think should not be necessary by a dean of instruction.

A great many of the people that came into teaching in the late Sixties and early Seventies had very poor training. I had many who would say, "Well, you make too many demands on the student. You want them to write two hours outside class, or study two hours outside class for every hour in class, and I never worked that hard when I was a student." The academic unit equates with two hours outside of class for every hour in the class. But most of the people coming through in the nineteen-sixties didn't understand that. So you had these negative factors going, and I was hired to bring the faculty up to the level of college teaching. So, yes, I came down pretty damn hard. It took till 'seventy-three to come up to where our students were at a plus transfer ratio, which they are, but there was a mean dean sitting here making demands that in many institutions aren't necessary. In the older institutions, a professional faculty set and maintained the standards and the new faculty had to come up to them.

C: I gather that another factor in your firing was the fact that you terminated a few people?

D: Oh, yes. I had faculty come to me and tell me this teacher is doing a very poor job. He's not assigning any legitimate work; he accepts papers written at a junior-high-school level with grades of A and B. He's not doing any actual content teaching, just rapping with his students. So I said, "Well, you know, with your help we can get rid of this person, because he is not holding to standards you think belong in your division." And they said, "Oh, my, no, you can't count on us for anything. The last time we took sides and got rid of a bad teacher, we were picked on by the rest of the faculty." Here I am, every member of the division coming in and telling me about this teacher, and yet not one person was willing to stand up and be counted.

C: So what happened?

D: I asked the members of the division to talk with this teacher. They said they didn't feel they could do that. So on several occasions I sat down and discussed step by step the responsibility for trying to help the students learn. The very next day I'd get feed-back that he had gone all over to the faculty and said I was abus-ing him again and making foolish demands.

After about a year of this, with the situation getting worse, and with students complaining, I fired the guy. You wouldn't believe the commotion that caused. We had student protests, and marches, and the faculty union filed court action. They had a petition claiming I was infringing on academic freedom, and some of the same faculty members signed it who had privately asked me to get rid of this guy. The state hearing officer backed me up on the firing, so all the protests eventually petered out.

C: Did you know in advance they were going to can you?

D: I heard warnings. I've got a lot of sympathetic buddies out there who said, "I hear you're going to get fired. Why the hell don't you ride along with the faculty?" "Well," I said, "I've got a president who wants standards established here. I'm not going to undermine him; he wants an institution with standards and that's the only thing I know." I don't need to sit here from an authoritarian position and do all this crap. I think it's stupid, I want the faculty to set the standards. But Christ, I had faculty say to me, "Why don't you come over on our side. If you help us get rid of the president, we'll back you with the board to make you president." I said, "I'll act like I never heard you. If you have something you don't like about the present institution, go to the board with it. Don't come here and try to get me to stab the president in the back."

There is a carryover of respect for the college professor from past times. Even my wife has this high degree of respect for their standards, their professionalism. In some cases that's still true, but it isn't universal, I'll guarantee you that.

Hell, there are certain institutions I absolutely won't even interview people from when a job opens up here. On the other hand, at certain schools I am well aware that the faculty have professional pride in what they are doing. At Berkeley, at UCLA, the faculty will clean house themselves. It's their own pride in their chosen lifework.

C: You claim some of your faculty aren't demanding enough. Do you know anything about high-school faculties?

D: Of course. When we had articulation with the area's high-school science faculty meeting with our science faculty here, we said, "Hey, your students are flunking chemistry and some of them got A's and B's in your courses." The answer was "Hell, if we didn't give them A's and B's they wouldn't stay in our courses and we'd be out of work." That was the ethic of the high-school science teacher.

    If a student really wants to go on to college, he should know what the hell the standards are. When they get here, they wouldn't have false expectations: I've been passed for twelve years, and, therefore, I'm eligible for college. Then we're under tremendous pressure to push them through, as are the state colleges. If we don't push them through, we're the failure.

C: Make a comparison between the amount of work demanded of the students in this institution, or in college, in terms of reading and writing, today versus 1960.

D. I'd say the demands are only about forty percent as great as they were at that time. You find a tremendous number of college students working full time now, going to college full time, and they're getting A's and B's. So what could the demands be? I see a tremendous number of college people. "How do you earn a living? Are you working part time?" "Oh, I work full time on the outside." "How many units do you have?" "I'm taking sixteen units." "I'm taking eighteen units." By the standards of colleges I knew in the Forties and Fifties if you came in and said you were taking a fifteen-hour load, that meant you were doing about thirty hours of studying on the outside.

C: Is that just at junior colleges?

D: No, four-year state colleges. I know a lot of students at State who have full-time jobs. Students are far less prepared today than they were ten years ago, fifteen years ago. I was last in the classroom eleven years ago, and I felt at that time a far higher percentage expected college to be rugged. They came in psychologically ready, knowing that they were going to have to work.

Now I'm finding that students are actually hostile that I assign research reading in addition to the textbook. When I flunk them for a junior-high-school level paper, they come and complain that I'm being unreasonable. In high school all they got was A's and B's—for nothing. The A or the B says you are doing adequate work, but they aren't.

C: What's the biggest problem confronting education today?

D: It's that the underlying goal of education itself is getting lost in the shuffle. What's happening to children's minds, to their intellectual development, hell, that's not even a minor issue. The principal is running around putting out a fire in the trash basket, handling discipline problems, dealing with the police. He's a damn errand boy. He's lost his function as an educational leader, someone to inspire and lead his faculty in the process of education. Many school districts I know of don't even have a superintendent of instruction, or they don't have any real importance or influence.

Administrators are so damn scared of this pressure group or that pressure group. It's almost funny. I have a friend, a black woman in L.A. I've known her for thirty years. Well, she was in charge of a training program to train teachers from Watts. She worked with students and helped get them through an L.A. junior college and then through State. She found out that the English faculty was lowering the standards for these students. She damn near tore the State College apart. "What the hell do you think you're doing?" "Well, I thought you wanted to get these students through?" "I don't want them to get through illiterate, I want them to get through and be highly literate so they can help people. Don't pass them, I want them taught." "Well, it may take them longer than a semester." "I don't give a damn if it takes three semesters to get them through English; it's going to be their toughest subject but you're going to get them through and you're going to teach them, you're not going to pass one of them below the standards of the university."

INTERVIEW 9

This next man teaches history in a pretty tough city school. He's an ebullient Italian, who's been teaching for fifteen years. I observed several of his classes. The man was teaching his heart out to students who were not even paying attention. After fifteen years, how does a man keep pouring it out to an unresponsive, resentful, unappreciative audience? I started off the questions by asking about any attitude shift he had noticed in his students. To put it mildly, I was rather startled by his answer.

C: Do you notice a difference between the attitude of your students in the early nineteen-sixties versus today?

TEACHER: The main difference in attitude that I've noticed is in myself. I remember when I was taking education courses, the emphasis was on the whole child. I went for that tooth and nail. I was the type of teacher who would try to be relevant. As time went on I noticed that this approach was not giving me the results that I was told to anticipate. So I've changed. As much as anything, I would guess it is teachers with attitudes like mine that actually caused students to produce less, learn less, and therefore not develop their skills.

C: So now you're saying that you are putting more demands on your students.

T: And as a result, I'm seeing an increase in what the students are able to produce. I also feel their resistance increasing, but that doesn't bother me that much anymore.

C: How would you compare the level of skill of students today versus the early nineteen-sixties?

T: As I said, you can't compare. It's like comparing high-school students with junior-high students. The disparity is pretty enormous. I really think it has to do with the level of teacher demands. Look at the racial thing. We've been bombarded for the last fifteen years with some kind of a notion of what racism is. I know I've been very conscious of this. I've been bending over backward not to be identified as a racist who's going to come down hard on black kids. There's a lot of teachers who do the same thing. This translates into lower demands, if you teach in integrated classes, for everybody.

There is this other thing that's going on in my mind too. When I got my teaching credential, one of the dogmas was and still is that you have to be a real human being. You have to share yourself, you have to love the children, you have to touch them. I went along with it to the point where I realized that what I was doing was loving the students and wanting to be loved, but I wasn't teaching that much. I see a lot of other teachers doing the same damn thing. If the students come up with a politically radical point of view, the teacher is somehow shirking his duty if he does not accept and project an equally radical point of view.

Another difference is that parents used to be highly interested in what their kids were doing. They knew what the homework was going to be. They knew what the student's assignment was going to be, and if it didn't meet their approval, they would let the school and the teacher know. There was a great competition for success among the students. Now it's a no-no to be seen taking books home. Then it was a no-no not to take books home. The students used to be angry if I had a class and I did not issue books immediately. They were angry because they did not have books to carry. Here you don't see students carrying books. I think what's happening is the school is so loose that the students who are going to be discipline problems just don't show up.

C: How do your students respond when you assign a fairly tough assignment?

T: I think there's almost a sense of pride: "Hey, this guy is really sticking it to us." Yesterday in world history there was a great deal of moaning, but there was a tone to the moaning that said, "Oh, boy, goody, goody, goody."

C: When did the change occur in your own attitude about increased work demands? Is that fairly recent?

T: Yeah, I can tell you exactly. It was five years ago when my younger son went into elementary school. I went to teacher's night and talked to the elementary-school teacher. The elementary-school teacher was not teaching my son diddle ding dong and she was saying all the things that I was saying. I just said, "Hey, wait a minute, that's me talking and look what's happening." As a parent, I'm not satisfied with what's going on. The kid's loving it, the teacher is being very modern, very current, very loving, very all the best things, but she's not teaching him. And I look at myself and that's what I'm doing.

INTERVIEW 10

The next teacher has been teaching business math and bookkeeping for seventeen years at the same school. He teaches in a suburban high school which serves an integrated, upper-middle-class professional community. His students are what used to be called commercial students, definitely not college prep. Physically he is a balding, chubby little man, but a dynamo. My impression was that he is extremely conscientious, but a little too nice for his own good. His colleagues feel that he is rather unsocial, because he spends his lunch hour in his class tutoring students. I was very interested in his analysis of where his students had experienced the greatest drop-off in skill.

C: How would you characterize the difference between kids today and in the early Sixties as far as their reading, writing, and math skills?

TEACHER: They're less willing to read and I think they're having a good deal more difficulty understanding what they do read.

C: You've been teaching the same subjects for fifteen years?

T: Seventeen years—business math, business investments, bookkeeping. Let's take, for example, a business-math class. The first few years that I taught I got practically through the whole book, which is about ninety sections, and gave tests and everything. In 1974–1975, I got through about thirty sections. I found that I had to explain things, whereas before I could say something once and people would understand it. For example, if I start talking about finding commissions, which is a percent of amount sold, then I say, "Okay, you take sixteen percent of this figure and you get your answer." They'd look at me and say, "What's percentage?" So I'd have to stop and show them how to change percent into a decimal, which they can then use to multiply. Because their backgrounds aren't as good, I'm forced to go into things that I don't particularly care to so they can do the work.

And I had even bigger classes then. Now we consider thirty students to be a big class. At that time I usually had over forty and we accomplished more because we worked together and the students were better prepared to receive what I was giving them.

C: What's lacking in the students' background? Is it because they can't do the basic operations—they don't know fractions, decimals, percents, multiplication?

T: Reading skills are the weakest.

C: Even more than math?

T: Yeah, oh, sure, more than math definitely. Except for what I consider to be many careless mistakes, their math is not too bad, they can add, subtract, multiply. I would say it's reading more than mathematical ineptitude that causes their problems. The biggest thing is they can't interpret a word problem and set up the computations, which I consider a reading problem, not math. A lot of them never had to do it until they took my class. When they're out in life and they're presented with a set of figures, nobody's going to tell them how to get the answer. They have a problem which involves math and they can be perfectly capable of doing the math, but if they can't size up the situation and know that they have to multiply 2 times 6 and then take away 3, what good does it do knowing how to do the arithmetic?

C: Could you give me a specific example of what you mean?

T: Well, okay, you go out and you buy something on credit. The cash price of the thing is $120; however, "Just because it's you, $40 down and $12 a month for a year, okay?" Very often the people who don't know better say, "Hey, I've got $40, I can make the down payment, and, hey, $12 a month, that's not bad; let's buy it." They don't think, well, the thing costs $120, if I put $40 down, I'm borrowing $80. If I pay $12 a month for a year I'm paying $144 back on $80. That's $64 interest; that's a lot of interest on a one-year loan of only $80.

Now the student can probably do all the arithmetical operations. He can subtract 40 from 120. He can multiply 12 times 12. He can subtract 80 from 144. But nobody's going to be there in real life telling him what to do. He's got to be able to set up the problem himself. School should give him practice with this type of thing.

C: Is there anything else inhibiting your ability to teach the subject matter?

T: Kids today, I think, aren't used to doing things, building things. They watch TV where somebody makes the picture for them instead of reading and making their own picture in their mind. They're very passive.

C: Is that the major difference in attitude, this passivity?

T: Learning what you don't know is work, and you have to be psychologically ready to walk in and say, "Okay, what are we going to do now? I'm willing to try." I've heard teachers say, "You can't give that class homework; they'll never do it." My classes are less willing to work, less willing to accept assignments without question, and do them. They just don't try as hard. They don't pay as close attention and take things as systematically as they can. People either assume (a) a kid's got the skills, or (b) he doesn't have the skills. One or the other. The truth is that a lot of students have skills but won't, or don't, use them. I think we're running into that a lot more now than we did fifteen years ago.

They look at a problem and in their mind they know, "God, that's going to take a lot of work and a lot of thinking; heck with it." A basic attitude that work isn't that important. I think in the society we're living in today the young people want instant results. They're not as willing to go through a set of steps to get somewhere.

INTERVIEW 11

The next conversation was recorded at an integrated city high school which sends about a third of its students to college. Two teachers participated in this talk with me. The first teacher, Don, is a history teacher with eighteen years of teaching experience. He is in his early forties, and has the reputation of being the scholar of the school. He is a big, thoughtful man, with an almost tangible sense of emotional and intellectual depth. The second teacher, Chris, is an attractive, vibrant woman in her early thirties, the chairperson of the social-studies department. The two teachers had an obvious camaraderie, and an evident concern for each other and their students. Again I started the interview around the issue of lighter teacher demands on students.

C: You said very definitely that students are reading less. Is that because you assign less?

Don: Do I assign less reading? Yes.

C: Yes, why?

Don: Because I've found it was pretty futile to ask students to do something that they wouldn't do.

C: Is it wouldn't, or couldn't?

Don: A few can't, most won't. It represents a different attitude on the part of the students. Their priorities, the importance of school, these things have changed.

C: So you're saying that you've accommodated to the change in their attitude.

Don: You have to. Fifteen years ago I used to assign one book report a quarter in an average class. About six years ago I realized that out of every four students I'd get one book report. And I'd gradually come to expect it, that was the part that shocked me.

Chris: There's something else too. Kids that were college-bound ten years ago were doing some reading. They didn't find it horrendous to read a book. Today, college-bound students are a little incensed that this is expected. I'm not talking about average students; the initial reaction of our sharper students to a reading assignment is to be incensed. Even my seminar kids.

C: Why?

Chris: I think partly it's because they've complained and teachers have responded, "Oh, well, I guess you don't have to." And those kids can read. The initial reaction of my seminar kids, I teach two seminars of gifted kids that are supposed to be really highly motivated, their automatic response is to complain. Juniors in history are saying things like, "This isn't going to get me a job." It's become a rhetorical thing they just kind of throw out. There's no sense that any of it really matters. There is very little long-range planning in our kids. They're very shortsighted, they go for immediate gratification only.

DON: Kids don't know how to sustain interest long enough to read anything as long as a short story, let alone a novel. You have to sit down a couple of days in a row to get from the beginnnig to the end of a novel. You can just turn on a TV program, *whip whop,* and it's done. All finished, let's go play hockey.

CHRIS: Our students are the first kids to be second-generation TV addicts. If you think about it, the parents were the transition culture, they watched a lot of TV, but they also had the older literacy culture values that reading was good, important. But their kids were exposed only to role models who were television addicts. When you combine that with our national syndrome of complete hypocrisy from our politicians, no wonder these kids are turned off to what they consider establishment values.

C: Is this restricted to one group of students? Are you referring primarily to black or Mexican-American kids? How about the white students?

DON AND CHRIS: Same.

DON: Perhaps even worse in proportion to the numbers. From my view I think blacks are more into studying and reading than my white students.

CHRIS: Definitely, particularly with the ten gifted students in my seminars.

DON: So are low-income whites more motivated.

CHRIS: But your middle-class white base, what this school was when I was a student here twenty years ago, your solid middle-class family that was going to send their kid to college, maybe fifty percent of us went to some sort of college; it's the kids from those families who are so turned off.

DON: We've just done a study that throws some light on these attitudes. A lot of students aren't interested in A, B, C, D, at all, they're interested in credits. A D is just as good as an A.

CHRIS: Because it means five credits.

DON: Why work hard for an A when I can get a D and get five credits for graduation? The only real control you have is the F.

They're delighted with a D.

C: What percentage of the students here aren't concerned with A, B, C, or D—they only care between D and F?

DON: The study indicated about one quarter, but personally I think a more accurate figure would be thirty to fifty percent.

CHRIS: The fury that is engendered in some students if you say, "I'm sorry, I'm not interested that you just come to occupy that seat, I expect something out of you." "But I'm here; I should get my five credits," Not "I should pass," but "I should get my five credits, I'm here."

DON: Bullshit.

CHRIS: Amen. I think too many teachers are malleable. The students can bully or talk them into passing them, and this affects other teachers. These kids are incredibly well-skilled at manipulation. All levels, bright, dumb, it doesn't matter. I coudn't believe one girl in my gifted seminar, she said, "I can't write out my ideas too well about the differences between Hamilton and Jefferson, so why don't we just talk about them." This is a kid who's perfectly capable of writing anything. They know how to work teachers.

DON: Last year we had an administrator question a relatively new teacher who failed a lot of students. The question supposedly was not the number of F's, but what he was teaching in the classroom.

CHRIS: The guy thought he was still a teaching assistant in Berkeley.

DON: No, I think he just didn't want to cave in to his students. Once he gives them that D for not doing anything, he knew they had him. I kind of admired his guts.

CHRIS: Maybe, but it made an impossible scheduling situation. None of the kids would sign up for him second semester.

DON: The big problem is the lack of uniformity. We all have different standards. The kids can play the teachers off against each other, the administrators against the teachers. They're experts.

C: What finally happened?

DON: He transferred to another school.

C: Do you have different types of classes here that are college prep?

DON: In the social-science department we are heterogeneous, with the exception of a very few who are taken out because they are emotionally handicapped.

C: Except for the gifted seminars, right?

CHRIS: Yeah, but those are less than twenty kids out of five hundred in the senior class. It's really pretty mixed here.

DON: We used to track, but what that does is put an onus on the kids in the lower tracks. You can call them, X, Y, Z, or butterflies, pigeons, and bluebirds, but the lower groups know what's happening. They might not be smart, but they aren't dumb.

CHRIS: You have to teach to the middle. Otherwise you'll go nuts. The resistance will drive you crazy if you try to teach to the top third, say.

DON: It's not fair to teach to the top third anyway. What are the bottom kids supposed to do? If you're good, you can use the top kids as motivators, sort of like spark plugs for the class.

C: What about your gifted seminars? Do the kids in them learn more history than if they were in the regular classes?

CHRIS: That is putting it rather mildly.

C: Would some of the smarter kids in the regular classes be able to learn more if they were put in the seminar, but the level of instruction was held the same?

CHRIS: Definitely.

DON: But then you're back to a tracking system, and that is unacceptable. It simply stops the development of the lower kids. What are you thinking about?

CHRIS: I just wondered if I locked my room, because my purse is in there.

C: How would you compare your students today with those ten years ago in terms of writing skills, reading skills?

DON: Very much less prepared. In math where they have to figure out percentages, figure out subtraction and addition, their basic math skills are a lot weaker.

CHRIS: I think writing skills are even lower.

DON: Yeah, if I compare the last five years with the early nineteen-sixties, the situation is an absolute disaster. Writing is not something that these students feel is of any importance. Somewhere in the grades down the line they do not practice it as a skill.

CHRIS: There's something else too. Getting kids to give speeches is like pulling teeth. "You say you have an idea, now tell me about it." "Well, I went into Berkeley on my school holiday." And you have to ask, "What did you do? Where did you go? Who did you see?" They don't understand the basic skills involved in the development of any thought.

DON: Or you'll ask them, "What's the major idea in this paragraph?" Now they can read the paragraph all right, I know because sometimes when they tell me they don't know the main idea I have them read me the paragraph out loud.

CHRIS: If the main idea is not written in a simple heading, "The West was developed by farmers," if they can't find that sort of sentence, they'll try and find a sentence that they think is like that. They'll read you a sentence that has no relationship to the question you asked.

DON: Which tells me that the answers that were required of them in lower grades were purely details. Fill in the blank. John Blank invented the snowmobile—fill in John's last name.

C: Let's get back to the volume of assigned writing. In English the rule used to be in the early Sixties that a kid was supposed to do a composition a week. Isn't that the way you used to do it in English?

CHRIS: Yes, I was laughing about how many compositions we give them here.

DON: I've been teaching since the early Sixties, one a week was the rule.

C: Okay, what's the rule now?

DON: Maybe one a semester.

CHRIS: We went through a large period at our school where everyone in English was going to be cool, relevant, and creative, and the thought of writing and spelling disappeared for a while. We're getting better, but we're worried about getting sentences and paragraphs.

C: So the question of how many compositions a time period is just not—

DON: It's really, it's not relevant for this school. A student may begin to get some paragraphs together that will eventually give him some skills, but that's about it. One more thing. When I began teaching, there was a rule in the black community, and it was also in the white community but not talked about as much. You don't cause any problems at school. Period. Or you're going to catch hell at home. That was one hundred percent in the black community.

C: When you say problems, what are you talking about?

DON: You cause any problem at school, discipline, truancy, whatever, you're going to have it double at home. We have a black dean here, and I was talking just yesterday with him, and I asked what percentage of the black parents still had that attitude. He guessed between forty and fifty percent. The point is that the home isn't backing up the school here anymore. You can't overestimate the problems that causes us.

INTERVIEW 12

The next interview is with one of the top people in reading and measurement in the world. His professional activities include the training of reading specialists, developing standardized tests and basal reading series for major educational publishers, evaluating USOE programs, and consulting for school districts in reading and measurement all over the country. At the beginning of the interview he is commenting on some of the problems in beginning reading instruction.

DOCTOR: Lots of teachers start to do their own thing. You get a lot of young teachers who have been convinced that basal readers are no good; all you need is good books in front of the kids and they're going to learn through some process. If you love kids, they'll learn —that's the philosophy. So you do a lot of loving, and you don't worry about the skills.

I think you've got another problem too. Suppose in the first grade the teacher is on a new program for the first time, and when the students get to second grade, their teacher is on a new program for the first time. In school districts that change programs frequently, this happens to a pretty sizable percentage of kids and creates tremendous problems.

C: You mean the fact that the teachers were brand-new to the system?

D: Yeah, because, as I said before, they don't study up on these things. I'm not that much against innovation, but I don't think you should innovate statewide all at once, or nationwide as they did on modern math. Modern math is a black mark on the entire education profession so far as I'm concerned. Imagine a whole country of this size going to a method which was essentially untried. It's incredible, absolutely incredible.

C: Actually, they tried it out at the junior-high-school and high-school level, and they had some favorable subjective responses by teachers.

D: Modern math started in the Greater Cleveland Mathematics Project. I was in Cleveland four or five years after they started it, and I sat down at lunch one day with the administrators of the Cleveland schools. So I was sitting next to the math consultant for the Cleveland schools. Here we had the cradle of modern math and here's the guy in charge of it. So I said, "I've been spending the morning looking at the achievement test results of Cleveland public schools—there's something I was looking for but I couldn't find it, and that is low scores in computation. Everywhere else that they're doing modern math the kids score low in computation, how come in Cleveland where you've had modern math longer than anybody your kids don't score low?" "Well," he said, "we test every year, and when we saw what happened to computational skills as a result of the modern math, we just added a twenty-minute-drill period every day to every classroom in the Cleveland public schools." He didn't tell anybody about it; it's not part of the program, but that's what they were doing in Cleveland. At the time nobody knew about it. He wasn't making any secret about it, but he wasn't writing big articles about it either.

That's what you've got to do. You've got to study your

programs; you've got to study the results. At least when you switch to new methods, if you test you've got some information to work with. I was over in Hawaii several years ago to look at their test results. I said, "How are your kids doing in computation?" "Well," he says, "I don't know, because we don't give a computation test." Well, you've got to have some data to work with. But when you're going on this innovative kick on the one hand, and at the same time going into the notion that tests don't tell you a damn thing, what have you got? What can you do to defend the kids against being experimented with unduly?

Take for example the _____ public schools. They were teaching ITA [Initial Teaching Alphabet] at some schools. I had two or three students who did master's theses on the results of that method, including one that looked up the spelling scores of ITA students versus non-ITA students at the third-grade level. The ITA students consistently scored higher than the non-ITA kids. The spelling differences were enormous. Well, here is an experimental program, ITA, with excellent results. The kids are doing very well. Then they had to switch because they couldn't get money to continue it. It was determined ITA was no longer innovative, so they were forced to switch to something else. The guidelines say you've got to be innovative.

C: You mean they had to abandon a successful program?

D: Right, right. They forced the schools to drop what was a good program. You know I could show you the most beautiful data you ever saw. This school district in Montana. The median for the district was very high, maybe the seventieth percentile, for the average, mind you. Practically no one was scoring badly. You know what they were using? Guess what program?

C: Dick and Jane?

D: How did you know? Did I tell you this story before?

C: Wild guess.

D: They were using the old Scott, Foresman, Dick and Jane series. Every year for fifteen years. Beautiful results. Those kids could read, I mean really read. And you know what, they felt guilty about using Dick and Jane and Spot; they felt guilty because they hadn't changed programs in fifteen years. The best damn data I have ever seen, and they feel guilty about their program. You know, Dick and Jane has been panned in the magazines, it's been made into a joke, everybody laughs at Dick and Jane.

C: Was it an upper-middle-class, intellectual district?

D: In Montana? Upper-middle-class intellectuals? No, it was working people, middle class, even somewhat of a depressed area. These people were very organized. They tested all the time. They found that the program was weak in phonics, so they appointed a master teacher to find the best available phonics supplements to the program, which she did. When she was satisfied she had that problem licked, they adopted the supplementary phonics materials in the whole district. Then a couple of years later they felt the students needed wider exposure to books, so they developed the best library of high-interest books you ever saw, and those kids read lots of books now as another supplement to the program.

C: It sounds very disciplined—slow to change, but at least in the right direction.

D: Absolutely. That's how you change. I go down, for example, to the _____ schools, and they're trying everything. You name it, they'll try it. Terrible schools, and the kids read very poorly. In the _____ school district down there, old-fashioned conservative schools, they score the best in California, and the whole district used Ginn until the state forced them to abandon Ginn. Then the whole damn thing switched to Harper and Row. The whole district. No big swings from one thing to another.

    You know it happens time and time again. You go into a school, and here is one teacher doing this program, one teacher doing that one; here's this learning carrel, here's that special playroom—something different is going on in every damn room in the school. Then the teachers and the principal say to me, "Where we really need help is for you to raise our reading scores." It happens with such regularity. Then you go into a school that has tremendous scores, and the teachers say, "What do you think we ought to be doing? We feel very old-fashioned in this school. We feel we're behind the times. We're still using this old program or that old program. Could you recommend to us what program we should change to?" This happens to me again and again. What are you laughing at?

C: You. You kid *me* about being old-fashioned.

D: Old-fashioned, up-to-date, is there a difference? Last summer I visited my son in Montana. We went for a drive one day; about every thirty minutes we passed one of these old two-room schoolhouses all boarded up. My son explained that they had recently consolidated all the old elementary schools into one big school in town. They're doing a lot of busing—some kids have to travel an hour and a half each way to get to school. The next day I visited the elementary school in town. They were all excited about this new innovative program they were trying out. They hired a big consultant who had them doing this new program. They couldn't stop talking about how wonderful it was. Guess what it was.

C: No idea.

D: Cross-grade grouping. Can you believe that?

You want a solution to our educational problems, go back to extremely small, local schools. One in every little neighborhood.

C: Do you really think we could go back to that?

D: I don't know. The thing is this, educational research in public schools, I think we'd be better off if the whole thing was abolished. It's so badly executed because there aren't any researchers. The notion of research or experimentation in public school is that you try something and then you ask the teacher at the end of the year if it works. It's really that loose. I don't think anyone should be allowed to experiment with kids. If they do, it should be done with a guarantee that it will be measured. I don't think anybody should be allowed to change programs without measurement. Unless you involve several hundred students with a carefully controlled study over several years, there is absolutely no educational point to all this change. It shouldn't be permitted.

INTERVIEW 13

The next interview is with a professor of education in the graduate reading department of a private university in California.

He trains reading specialists and consults extensively in school districts throughout the state. I've known this man for a number of years and used him as a consultant for several programs which I have developed. He is one of the most brilliant, competent, and productive people I know. Because I respect his judgment so highly, I was doubly disturbed by some of the things he had to say.

C: How important is stability in the basic reading program, grades one through six? If the school changes program, does it affect the acquisition of basic skills?

PROFESSOR: It depends on the extent of the changes and on the type of kids. I don't think it's a good thing for kids to go through any major program changes in the first three grades, and preferably the first six. To give you an example, I was recently called to consult in a district where the kids had been through Distar in kindergarten, Harper and Row in first grade, an individualized language experience approach in second grade, Sullivan in third grade, the Santa Clara developmental task inventory in an overlaid management system throughout. These kids didn't know whether they were coming or going.

C: That's incredible.

P: No, it's normal. Many school districts that have access to a lot of federal money put their kids through the same kind of circus.

C: It seems to me that a good reading person at the district level could put a stop to that. Don't most districts have somebody good in reading in a decision-making position?

P: You're asking me something I don't think anybody knows. All I can say is that I work with a lot of districts, and I could list off a good half-dozen that are in at least as bad a shape as the one I just described.

C: You're the guy that credentials these reading specialists. How good are they?

P: The biggest problem in public education is that we don't have the quality of human being that goes into law, goes into engineering, goes into medicine. They just aren't professional. They don't prepare at home. They don't get involved in in-service education unless they have to. They don't take additional courses. They don't read at all. In in-service sessions I get comments and questions from first-grade teachers who have been teaching for ten to twelve years that absolutely flabbergast me.

C: Like what?

P: A week ago a woman actually spent ten minutes arguing with me in front of the group that there was no difference between a blend and a digraph. That's not important for a layman to be knowledgeable about, but it's sort of like a doctor saying, "Oh, well, there's no difference between a spleen and a liver—they're both inside your body." A professional teacher of first grade needs to know that digraphs are different, that they need to be taught differently. She didn't know that, and not only did she not know it, she was adamant in her ignorance. The next time you come back, I'm going to dig out some of my old exams so that when I tell you a story like I'm going to tell you, you'll believe it. I have an exam question from my advanced graduate-level course; the students are all experienced teachers, and the question goes like this: Which should be taught first, the vowels or the consonants? And why? Brief paragraph answer. I have got some answers that would make your hair stand on end. All of which indicate, believe it or not, that experienced teachers do not know the difference between a vowel and a consonant. One teacher said, "Teach the vowels first because they are all words of three letters or less."

C: Isn't it true that one of the things teachers have to deal with now is that they have lost a lot of support from the home?

P: Sure. When I taught school, and I taught school in the inner city, parents would come in and before I could get a nice word out about their kids, they'd say, "My kid gets out of line, you whop him good." I don't think that goes on too much anymore. Now the kid looks at the teacher and says, "You and I don't get along and my old man will have your job." A lot of teachers are really intimidated by kids.

C: What is your solution to the problems in inner-city schools?

P: The same as my solution to problems in middle-class schools. If you really want to do the job, ultimately push is going to come to shove, and you're going to have to talk about getting rid of people. I realize that in some cases it is difficult, teachers fight and go to court and all that, but in most cases I don't think it's difficult at all to get rid of a teacher. I think people just don't have the balls to do it. If you confront most teachers with their own inadequacy and make them uncomfortable, they will voluntarily get out because they're not that well paid, it's not that easy a job even if you're lousy at it. It's a hard job.

You've got a weak teacher, what's usually done with that weak teacher? You give him the easiest assignment and the sweetest kids. I think just the opposite should be done. I'm talking about someone who's gone beyond the point of help. First you try to help him, that's the other thing, that's never done. Damn it, the principal's responsibility is not to order books, or to attend PTA meetings or join the Kiwanis Club; his responsibility is to be in the classroom showing teachers how to be good teachers. I'll show you how to do it, you do it wrong, then I tell you how to do it right. Then you demonstrate for me that you can do it right and then we go on to the next thing. That's what ought to go on with teachers and principals, but, oh, do principals fight that. When I consult, I do that, and the teachers beg for it. They say, "Why doesn't the principal ever come visit?" They really want it. It's a very unusual principal that spends an hour a day in the classroom. Typically, elementary-school principals have never even taught in elementary schools. Certainly not the primary grades; very few primary teachers would go into administration. Of course, that's where the biggest reading needs are. Most often weak elementary principals are former junior-high or senior-high P.E. teachers.

C: Describe a good principal.

P: I'll describe two real ones I know. They can talk to teachers; they can talk to kids; they can talk to parents. They can resolve conflicts without screaming and yelling, and they can deal with teachers without putting them on the defensive, without alienating them. They have the trust and support of the people that they deal with. They have courage, and some convictions and integrity. In my experience as a teacher that was the one thing that was lacking in every single principal I ever worked under. That really jaded me.

C: No courage?

P: No integrity. Not exactly the same thing.

C: What's the difference?

P: They might fight, but sometimes for the wrong thing. They might fight for their own salary or something like that. No integrity. When the going got tough they got going in the wrong direction

C: Give me an example.

P: Just take some of the principals I worked with this year. There's the principal that authorized the whole staff to go out to a free dinner and bring their husbands on Title I funds for in-service. Another principal that authorized three or four teachers to go to Miami, Florida, for the IRA conference, again, on in-service funds.

Another principal I worked for this year was never on campus, she was too busy running around doing other things.

C: What was she doing?

P: She was a member of the board of education of another school district, member of the board of trustees of a junior college, on every committee that she could get on. She was a politician. That's what she wanted to do. She never was available to her teachers. She was incompetent and her secretary covered her trail. She couldn't write a letter, couldn't keep an appointment, couldn't remember anything, couldn't make a schedule, couldn't do an agenda for a teachers' meeting. She fooled you on the surface; she would appear very bright and very in control, but she was largely incompetent.

Or another school that's wasted thousands of dollars on me, because the principal is so totally inept. There was one day I didn't work thirty minutes, and it wasn't by my choice because I hate sitting around when I'm getting paid. I would go there and, honest to God, I would spend hours trying to find people, trying to find the room where we were supposed to meet. I would order video-tape equipment; the equipment wouldn't be there. It was amazing.

This was a school that I was in one hundred hours over two years as a consultant. And in one hundred hours I never had a conversation with the principal. There were not five hundred kids in that school. Never had a conversation with that principal. The principal of this particular building is so ill equipped to be principal that I have nothing but pity for him. He's physically ill. He's stupid. He's poorly educated. He can't do anything, I mean anything. He gets no respect from the children or the staff. I can't name that district on this tape, but I know that the superintendent of that district is as aware of that situation as I am. You cannot have integrity and be a superintendent of a district that has this man as a principal.

The worst thing of all in this particular school is that the parents put up with it. You don't have to be an educational expert to see what's going on; all you have to do is walk around the campus and hear the teachers screaming and swinging boards and humiliating children. They're crazy, sick teachers.

C: It seems to me that the key is that the principal has to back up his teachers.

P: No, I think it's just the opposite. Yeah, back up the good ones, but there are very few of those. I think where they lack the guts is in confronting the bad ones.

Let me tell you about a sixth-grade teacher I supposedly trained this year. I walked into this teacher's room, she's young, under thirty, she's got long hair and looks a little bit like she likes organic food. We'll call her Miss Jones.

C: White?

P: Yes, happened to be white although I don't hold that against her, or the organic food. Her room is in a portable which should have been burned forty years ago. That's another thing, they've got money that they throw away left and right, and they've got a physical plant that I wouldn't piss in. It breaks all kinds of codes, I'm sure, not the least of which is the fire code.

The first time I was there it was a zoo parade. Kids running around, one kid broke my Thermos bottle; rough day. One of the things I do is I tell the school, you must have a sub here every day when I come. I want the sub to follow me around, and as soon as I'm done observing, I grab the teacher and go out for a conference and the sub takes over. I'll usually see two teachers in the morning and two in the afternoon. And then I need a place to conference. This was a school where they never ordered a sub, all they had to do was lift up the phone and make a phone call. They never had a sub there. "Oh, well, we forgot." They couldn't seem to get a conference room for me either. I'd go in whatever room they assigned, and the safety patrol would be in there.

So here I am, I'm trying to draw it out of her. She has to ask me for help, admit she's got problems. She doesn't. I don't want to say, "My God, you need to get control of your kids." For two sessions it went like that. Finally, by the third session, I said, "Look, you don't seem to think you have any problems. You feel there is nothing I can help you with, so I'm going to have to go somewhere else."

And she says, "Well, I'm a good teacher." And I didn't say anything, I bit down real hard. Then she said, "Don't you think I'm a good teacher?" Rhetorical question.

So I thought about it for a second, a very short second, and said, "No! I think you're a terrible teacher." And her whole face dropped and she started crying, which doesn't bother me a bit because in my business I go through three boxes of Kleenex a year. If you teach first grade, they wet their pants, and if you teach college, they cry.

So she says, "What do you mean, how can you say that?" Oh, her room, nothing on the walls, totally barren, blank, nothing. All she did was pass out dittos all day. Unreadable dittos. And the kids didn't even do those.

Incidentally there were three adults in addition to me in the room. She's got a full-time aide and there's a resource teacher in there too, full time.

By the third session in her class I was doing task time-charts. I'm sitting in the back of the room and she's trying to do what you might generously call a directed workbook lesson, going over the workbook that the kids were supposed to have done the previous hour, which, of course, none of them had done. She's up in the front of the room with a few little sweet girls, and the rest of the kids are doing things like throwing paper airplanes, pulling the shades up and down, fighting, swearing, cussing, you know. The kids were so miserable, and the weaker kids were just so intimidated that they literally sat with their arms over their heads.

I just take a very general assessment of what the kids are doing when they're supposed to be doing something. If the teacher's talking, are they looking somewhere in the direction of the teacher so that they might presumably be listening to the teacher? If they're reading a story silently, are they reading the story silently? If they were given a ditto to do, a map, a page of math problems, are they doing that? And so forth. She had a small class too, she had only twenty-four kids, and about a third of those were never there. I never got more than three kids on task at any time, three on task! It was that bad, it was that outrageous, eighty to ninety percent of the class were pulling on the shades, flying airplanes, walking around, kicking the wastebasket. It was really that bad.

So I confronted her with that and I said, "I'll tell you right now if I were a parent of these kids I'd go for your job." I looked her right in the eye and I told her, "I'd tear you apart, I'd kill you. Those are children in there. And if there's anything that frustrates me more than that, here you have an opportunity to take advantage of my skill in helping you deal with your problems, and you don't even want to deal with them."

So after she stopped crying, she says, "Oh, you're right, I'll do it, I'll try, blah blah." Walked her back to the classroom, patted her on the shoulder. "Don't worry, these things can improve, a lot of teachers go through this, blah blah blah." I'm really a gentle person, you know, I really don't like to hurt people.

Well, she had second thoughts. The next time I came, the vice-principal tells me, "I want you to know you're not going to

Miss Jones today. She requested that you work with some other teacher instead." "Well, that's fine. I don't want to see people if they don't want to see me. But what are you going to do about her?"

What had happened, you see, was that Miss Jones had gone to the principal and told him she wanted to quit, that she was incompetent. All I'd really done was prick a level of her own consciousness. A bad teacher's aware of it.

What do you think happened? Dumbshit principal, who had given her tenure, and the vice-principal coddled her. They sat her down and went through the whole litany. "Aw, those kids need you, you're so dedicated. Oh, don't listen to him." And they talked her out of retiring. That's the upshot. That's lack of integrity. I had done their dirty work for them and they wouldn't follow through. I'd done what they should have been doing even before I got there.

A good principal would be going in to a teacher like this every day for five minutes. "Where are your lesson plans? Where's your seating chart?" Needling, not antagonistic, always with a smile. "Oh, I see you're teaching reading today. How many groups do you have? Oh, I see, what books are you in? Oh, could I see their workbook pages, have you corrected their workbook pages? What are your plans for the rest of today?"

There's another teacher in this school. Now you're not going to believe this, but I saw this every day I was there, and it's a fact. He has no books in his room; he got rid of all the books. I don't know why, usually a bad teacher's given a lot of books. The bulletin boards are cork, there's not even a scrap of paper on them. There's nothing there, the desks are in rows. Every afternoon, precisely at one o'clock when the bell rings in the afternoon, he sends his kids outside to play kickball, and they play kickball until it's time to go home. They play very well. They're good kickball players. Doesn't even come out of the room; he stays in there. I don't know what he does in there, and that's a fact.

C: What does he do between nine and one?

P: He lectures, and passes out some dittos and writes things on the board for them to do. But it's worse than that, because he humiliates and he degrades those children. Yeah, that school's a mess.

Another teacher, same school. She had a grant from _____ Corporation, to teach her kids how to manage their own mini society. I was in there just after her kids had gone wild, throwing things, bouncing off the walls, killing each other, and in march about a dozen button-down three-piece young executives, come to observe the results of their grant.

She got all sorts of credit, and recognition, and probably money, and was supposed to set the kids up into a mini society. Give them money, teach them how to handle certain affairs, and they would run their own society and have a court, you know, all these wonderful ideas. Of course all they had was chaos. This was the mini *Lord of the Flies* society. You've read *Catch-22*— I felt like Yossarian sitting in the tree looking down. You've got to picture these dozen button-down guys with their briefcases and their ties, walking into this school, thinking, Here's our great grant of money to do something for these little black kids. And here's their pathetic, hopeless white teacher, can't even get the kids to stop burping at each other. They sit there and burp at each other, they're so desperate for humor. Oh, she was so awful.

Or, take another incident from the same school. This was a mandatory in-service session for all faculty, a half-day of school just for this purpose. Half the teachers didn't show up! Only one teacher had a pencil in her hand the whole session. The teachers came strolling in late, strolled out early. I found out the kindergarten teacher goes home every day at noon. She's supposed to be there a full day; she's paid for eight hours—she doesn't feel like paying a babysitter!

Some of the other teachers were out at the racetrack. I found out some of them leave their classes a couple of days a week at lunch break to go to the track and just don't return. Just turn their classes over to their aides. It's unbelievable!

And their reading specialist, my God! This lady was so ignorant I don't know where they found her. She didn't know anything about reading, and she was too stupid even to pretend.

She didn't know how to teach anything. Vowels, consonants, sight words, structural analysis, phonograms, phonic generalizations, she'd never even heard of these things. And the teachers were just sort of snickering that I thought all that stuff was important.

C: How many inner-city public-school teachers are as bad as the ones you're describing?

P: I'd say ninety percent.

C: I don't believe it. That's too high.

P: Oh, some of them could function in a middle-class school, but as far as being able to do the job in the school they're in, ninety percent aren't making it. So many teachers I know who are certainly in the upper groups, good or at least adequate, immediately dropped to the bottom in an inner-city school. They can't handle those kids. They can't handle the demoralization, the incompetence, the aides, the chaos, the lack of cohesion, of direction.

By the way, in inner-city schools it's not just the teachers, it's the teacher's aides. They have what they call permanence, which is tougher to get rid of than tenure. These teacher's aides are permanently in their jobs, and many of them are terrible, doing damage to children, and they're supposed to be helping them.

And you can't get a decent person to be a principal of those schools. No one in their right mind can be a principal at a school like that.

C: Why?

P: Oh, the problems are so severe. Do not get me wrong, I am not talking about the kids, and only to a small degree am I talking about the parents. I'm talking about the teachers and the aides. The teachers are so bad and so out of control that no healthy or competent human being is going to take $23,000 to go in and deal with that. They end up with weak-kneed principals who look the other way and have no integrity whatsoever, or they end up with people who have some backbone but are so incompetent they don't know how to walk through a door without walking into it.

And there is another thing too which is simply never, ever

discussed in public. Inner-city schools have done a lot of recruiting of black and other minority teachers; a lot of these people are from the South, and are virtual illiterates. They can be nice people, but put an illiterate in charge of an educational program, in an alien culture, and as often as not he'll turn into a monster.

C: It's really tragic we have so many bad people in those schools.

P: Now I didn't say bad people, bad *teachers*. They're not bad people, they're usually decent people. Take my neighbor down the street. He's a high-school teacher. During the year he's really grouchy, really irritable; he really hates teaching. But when the summertime comes, he's a split personality. All of a sudden there's this big huge grin on his face. He gets burned out. It's a really hard job.

Unless you're a very special person, teaching is really a tough job. I've done it. Thirty kids year after year all day long can really take a toll on you. Teachers are so absolutely unappreciated. They get shit from the principal, they get it from the kids, they get it from the parents, they get it from the school district.

Why does society expect them to be so goddam different from any other class of people? You take working people—plumbers, janitors, anybody—they come and they punch in and, boy, that's it. The teachers are not only expected to put in a number of hours per day, but are also expected to do all the stuff at home, and also expected to assume all the other roles from school psychologist to nurse to welfare aide, and always be cheerful and pleasant and be able to deal with parent problems and you name it, for very mediocre salary.

The other thing is status. Teachers hold very little status. Since I went from fifth-grade teacher to a professor, my status level's gone way up. When I talk to a travel agent, I get better service. When I go to the gas station, I get better service. If I hustle my doctorate, I get super service. You go to Europe and tell them you're a teacher, they call you "sir"; you're given great status. I think that affects teachers a lot, the lack of status that they have.

The one other thing that is absolutely true is they never get any help. I had a graduate student recently, a professional teacher for twenty years, come back to get her master's. As a favor I went out to her school to observe her teach. I don't do it on a long-term basis, but I'll go and visit them once or twice in the school and critique them and give them some feedback.

I spent all morning in her classroom and was appalled. She was a straight-A student, very, very good student, a wonderful person, extremely dedicated in her work and writing. She had so much planned, which is so diametrically opposed to some of the things that I see in some schools. All these really neat, exciting things for these kids. It was an upper-middle-class school, well-off kids, but she didn't know how to handle them. They were just making a fool of her. Hell, kids will eat you up if you let them. It wasn't chaos, but they were just so rude, and so silly and dumb. She was just taking all this guff from these kids.

So we went to lunch; she got someone to cover for her and we spent ninety minutes or so. Nonstop I started talking and she started listening and writing. I said, "Joanne"—I knew her pretty well—"do you think you can take this?" "Yeah, yeah, yeah." "Okay, here we go." I described the problems, the lack of control, and I told her all the good things she was doing, and there were a lot of them. I asked, "Do you want to dwell on the good ones or do you want to dwell on the problems?" Oh, she wanted help, fine. "Here's what you need to do." I gave her specific things. I told her how to discipline kids, basic stuff, I couldn't believe it, it was like talking to a student teacher.

When it was all done, her eyes welled up with tears. I said oh, oh, and she said oh, no, she was so happy. Twenty years, never had any help. No one had ever, ever given any constructive feedback to her, critical or otherwise as a teacher. And then she wrote me a nice letter reaffirming that same statement. Here's a teacher with all the talent in the world, functioning at about fifty percent because she's never had a principal do what I had done as a favor.

This woman, by the way, is an example—if she were in an inner-city school, in a year or two she'd be as awful as any of them.

Yet, honest to God, if I were her principal and I could go in there intensively and follow up with this, I could make her into a top-category teacher. I know I could, because she's bright enough, and receptive, and dedicated. She's creative, her room is magnificent, the things that she does. The other part of that letter was "I've been doing everything you said and my kids are being real good. I hope I have the courage to maintain it." These teachers have the right, and we owe them the help to learn the skills of being a teacher.

INTERVIEW 14

The elementary-school principal in the final interview meets many of the criteria listed earlier for an excellent principal. I had heard about him for over a year before I actually met him. A friend of mine in the test-publishing industry kept telling me about a school where the test results violated the conventional wisdom regarding the relationship between achievement and socioeconomic status. Over a third of the school's students came from families on welfare; the average socioeconomic level was below average; the average IQ of entering first-grade students was below average. Yet by fourth grade over seventy-five percent of the students were reading above grade level, and by the end of sixth grade the average student was reading two years above grade level. My friend claimed that the school's teaching staff was adequate but not exceptional, and that the best explanation for the high test scores was the curricular leadership supplied by the school's principal.

When I finally met him, the principal turned out to be an easygoing man in his late fifties. While he acknowledged that he provided the school with curricular direction, he insisted his teaching staff deserved the credit for the students' learning. He had been the school's principal for twenty years, and had focused his staff on the overriding importance of reading for the past dozen. My initial questions dealt with the reading program he and his staff had developed.

C: Why did you first start working on reading?

PRINCIPAL: I sat down and thought, What is the most important thing for us to accomplish? Okay, reading is the most important, this is the cause for discipline problems, this is cause for dropouts, this is the foundation for learning. So we had a teachers' meeting and the first thing that comes up, "Okay, what about science and health and all the other things that the state requires us to do?" I says, "The hell with that, that's my responsibility. We're going to solve the reading, and then we're going over to the other things."

I think this is one of the big problems. We have to fight all the time to stay on the objective. For instance, right in the middle of this, the new math came in. Everybody got involved in the new math and we were going to all kinds of meetings and taking classes.

C: How long did you get off the track?

P. We went off the track about a year and a half. We came to the conclusion after the first year that the new math was not exactly what it was cut out to be, so we went through the book and threw out about fifty percent of it in the primary grades. But that detracted from the reading emphasis. In my opinion you have to set a goal and then don't fall for all these other things that are being pushed on you.

C: Have you always had these good results with the average sixth grader coming out at the high eighth-grade level?

P: No, I think after we really started emphasizing it, nothing happened to the test scores for three years. They were about average at that time, mid-1960's to late 1960's. We started making some progress in the fourth year. We didn't change anything, all of a sudden we just started getting results. I don't really know why we had that time lag, but we did. One thing we did that was very important about the fifth or sixth year, we went into the Stanford Diagnostic Testing.

C: How do you use it?

P: We group the kids according to their skill needs. In the morning from nine to nine-thirty-five each teacher teaches a specific skill in reading. In other words, she's going to become a pro in this one particular skill, whether it's syllabication or whatever it is. First, second, and third graders are grouped together, and fourth, fifth, and sixth graders.

C: So you'd have a group of thirty kids who need syllabication skills, all taught by one teacher?

P: Yes. They would go to the one teacher for thirty-five minutes. But I don't think the organization was the most important. I think the most important thing was that fourth-, fifth-, and sixth-grade teachers learned how to teach reading, and it affected their teaching the rest of the day.

C: Who decided which teachers would teach which skill?

P: I had each one pretty well decided. I thought we'd have a big battle then, but they all agreed that they'd teach what I had there, so I gave them the materials for it.

C: Where did you get the materials?

P: Some of them were what the Stanford test recommended, and other things that we had on hand. We've switched around many times since. Someone would have comprehension down, and then we'd do some switching. They didn't mind. They wanted to learn to teach reading too. I think the key is not that we do such a whale of a job in the primary grades, we just do a better job than the other people in fourth, fifth, and sixth grade, because we still keep emphasizing reading.

C: Do you have a young staff or an old staff?

P: Until the last three or four years we were known as the menopause set, but now we have a younger set.

C: Didn't you get resistance from teachers about taking the added responsibilities?

P: There's some resistance to getting out of your classroom because it's another preparation, it's more work, and especially a fourth-grade teacher getting sixth-grade kids into the program. Maybe the sixth-grade kids are going to test the fourth-grade teacher. But I'm real enthusiastic about the program and I think maybe that's part of it. I did a good sales job on the staff, and then, of course, the results started coming in. I'm the old-fashioned type anyhow, what I say, in my school, goes.

C: How about union, are they unionized here?

P: Some of them are, about half the faculty are union, but we don't have any cliques. We all work together here. You know, it's interesting, I don't know how I do it, but a psychologist came down here once and tried to explain how I keep the cliques from forming. When it comes right down to it, it's a matter of not being wishy-washy. If you're going to do something and it's worthwhile, and you think it through, well, you might have to sell it to a few people. But if it's good for kids, I don't think you have much of a job selling it to people. If they're at least average teachers, have an average interest in kids, why, if you come up with something that's going to be good for kids, you don't have much trouble selling it.

C: What's your philosophy on discipline?

P: I think I'm a real strong disciplinarian. It's a privilege to go to school. The best thing I ever did is to have automatic exclusion.

C: How do you get away with it? How come the parents don't come down on you? "What right do you have to send my kid home?" First question they would ask you.

P: I don't get that too often. I tell them, "These other kids have a right to learn, and your child's not taking that right away from them."

C: How about the Supreme Court decision that says you have to offer due process?

P: I'm offering them due process, I'm telling him why. All I have to do is tell him why. He knows why. The biggest thing that I'm interested in, every kid has a right to learn and one kid in a class can ruin that.

C: The parents cooperate? They don't argue?

P: They argue sometimes. They'll come in here madder than a wet hen. Another thing too, I think it's real important, the teachers back me up.

C: Who calls the parents? Do you do it, or do you have a vice-principal who does that? You seem to have a special system here.

P: I do the calling.

I have a system that I couldn't run a school without. If

a kid is a real problem, and he disrupts the class all the time, I call the parents in and discuss the situation. They set up a place where the student can always go. It's a process you set up with the teacher, you set it up with the secretary, you set it up with everyone concerned. What happens is the kid can come to school and he can do anything he wants to, but anytime he doesn't have perfect behavior the teacher has a little signal, she goes by and taps his hands or touches the top of his head or something. He gets up, comes into the office, we pick up the phone, we'll only say four words, "He's on his way." He goes home and the parents cannot talk to him at all about what happened at school, or anything like that. He can play with his toys, but he has to stay within the confines of his yard till school is out. That's the only stipulation, and he can come back each day and start over again. It's his job to see how long he can stay in school, see, and he can feel good about it because he's doing it.

You ask a kid whose job it is to make them behave. They'll tell you everybody but themselves, because they don't think it's their job to behave. Consequently, they can't feel good about it when they do behave.

C: And this system works.

P: I have one kid in sixth grade now, when he was in fourth grade he was one of the biggest problems I've ever seen in this school. Last year he did an about-face, and this year he's been a fine kid. I don't know what happens with them. I've had kids that played truant. Had a big kid in sixth grade one time that was staying with his grandmother and he played truant. I put him on automatic, and every time he came in to go home he bawled like a baby. One day I called him in and I said, "Look, what's the score, I'd like to know? Here you play truant, and then we send you home, and then you cry. I can't understand it." And he didn't know, he says it's just different, it was the only thing he could say.

Another thing that happens is it cuts out a lot of fighting in the home. In the past, the kid gets sent home and the mother says, "Wait till your father gets home." Father comes home feeling good, and then has to discipline him. Pretty soon the kid's playing one parent against the other. This way there's no way he can work one against the other.

By the way, if both parents work, or there's just one parent and she works, we insist there are two babysitters in case one isn't home. We go to a lot of trouble to set it up right.

C: I would think that this discipline that you're talking about is probably just as important as the reading, as far as your results here. You can't teach if you don't have their attention.

How do children feel about you, do they feel a little scared of you or do they think you're the kind old principal?

P: Stay away from the world "old," will you? Of course, the kids that you give the bad time to, that you have trouble with, they're the ones that think the most of you. They're the ones who come back and see you, and they come up and say hi to you and give you a present at the end of school, all that stuff.

C: Sure, because when you act as disciplinarian that means you care for them.

P: That's right. They know that. Children automatically identify discipline with love. It's the same thing in their mind.

C: How do you keep your teacher quality high? What if the district assigns you a teacher you don't think can do the job?

P: Well, I had one last year. She'd been in the district around eight years, I guess. I just went over to the superintendent and says, "I'm not going to have her, no way." She's in another school now.

C: But if every principal did that—

P: You've got to be stronger than the other ones.

C: Well, how come that other principal got stuck with her?

P: I don't know, that wasn't my problem. She might have been all right somewhere else, but she wasn't a diagnostic/prescriptive-type teacher. She didn't, and wouldn't, fit into what we wanted and what we required.

C: And she wouldn't learn it?

P: It takes two things: it takes some brains and it takes some willingness to really work. Most anybody can do it if they're willing to work. That's the only requirement. They're drawing the money,

I expect them to work. That's the old school theory, see.

Now you have some real good teachers coming out, whereas there was a time when we were hiring them if they were warm. You had to have a body. You know, right after World War Two. A lot of these people are still in it, and they've got tenure.

C: I assume you've never had to fire a tenured teacher?

P: Got rid of them. They quit, or request a transfer out of my school.

C: How'd you get rid of them?

P: Well, you talk to them, and say you have your evaluations. I think if they're dead weight they know they're dead weight. If you have a school that's functioning and they're off in left field somewhere, I think that's where the pressure comes. They're not cutting it. And I think it's my responsibility to tell them that they're not cutting it.

C: What reading program do you use, Harper and Row?

P: No, Scott, Foresman.

C: Is that an integrated program that starts with first grade and goes all the way to sixth?

P: Right, all the way through and everybody uses it too.

C: You don't have one teacher using her own system?

P: I had one that was trying to.

C: But they're not using it anymore?

P: Not anymore.

C: How about this new state law in California that says you've got to buy a new program every six years?

P: Buy the same thing over again. You've got to play games. I've been in this Title I program for years. I had a Title I auditor come out and tell me I had some students scoring over the fiftieth percentile who were in a reading class paid for out of Title I funds. I told him the kids needed improvement in that area of reading, but he said it violated their rules to help these particular children. So I told him the students weren't actually in the class, they were just observing that day.

C: Any final words of wisdom?

P: You've got to have a climate of respect for education, with dis-cipline at the basis. Then the teacher can function, and can be happy functioning. If you don't have that then the kids aren't going to accomplish anything. The first thing you've got to do is establish discipline. It's going to be real tough, but I think it can be done. I think kids basically want to go to school.

What we need to do is to get back to the idea that it's a privilege to go to school. If you can work that around, you've got it made.

I believe these interviews accurately reflect the educational history of our public schools over the past dozen years. Starting in the middle to late 1960's, there was an increase in student resistance to assigned schoolwork. Many teachers, especially the young, less experienced ones, accommodated to this change by reducing their standards and assignments. When the older teachers tried to maintain their standards, school administrators subverted their authority by pressuring them not to fail students, and by letting students choose their teachers or drop their courses halfway into the semester. Thus, the older teachers were all forced to drop their standards and work demands.

Whenever I reread these interviews, I am struck by the fact that the teachers and administrators I talked to are extremely talented and competent human beings, but our schools do not permit them to utilize their ability. Our schools function in such a way as to drag their best teachers down to the functional level of the mediocre. Our young people desperately need teachers and educational leaders with standards and courage, but as these interviews indicate, the political and social environment of public education precludes that possibility.

The great majoirty of teachers are not superb, and they especially need to work in schools that back their authority, and provide inspiration, leadership, and training. Instead, most teachers are left to rely almost completely on themselves. An institution maximizes its output when it fully utilizes its resources. Our schools are wasting the potential and the talent of their primary resource, their teachers, and I attribute the achievement decline of the past dozen years directly to this fact.

Author's Note

EVERY MONTH I RECEIVE DOZENS OF LETTERS REGARDING MY BOOK and my work. Following are the three most frequently asked questions, and answers:

1) Is there an organization I can join that will keep me informed on public education issues?

Yes. Join the Council For Basic Education, 725 15th Street N.W., Washington, D.C. 20005. It is a responsible group of scholars and professional educators who publish a monthly newsletter on educational issues. It acts as a clearinghouse for information on various topics, such as 3R schools and minimum competency testing, which it will share with anyone who asks.

2) Do you speak or consult?

Yes. I've testified before U.S. Senate and House subcommittees, keynoted annual conventions of numerous professional groups, and consulted for school districts, universities, and State Departments of Education. If you would like a copy of my Senate and House testimonies, plus a technical analysis of the decline in achievement (published in the June, 1979, *Phi Delta Kappan*), send $1.00 with a stamped, self-addressed envelope to me c/o Institute of Reading Development, 4630 Geary Blvd. #303, San Francisco, California 94118. Address all personal correspondence to me at this address.

3) What does your organization, the Institute of Reading Development, do? Do you work outside of California?

The Institute teaches speed reading and comprehension training programs to junior high, high school, and college students, and adults. We have contracts with universities, school districts, corporations, government agencies, and individual students and parents. The Institute has offices in San Francisco, Berkeley, Palo Alto, San Jose, Orange County, and San Diego. Starting in 1980, the Institute will open up franchises nationwide. If you are interested in a California program, write the nearest Institute. If you are interested in information regarding an Institute franchise, write me at the address above.

REFERENCES

1. "A 1976 Declaration of Independence by the Presidents of the American University, the Catholic University of America, George Washington University, and Georgetown University." *The Chronicle of Higher Education,* April 19, 1976, p. 5.

2. *Administrative Regulations of the California State Board of Education.* Title 5, Section 3931, 1973.

3. "All Kinds of Crime." *U.S. News and World Report,* December 16, 1974, pp. 33, 34.

4. American College Testing Program, Iowa City, Iowa, Personal Communication (Table S-2.5), January, 1977.

5. *The American Freshman: National Norms.* Los Angeles, California: American Council on Education, Cooperative Institutional Research Program and the Graduate School of

Education, University of California at Los Angeles, annual reports, 1966–1977.

6. *An Analysis of the Evaluation of State Educational Programs.* Sacramento, California: Office of the Legislative Analyst, September, 1975.

7. Anastasi, A. *Psychological Testing.* London: Macmillan, 1968.

8. Armbruster, F. *The U.S. Primary and Secondary Educational Process.* Croton-on-Hudson, New York: Hudson Institute, July, 1975.

9. Armor, D. "The Evidence on Busing." *Public Interest,* 1972, *28,* 90–126.

10. *Assessment of Reading Activities Funded Under the Federal Program of Aid for Educationally Deprived Children.* Washington, D.C.: U.S. General Accounting Office Report Number MWD-76-54, December, 1975.

11. Averch, H., Carroll, S., Donaldson, T., Kiesling, H., Pincus, J. *How Effective Is Schooling?* Englewood Cliffs, New Jersey: Educational Technology Publications, 1974.

12. Ball, S., and Bogatz, G. *The First Year of Sesame Street: An Evaluation.* Princeton, New Jersey: Educational Testing Service, 1970.

13. Bandura, A., Ross, D., and Ross, S. "Imitation of Film-mediated Aggressive Models." *Journal of Abnormal and Social Psychology,* 1963, *66,* 3–11.

14. Bauernfeind, R., and Blumenfeld, W. "A Comparison of Achievement Scores of Public School and Catholic School Pupils." *Educational & Psychological Measurement,* 1963, *23,* 331–336.

15. Baumrind, D. "Authoritarian vs. Authoritative Parental Control." *Adolescence,* 1968, *3,* 255–272.

16. Baumrind, D. "Coleman II: Utopian Fantasy and Sound Social Innovation." *School Review,* 1974, *76,* 279–303.

17. Bender, L. *Federal Regulation and Higher Education.* Washington, D.C.: The American Association for Higher Education, 1977.

18. Bennett, N. *Teaching Styles and Pupil Progress.* London, England: Open Books, 1976.

19. Blackburn, R., Armstrong, E., Conrad, C., Didham, J., and McKune, T. *Changing Practices in Undergraduate Education.* Berkeley, California: The Carnegie Council on Policy Studies in Higher Education, 1976.

20. Blackmore, E., et al. *Early Childhood Education: Report of the Task Force on Early Childhood Education.* Sacramento, California: California State Department of Education, 1972.

21. Bloom, B. "The 1955 Normative Study of the Tests of General Educational Development." *School Review,* 1956, *64,* 110–124.

22. Bower, R. *Television and the Public.* New York: Holt, Rinehart and Winston, 1973.

23. Bronfenbrenner, U. "Is Early Intervention Effective?" *Teachers College Record,* 1974, *76,* 279–303.

24. Bronfenbrenner, U. "The Roots of Alienation," in U. Bronfenbrenner (ed.), *Influences on Human Development.* Hinsdale, Illinois: Dryden Press, 1972.

25. Bulletins 89–101, *Testing Programs in Independent Schools. Summary and Normative Data.* Framingham, Massachusetts: Educational Records Bureau, annual reports, 1966–1975.

26. Carnegie Foundation for the Advancement of Teaching. *Missions of the College Curriculum.* San Francisco: Jossey-Bass, 1977.

27. Chall J. *Learning to Read: The Great Debate.* New York: McGraw-Hill, 1967.

28. Christenson, R. "McGuffey's Ghost and Moral Education Today." *Phi Delta Kappan,* 1977, *58,* 737–742.

29. "City Schools in Crisis." *Newsweek,* September 12, 1977, 62–70.

30. Cleary, A. "Test Bias: Prediction of Grades of Negro and White Students in Integrated Colleges." *Journal of Educational Measurement,* 1968, *5,* 115–124.

31. Clifford, G. *The Shape of American Education.* Englewood Cliffs, New Jersey: Prentice-Hall, 1975.

32. Clymer, T., et al. *Reading 720.* Lexington, Massachusetts: Ginn and Company, 1975.

33. Coleman, J., Campbell, E., Hobson, C., McPartland, J., Mood, A., Weinfeld, F., and York, R. *Equality of Educational Opportunity.* 2 volumes. Washington, D.C.: Office of Education, U.S. Department of Health, Education, and Welfare, U.S. Government Printing Office, 1966.

34. *College Bound Seniors.* New York: College Entrance Examination Board, annual reports, 1972–1977.

35. Committee on College Composition and Communication. "Students' Right to Their Own Language." *College English,* 1975, *36,* 709–726.

36. Dale, E., and Chall, J. "A Formula for Predicting Readability." *Educational Research Bulletin,* 1948, *27,* 11–20; *28,* 37–54.

37. Denholm, R. *Math for Individual Achievement.* Boston: Houghton Mifflin, 1974.

38. Denny, E., Nelson, M., and Brown, J. *Nelson-Denny Reading Test, Form A.* Boston, Massachusetts: Houghton Mifflin, 1960.

39. *Digest of Educational Statistics.* Washington, D.C.: National Center for Education Statistics, 1977.

40. Divorky, D. "Opting for an Old-fangled Alternative." *Education Yearbook 1974–75.* New York: Macmillan Educational Corporation, 1975.

41. Dyne, L. "The Free-Tuition Fight Is Lost, The New York Tragedy—2." *The Chronicle of Higher Education,* September 20, 1976, pp. 4, 5.

42. Ebel, R. "Educational Tests: Valid? Biased? Useful?" *Phi Delta Kappan,* 1975, *57,* 83–88.

43a. *Education Code of the State of California.* Sections 6445 and 6446 4 (h).

43b. *Education Code of the State of California.* Section 9465.

44. *Education of the Disadvantaged.* Washington, D.C.: Office of Education, U.S. Department of Health, Education, and Welfare, OE-37013-68, U.S. Government Printing Office, 1968.

45. *Education Yearbook, 1974–75.* New York: Macmillan Educational Corporation, 1974.

46. *The Effectiveness of the Early Childhood Education Program: An Analysis of 1974–75 State-level Evaluations.* Sacramento, California: Office of the Legislative Analyst, February, 1976.

47. Erickson, B. "School Board Says Never Again." *The Independent,* Richmond, California, April 29, 1976, p. 1.

48. Eron, L. "Relationship of TV Viewing Habits and Aggressive Behavior in Children." *Journal of Abnormal Psychology,* 1963, *67,* 1973–1976.

49. *Evaluation of the Impact of ESEA Title VII Spanish/English Bilingual Education Program: Interim Results.* Washington, D.C.: Office of Education, U.S. Department of Health, Education, and Welfare, April, 1977.

50. Farr, R., Tuinman, J., and Rowls, M. *Reading Achievement in the United States: Then and Now.* Indiana University, Bloomington, Indiana, August, 1974.

51a. *Federal Register, Volume 41, Number 189, Tuesday, September 28, 1976.* Paragraphs 116.40 and 116a.22b.

51b. *Federal Register, Volume 41, Number 189, Tuesday, September 28, 1976.* Paragraph 116A.25.

51c. *Federal Register, Volume 41, Number 189, Tuesday, September 28, 1976.* Paragraphs 116A.2 and 116A.21e.

52. Ferguson, R., and Maxey, E. *Trends in the Academic Per-*

formance of High School and College Students. American College Testing Program Research Report Number 70, Iowa City, Iowa: American College Testing Program, January, 1976.

53. Fernandez, C., Espinosa, R., and Dornbusch, S. *Factors Perpetuating the Low Academic Status of Chicano High School Students.* Stanford University, Stanford, California, July, 1975.

54. Flesch, R. *Why Johnny Can't Read.* New York: Harper and Row, 1955.

55. "Flood of Testimony Asks for Changes in Title I." *Kappan,* 1977, *59,* 283.

56. Folgar, J., and Nam, C. *Education of the American Population.* Washington, D.C.: Bureau of Census, 1967.

57. Fredericksen, N., and Schrader, W. *Academic Achievement of Veteran and Non-veteran Students.* Washington, D.C.: American Psychological Association, Psychological Monographs: General and Applied, 1952.

58. Gates, A. *Reading Attainment in Elementary Schools: 1957 and 1937.* Teachers College, Columbia University, New York, 1961.

59. *Goss v. Lopez,* 95 S. Ct. 729 (1975).

60. *Handbook on Women Workers.* Washington, D.C.: U.S. Department of Labor, 1975.

61. Hansen, D., National Institute of Education, and several officials, California State Department of Education. Personal communications, October, 1976.

62. Heller, L. *The Death of the American University.* New Rochelle, New York: Arlington House, 1973.

63. Herndon, T. "Standardized Tests: Are They Worth the Costs?" Address to the Commonwealth Club, San Francisco, California, December 19, 1975.

64. Hieronymus, A., and Lindquist, E. *Manual for Administrators, Supervisors, and Counselors, Forms 5 and 6. Iowa Tests of Basic Skills.* Iowa City, Iowa: University of Iowa, 1974.

65. *Hobson v. Hansen*, 269 F. Supp. 401 United States District Court, D.C. Cir. (1967) aff'd sub nom Smuck v. Hobson 408 F. 2d 175 (D.C. Cir. 1969).

66. Hockman, C. "Black Dialect Reading Tests in the Urban Elementary School." *Reading Teacher*, 1973, *26*, 231–233.

67. Holt, J. *How Children Fail.* New York: Pitman Publishing Corporation, 1964.

68. *Hoover Structured School.* Palo Alto, California: Publication of Hoover Structured School in the Palo Alto Unified School District, 1976.

69. Howe, L., Simon, S., and Kirschenbaum, H. *Values Clarification.* New York: Hart, 1972.

70. "Illiteracy Among Recruits Threatens to Sink U.S. Navy." *Palo Alto Times,* June 23, 1977, p. 1.

71. *Impact of Educational Innovation on Student Performance: Executive Summary.* Palo Alto: American Institutes for Research, 1976.

72. *Instruction Guide, Tamalpais High School.* Mill Valley, California, December, 1975.

73. Jackson, R. *A Summary of SAT Score Statistics for College Board Candidates.* Princeton, New Jersey: Educational Testing Service, December, 1975.

74. Jacoby, S. *Inside Soviet Schools.* New York: Schocken Books, 1974.

75. Jencks, C., Smith, M., Acland, H., Bane, M., Cohen, D., Gintis, H., Heyns, B., and Michelson, S. *Inequality.* New York: Harper and Row, 1972.

76. Jones, E., Supervisor, Subject A, University of California at Los Angeles, Personal communications, 1975 and 1976.

77a. Juola, A. *Grade Inflation (1969–1973) A Preliminary Report.* East Lansing, Michigan: Office of Evaluation Services, Michigan State University, August, 1974.

77b. Juola, A. *Grade Inflation—1975 Is It Over?* East Lansing, Michigan: Learning and Evaluation Service, Michigan State University, August, 1976.

78. King, E. M., and Hieronymus, A. N. *Canadian Tests of Basic Skills Manual for Administrators, Supervisors, and Counselors, Forms 3 and 4.* Ontario, Canada: Thomas and Sons Limited, 1974.

79. Kirkendahl, R. "The Status of History in the Schools." *The Journal of American History,* 1975, *62,* 557–570.

80. Koerner, J. *The Miseducation of American Teachers.* Baltimore, Maryland: Penguin, 1965.

81. Koerner, J. *Who Controls American Education: A Guide for Laymen.* Boston: Beacon Press, 1968.

82. Kohl, H. *36 Children.* New York: Signet, 1967.

83. Kohl, H. *The Open Classroom.* New York: Random House, 1969.

84. Kohl, H. *Reading, How To.* New York: Dutton and Company, 1973.

85. Kohn, S. "The Numbers Game: How the Testing Industry Operates." *The National Elementary Principal,* July/August, 1975, *54,* 14.

86. Kurzman, M. "The Reading Ability of College Freshmen Compared to the Readability of Their Textbooks." *Reading Improvement,* 1973, *11,* 13–25.

87. Kvaraceus, W. "Reading: Failure and Delinquency." *Discipline in the Classroom.* Washington, D.C.: National Education Association, 1974.

88. Ladd, E., and Lipset, S. "The Faculty Mood: Pessimism is

Predominant." *Chronicle of Higher Education,* October 3, 1977, pp. 1 and 14.

89. Lennon, R., and Mitchell, B. "Trends in Age-Grade Relationships: A Thirty-Five Year Review." *School and Society,* 1955, 123–125.

90. Lesher, J. "The Literacy Victims." *California Living Magazine,* May 22, 1977, 7–9.

91. Lesser, G. *Children and Television.* New York: Random House, 1974.

92. Liu, S. "An Investigation of Oral Reading Miscues Made by Nonstandard Dialect Speaking Black Children." *Reading Research Quarterly,* 1975–1976, *11,* 193.

93. Magrath, P. "Colleges and Washington Need to Sign a Peace Treaty." *Chronicle of Higher Education,* July 6, 1976, 32.

94. Mayer, M. "Higher Education for All? The Case of Open Admissions." *Commentary,* February, 1973, *55,* 37–47.

95. McKee, P., Brzeinski, J., and Harrison, M. *The Effectiveness of Teaching Reading in the Kindergarten.* Denver, Colorado: Denver Public Schools, 1966.

96. McLaughlin, M. *Evaluation and Reform: The Elementary and Secondary Education Act of 1965, Title I.* Cambridge, Massachusetts: Ballinger Publishing Company, 1975.

97a. McMurdy, J., and Speich, I. "Student Skills Decline Unequalled in History." *Los Angeles Times,* August 15, 1976, pp. 1, 3, 23, 26.

97b. McMurdy, J., and Speich, I. "School Standards Also Decline, Fewer Basics, More Electives Lead to Drop in Student Scores." *Los Angeles Times,* August 16, 1976, pp. 1, 3, 18, 19.

98. "Med Schools Forfeit $11 Million." *San Francisco Chronicle,* November 28, 1977, pp. 1, 22.

99a. Metropolitan Achievement Test Special Report, 1970 Edition,

Report Number 15. *Equivalent Scores for Metropolitan Achiement Tests, 1970 Edition, and Metropolitan Achievement Tests, 1958 Edition in Terms of Metropolitan 1958 Modal-age Grade Equivalent.* New York: Harcourt Brace Jovanovich, 1971.

99b. Metropolitan Achievement Test Special Report, 1970 Edition, Report Number 16. *Equivalent Scores for Metropolitan Achievement Tests, 1970 Edition, and Stanford Achievement Test, 1964 Edition in Terms of Stanford 1964 Grade Equivalent.* New York: Harcourt Brace Jovanovich, 1971.

100. Metropolitan Readiness Tests Research Report Number 2. *Relation Between Scores on 1964 and 1976 (Level II) Editions of the Tests.* New York: Harcourt Brace Jovanovich, 1976.

101. Miller, N., and Gerard, H. "How Busing Failed in Riverside." *Psychology Today,* 1976, *10,* pp. 66–67, 69–70, 100.

102. Miller, W. B. *Violence by Youth Gangs and Youth Groups in Major American Cities.* Cambridge, Massachusetts: Harvard Law School, Center for Criminal Justice, April, 1976.

103. Modu, C., and Stern, J. *The Stability of the SAT Score Scale.* College Entrance Examination Board Research and Development Report RDR-74-74, Number 3, Princeton, New Jersey: Educational Testing Service, 1975.

104. Moore, R., and Moore, D. *Better Late Than Early.* New York: Reader's Digest Press, 1975.

105. Mosteller, F., and Moynihan, D. (editors). *On Equality of Educational Opportunity.* New York: Random House, 1972.

106. Munday, L. *Declining Admissions Test Scores.* American College Testing Program Research Report Number 71, Iowa City, Iowa: American College Testing Program, February, 1976.

107. Narss, J., and McGauvran, M. *Metropolitan Readiness Tests.* New York: Harcourt Brace Jovanovich, 1974.

108a. National Assessment of Educational Progress. *National Assessment of Science, 1969 and 1973*. Science Report No. 04-5-00, Washington, D.C.: U.S. Government Printing Office, February, 1975.

108b. National Assessment of Educational Progress. *Reading in America: A Perspective of Two Assessments*. Reading Report Number 06-R-01, Washington, D.C.: U.S. Government Printing Office, September, 1976.

108c. National Assessment of Educational Progress. *Writing Mechanics, 1969–1974*. Writing Report No. 05-W-01, Washington, D.C.: U.S. Government Printing Office, October, 1975.

108d. National Assessment of Educational Progress. *Changes in Political Knowledge and Attitudes, 1969–1976*. Citizenship Report No. 07-CS-02, Washington, D.C.: U.S. Government Printing Office, February, 1978.

109. National Committee for Citizens in Education Commission on Educational Governance. *Public Testimony on Public Schools*. Berkeley, California: McCutchan, 1975.

110. Neill, A. S. *Summerhill; A Radical Approach to Child Rearing*. New York: Hart Publishing Company, 1960.

111. Neill, A. S. *Freedom—Not License!* New York: Hart Publishing Company, 1966.

112. Nisbet, R. *The Twilight of Authority*. New York: Oxford University Press, 1975.

113. Norris, W. "Via Technology to a New Era in Education." *Phi Delta Kappan*, 1977, *58*, 451–453.

114. Northcutt, N. *Adult Functional Competency: A Summary*. The University of Texas, Austin, Texas, March, 1975.

115. *On Further Examination: Report of the Advisory Panel on the Scholastic Aptitude Test Score Decline*. New York: College Entrance Examination Board, 1977.

116. Osterndorf, L. *Summary of Offerings and Enrollments in Public Secondary Schools.* National Center for Education Statistics, U.S. Department of Health, Education and Welfare, U.S. Government Printing Office, 1975.

117. *Our Nation's Schools—A Report Card: "A" in School Violence and Vandalism.* Preliminary Report of the Subcommittee to Investigate Juvenile Delinquency to the Committee on the Judiciary, United States Senate. Washington, D.C.: U.S. Government Printing Office Report Number 67-589-0, 1975.

118. Piaget, J. *The Child's Conception of Number.* New York: Humanities Press, 1952.

119. Piccariello, H. "Evaluation of Title I," in Froomkin, J., and Dugan, D. (editors). *Inequality: Studies in Elementary and Secondary Education.* U.S. Office of Education, Department of Health, Education, and Welfare, June, 1969.

120. *Predicast,* Number 68, January 28, 1978.

121. "Preschoolers—Pawns in the Latest Education Battle." *U.S. News and World Report.* June 14, 1976, pp. 41, 42.

122. *Project Head Start: Achievements and Problems.* Washington, D.C.: U.S. General Accounting Office Report Number MWD-75-51, May, 1975.

123. Pulliam, J. *History of Education in America.* Columbus, Ohio: Charles E. Merrill Publishing Company, 1968.

124. Pursell, W. *A Conservative Alternative School: The A+ School in Cupertino. Fastback 67.* Bloomington, Indiana. The Phi Delta Kappa Educational Foundation, 1976.

125. *Putting Early Childhood and Day Care Services into the Public Schools.* The AFT Task Force on Educational Issues. The American Federation of Teachers, Winter, 1976.

126. Rapoport, D. "Street Gangs Are Back with Guns." *Parade Magazine,* May 2, 1976, p. 20.

127. Raybin, R. "Minimum Proficiencies in Pasadena's Secondary Schools." *Phi Delta Kappan*, 1977, *59*, 128–130.

128. *Report of the 1974–75 Michigan Cost Effectiveness Study*. Prepared by the Research, Evaluation and Assessment Services of the Michigan Department of Education. Washington, D.C.: Educational Resources Division, Capitol Publishing, Inc., 1976.

129. Rubin, R. "Reading Ability and Assigned Materials: Accommodation for the Slow but Not the Accelerated." *Elementary School Journal*, 1975, *75*, 373–377.

130. *School Suspensions: Are They Helping Children?*: Washington, D.C.: Children's Defense Fund of the Washington Research Project, 1975.

131. Scriven, M. "Problems and Prospects for Individualization," in Talmadge, H. (ed.). *Systems of Individualized Education*. Berkeley, California: McCutchan Publishing Corporation, 1975.

132. Scully, M. "Plainer Talk for Textbooks." *Chronicle of Higher Education*, October 15, 1974.

133. *Serrano v. Priest* 96 Cal. Rptr. 601 487 p.2d 1241.

134. Sherman, M. "Anti Intellectualism and Civil Rights." *Change*, 1976, *8*, 34–40.

135. Silberman, C. *Crisis in the Classroom: The Remaking of American Education*. New York: Random House, 1971.

136. Smith, A. *Summary of State Activity Related to Basic Skills Testing*. Princeton, New Jersey: Educational Testing Service, July, 1976.

137. Smith, R. "The Fall 1973 Survey of the Composition Requirement: A Summary of Results." *College English*, 1975, *36*, 589–593.

138. Spache, G., and Spache, E. Chapter Two in *Reading in the Elementary School*. Boston: Allyn and Bacon, 1973.

139. Stanford Research Report, Number 5, *Equivalent Scores for the 1973 Edition of Stanford Achievement Test and the 1964 Edition of the Stanford Achievement Test, in Terms of Grade Equivalents.* New York: Test Department, Harcourt Brace Jovanovich, 1973.

140. Start, K. B., and Wells, B. K. *The Trend in Reading Standards.* Slough, England: National Foundation for Educational Research, 1972.

141. *Statistical Abstract of the United States, 1976.* Washington, D.C.: Department of Commerce.

142. Stebbins, L., St. Pierre, R., Proper, E., Anderson, R., and Cerva, T. *Education as Experimentation: A Planned Variation Model.* Cambridge, Massachusetts: Abt Associates, 1977.

143. Stewart, E. *The Stability of the SAT–Verbal Score Scale.* College Entrance Examination Board Research and Development Report RDR-66-7, Number 3. Princeton, New Jersey: Educational Testing Service, July, 1966.

144. Sticht, T., and McFann, H. "Reading Requirements for Career Entry." In D. M. Nielsen and H. F. Hjelm (editors), *Reading and Career Education,* International Reading Association, 1975.

145. *Student Achievement in California Schools, 1976–77 Annual Report.* Sacramento, California: California State Department of Education, 1977.

146. *Summary Reports of Statewide Testing Program.* Office of Instructional Services, Evaluation Section, Testing Unit, Department of Education, State of Hawaii, annual reports, 1970–1974.

147. Suslow, S. *A Report on an Inter-institutional Survey of Undergraduate Scholastic Grading, 1960's to 1970's.* Office of Institutional Research, University of California, Berkeley, California, February, 1976.

148. Thorndike, R. "Mr. Binet's Test 70 Years Later." *Educational Research*, 1975, *4*, 3–7.

149. *Tinker v. Des Moines Independent Community School District.* 393 U.S. 503, 89 S.Ct. 733, 21 L.Ed. 2d 731, 1969.

150. Trace, A. *What Ivan Knows That Johnny Doesn't.* New York: Random House, 1961.

151. Tuddenham, D. "Soldier Intelligence in World Wars I and II." *American Psychologist*, 1948, *3*, 54–56.

152. U.S. Office of Education. First Grade Reading Studies. *The Reading Teacher*, 1966, *19*, 563–675; 1967, *20*, pp. 6–42, 541–545.

153. "U.S. Students Beaten by Refugees in Tests." *San Diego Evening Tribune*, December 31, 1975, p. 61.

154. "The Valedictorian." *Newsweek*, September 6, 1976.

155. Vetterli, R. *Storming the Citadel: The Fundamental Revolution Against Progressive Education.* Costa Mesa, California: Educational Media Press, 1976.

156. von Hoffman, N. "Hire a Drunk." *San Francisco Chronicle Sunday Punch*, July 31, 1977, p. 3.

157. Walters, R., Thomas, E., and Acker, C. "Enhancement of Punitive Behavior by Audiovisual Displays." *Science*, 1962, *136*, 872–873.

158. Weber, G. "Inner-City Children Can Be Taught to Read." *Four Successful Schools.* Council for Basic Education, 725 Fifteenth St., N.W., Washington, D.C. 20005. October, 1971.

159a. Weber, G. (editor). *Bulletin: Vol. 21, No. 4, December 1976.* Washington, D.C.: Council for Basic Education, 1976.

159b. Howard Jr., J. (editor). *Bulletin: Vol. 21. No. 6, February 1977.* Washington, D.C.: Council for Basic Education, 1977.

160. Wegmann, R. "White Flight and School Resegregation: Some Hypotheses." *Phi Delta Kappan,* 1977, *58*, 389–393.

161. Weinman, J. *Declining Test Scores: A State Study.* Massachusetts: Massachusetts Department of Education, 1977.

162. Westinghouse Learning Corporation. *Impact of Head Start Experience: An Evaluation of the Effect of Head Start on Children's Cognitive and Affective Development. Volume 1 Text and Appendices.* Ohio State University Report to Office of Educational Opportunity, Clearinghouse for Federal Scientific and Technical Information, Washington, D.C., 1969.

163. West Virginia State County Testing Program. Personal communication. West Virginia State Department of Education, 1975.

164. Wiley, D. "Another Hour, Another Day. Quantity of Schooling, a Potent Path for Policy." *Studies of Educative Processes,* Number 3, University of Chicago, July, 1973.

165. Wiley, D., and Harnischfeger, A. *Achievement Test Score Decline: Do We Need to Worry?* Chicago, Illinois: Cemrel, Inc., 1975.

166. Wiley, D., and Harnischfeger, A. "Explosion of a Myth: Quantity of Schooling and Exposure to Instruction, Major Educational Vehicles." *Educational Researcher,* 1974, *3,* 7–12.

167. Winkler, K. "Proliferating Federal Regulations: Is Government Now 'The Enemy'?" *Chronicle of Higher Education,* December 13, 1976, p. 3.

168. Wolynski, M. "Confessions of a Misspent Youth." *Newsweek,* August 30, 1976, p. 11.

169. *Wood v. Strickland,* 420 U.S. 308 (1975).

170. Zirkel, P. "The Legal Vicissitudes of Bilingual Education." *Phi Delta Kappan,* 1977, *58,* 409–411.

INDEX

Ability grouping, high school, 85–89, 109
Academic achievement, 28–50
  establishment and development of public school system, 30–31
  family, importance of, 53, 54
  minority groups, 117–135
  peer groups, importance of, 53
  post-*Sputnik* era, 34–37, 44
  quantity and quality of education and, 54
  renorming studies, 32–37, 42–45
  society, importance of, 54
  socioeconomic class, importance of, 53
  students' work habits and attitudes, 155–159
  1800's to early 1900's, 30–32
    percentage of age groups in school or completing school, 30–31
  early 1900's to mid-1950's, percentage of age groups in school or completing school, 32–33
  1937, 33
  1956, 36–37
  1957 to early 1960's, 34–37
    gains in academic achievement, 35–36
  1964, 36–37
  early 1960's to mid-1970's, 37–50
    elementary-school students, 42–44
    high-school graduates, 37–42
    national pattern in, 44–50
    secondary-school students, 42–44
  See also Testing
Academic deterioration, authority breakdown and, 185–186
Addison-Wesley Publishing Company, 82
Adult Performance Level (APL) study, 23, 47–48, 108, 117, 140
Adults, statistics on competence of, 47–48
Agriculture, Department of, 173, 174
Alabama, 49
Alcohol, 178
American Association of Higher Education, 189
American Association of School Administration, 143
American College Testing Program (ACT), 41–42, 49, 103, 117, 135
American Federation of Teachers, 194, 212
American Institutes of Research (AIR), 74, 121–122

Amphetamines, 178
Aptitude tests, 135
Arithmetic aptitude, *see* Mathematics
Armbruster, Frank, 50
Army Tests of General Educational Development (G.E.D.), 34
Association of American Publishers (AAP), 83
Audio cassettes, readability level and, 84
Auditory discrimination, importance of, 56–57, 60
Authoritarian parents, 163
Authoritative parents, 163
Authority
   natural, 148–150
   training agents and, 149
Authority breakdown, 147–181
   academic deterioration and, 185–186
   bureaucratic overregulation, 173–175
   busing, 171–172
   democracy and, 150–151
   drug usage and, 178–179
   educators and, 159–160
   gang activity in schools, 177–178
   lowering of educational standards and, 151–152, 155–159
   parental responsibility and, 151, 154, 160–161
   parent-child interaction, recent history of, 161–163, 165–168
   political, community, and professional organizations, 169–170
   school administrators and, 160, 178
   school violence and crime, 176–177
   secondary functions assigned to education, 175–177
   student resistance to authority, 168–169

Baumrind, Dr. Diana, 163–165
Bender, Louis, 189
Bennett, Neville, 69–70, 211
Berkeley Institute, 71
Berntson, Lynn, 19
Beveridge, Bob, 20, 22, 80
Bilingual educational programs, 170–171
Black, Justice Hugo, 172–173
Boston
   educational tests
      1845, 32
      1853, 32
      1919, 32
      1929, 32
Brigham Young University, 188
Bronfenbrenner, Dr. Urie, 59, 165, 166
Burns, Robert E., 80
Busing, 171–172

California, 44–46, 50
   banning of group IQ tests, 135
   English curriculum, 96, 97
   formal systems of individualized instruction, 74
   readability levels, 82–84
   reading programs, 125
California, Universitiy of, 41, 101, 106–107, 113, 188
California State Department of Education, 129, 130, 132–133
Canada, decline in academic skills, 44
Carnegie Commission, 68
Carnegie Council on Policy Studies in Higher Education, 115
Carnegie Foundation for the Advancement of Teaching, 107–108, 113
Chall, Jeanne, 22
Chicago, University of, 50, 54, 121, 188
Children's Defense Fund, 169
City University of New York (C.U.N.Y.), 83, 107, 110
Civil Service Commission, 173, 174
Civil-rights movement, 86, 87, 109, 110
   on standardized testing, 138–141
Cleveland
   educational tests
      1848, 32
      1947, 32
Cocaine, 178
Coleman report, 53, 121
College Entrance Examination Board (CEEB), 37, 40, 80–81, 101–102
College and university, 106–117
   academic turmoil, 107–108
   admissions, 37–42
   course requirements for a degree, 107–108
   deterioration of the curriculum, 107–117
   elective-oriented curriculum, 107–108
   English, 107, 108
   foreign language requirements, 107
   governmental attack on, 148
   grade inflation, 112–117
   grade-point average (1960–1975), 114
   history, 107–109
   inflation and, 148
   literature, 109
   mathematics, 107
   as meritocratic institutions, 111
   minority groups, 109, 110, 111, 112
   open admissions policy, 109–112
   Pass/No Credit (P/NC) grading, 115–116
   reading, 83, 108, 111, 112, 137
   science, 109